Bres

Welcome to the

Quilting Circle

Mel Janoy

12-04-2019

COMMAND AT DAWN

COMMAND AT DAWN

a novel

MEL CARNEY

Deeds Publishing | Athens

Published by Deeds Publishing in Athens, GA
www.deedspublishing.com

Printed in The United States of America

Cover design by Mark Babcock. Text layout by Matt King.

ISBN 978-1-947309-95-1

Books are available in quantity for promotional or premium use. For
information, email info@deedspublishing.com.

First Edition, 2019

10 9 8 7 6 5 4 3 2 1

To my wife Barb
and all of my family

And the men in
Company B 1/6th Infantry 198th LIB

And a special thank you to Patrice Ludwig for her
dedication and work on Command at Dawn.

In Flanders Field

... Take up our quarrel with the foe
To you from our failing hands we throw
The Torch; be yours to hold it high
If ye break faith with us who die
We Shall not sleep, though poppies grow
In Flander's fields.

—Lt. Col. John McCrae, MD

Contents

Preface

Vietnam, June 1, 1968: Lt Scott Ledbetter followed the mandate set down in the last stanza of "In Flanders Field.' He had to pick up the torch that had been "thrown" to him from failing hands.

Mortar round explosions were moving across his perimeter like the wind and no artillery was being fired by his Forward Observer. Knowing that something was wrong, Scott ran toward a zeroed-in Command Post. The carnage in the CP was overwhelming. The Forward Observer and his radioman were dead, lying with open mouthed stares against a wall of stone. The captain and several others were lying on the ground, wounded or dead.

Mortars rained down as Scott battled for the radio mic that was in the Forward Observer's death grip. Explosions were everywhere as he worked feverishly to get the mic released. When he had it in his hand he stopped and became as calm as humanly possible before starting to call in artillery on a determined enemy.

At daybreak, Scott moved what was left of his new

command off the Castle Hill, towards the rest of the war. While he could not bring them back, he knew that he had not broken faith with those who had given their lives for a small chunk of Vietnam real estate.

—Mel Carney

"Fear
is a Reaction.
Bravery
is a Decision."

—Winston Churchill

Day One — Plus One

Command at Dawn

"His heart went out to the five men killed and the twen-
ty-seven wounded, who were Medevac'd
off the Castle Hill."

Greasy sweat poured down the face of Lt. Scott Ledbetter
of the 6th Infantry. Like every day in the jungle, each man
of Company B moved through the jungle simply by pushing
one foot in front of the other. Today the task was made par-
ticularly onerous as last night's mortar barrage had cost too
many friends. The zeroed in mortars had started in the Command Post and spread across the hill like the wind.

As they walked away from that hill, the excessive heat
and smell of rotting vegetation burned at the nostrils and
wore deep into the very being of each man. On the western
side of last night's mountain, a wide stream was nose high to
Scott. The cool water gave a few minutes respite to the men

who lived with one-hundred-degree heat twenty-four hours by seven. Within steps of the cool stream, sweat was back on each man, with a vengeance.

The company was moving across a wide valley to a range of mountains that sat next to the Laotian border. Their only check point for the day was at the top of a mountain they could see as they walked. The sun was directly overhead as they worked their way up the near vertical mountain, a mountain four hundred feet tall with no trail to follow. To move up the mountain, each man had to use small rocks and trees to pull himself up.

As Scott reached the top, he stepped out of the line of men. He then greeted each man with a nod. This was the first time that he had a chance to assess the damage to the company after last night's mortar attack. The result of that attack showed in every face as forty plus men clambered over the top of the mountain. All worn slick by the climb, the jungle, and last night.

When Sergeant Bishop, Scott's Platoon Sgt, got to the top of the mountain he stopped to talk. After a pull on his canteen, Bishop stood there with sweat dripping off his nose as he tried to catch his breath. The two men talked about the night before and how the sergeant had made it through. The sergeant had learned that the Artillery FO and his radioman had been killed, but he did not know who had fired artillery long into the night. Scott told him he was the one who had done the firing, the scariest On the Job Training session he had ever been through.

The two men walked the mountain top to determine a night laager perimeter, then Scott left the job of setting the company to his platoon Sergeant He walked back and sat down where they had crested the mountain and looked back at the Castle Hill where they had gotten mortared the night before.

He pulled off his helmet and dropped his backpack and dug into his pack to find a pack of cigarettes. His search yielded a flattened pack of Pall Malls that were not smokable cigarettes. He did locate his mirror. He seldom took time to see what he looked like, because nothing ever changes in combat.

Looking at himself for the first time in days, he was startled by the image staring back at him. His face wore a scruffy beard and dirt stained sweat streaks ran down to his chin. His once blue eyes were gray and very deep set into his head. His cheeks were sallow, and his face gaunt. His hair was matted from months inside of a helmet. Across his forehead was a crease from his helmet liner. It looked like it was going to be there for the rest of his life.

The image that reflected from the 2"x 3" mirror was a far cry from the young man who had landed in Da Nang at the beginning of the TET offensive on February 4, 1968. In four months, he had been transformed into a combat infantryman. He appeared much older than his twenty-three birthdays would indicate. He considered that perhaps combat months were like dog years. Each month in the jungle made him a year older and it felt like he had been in the jungle forever. His soul felt heavy with the sense of combat and today his shoulders were slumped with his new command position.

This morning, as the predawn light permeated the night laager, Scott had gone looking for Lt. Fredericks. With

Captain Reeds being wounded in the mortar attack Fredericks had the most time in grade. That made him the new company commander. While the two men were not buddies, they had to work together. Scott wanted to talk with him after last night's mortar attack and the hours of firing artillery.

The first person he ran into was Doc "B" and he looked like he had been through seven kinds of hell since they saw each other during the mortar attack. Doc told him that they had five KIA and twenty-seven WIA. A quick count gave Scott the number of men left on the mountain, forty-four.

Scott asked, "Have you seen Lt. Fredericks?"

Doc, assuming Scott knew, was surprised at the question, "Yes sir, I medevaced him last night with wounds from a mortar round.

Scott, was not ready for this information, and asked, "Was he hit bad?"

"No sir, but he caught shrapnel in his back and I medevaced him."

That news hit Scott like a bolt of lightning! As the only officer standing, he knew that he was now the company commander. This was not what he was expecting. He enjoyed having his own platoon and having someone else in command. Now he knew that that someone else was him. He was trying get his arms around being the commander of a field unit when the third platoon sergeant walked up and asked, "Has anyone seen Lt. McAllen?"

Scott spun his head to look at the sergeant saying, "McAllen, was he in the field?"

The sergeant answered, "Yes sir, he came in the Slick that brought Doc back to the field."

This was all going too fast. He had not been told that the man was even in the field and now the platoon sergeant had no idea where the hell he was.

Doc "B" spoke up, "I was putting the last WIA on a medivac and I had several men loading a slick that had just come in for the KIAs. McAllen had talked to me about Shell Shock, but I had not addressed his issue. As the slick with the KIAs was lifting off, I turned and saw him sitting on the canvas seat in the back of the chopper and he was gone."

The sergeant looked at Doc and said, "Are you serious? He was claiming Shell Shock! When he left our area he told me that he was going to go check on the Command Post and God Dammit, I just realized that he had on his backpack! That sorry son of a bitch! I assumed he came back and bedded down, the son of a bitch! The sorry assed son of a bitch!"

McAllen had been in the field for less than a day before claiming shell shock and putting himself on a chopper that was carrying men who had been killed. He was now in some rear Landing Zone, safe. It seemed that Scott's world was raining down on him. His stomach took this latest news like a heat stroke. He had a pain in his gut and his breathing was coming hard.

McAllen knew, like Scott knew, that they were about to be overrun. When Scott started calling in artillery, he understood that the size of the company was no match for a battalion sized NVA unit. He knew that when the attack happened that they would not walk off this hill. To keep that attack from happening, he had fired hundreds of artillery rounds and the NVA did not attack. This morning forty-four men would walk off this mountain.

Fido

While Scott was wounded down deep in his soul, he was now the commander and he had to keep on moving. An old army expression fit the situation like a glove: FIDO: Fuck It, Drive ON! He felt for Lt. Fredericks being wounded and sad that McAllen had "Shell Shock." As for himself, he had forty-four men in his command, and every one of them wanted off the fucking mountain.

He wondered where Captain Ken was when he really needed him. Captain Ken had been the company commander when Scott first came to the field. Scott had so much respect for him as he really understood commanding field infantrymen. They had pulled him out of the field for a new position two months before. Scott wondered what he would do and deep down he knew that he would simply, Drive ON!

Battalion called and gave Scott a single checkpoint for the day: it was at the top of a mountain that sat across the valley, west of the Castle Hill. They would be crossing a large area filled with jungle. Scott asked Yancy, his radioman, to call in his Platoon Sgts so he could give them the objective for the day and to remind them that they were now platoon leaders.

With all the platoon Sgts present, they discussed the lack of any significant terrain between here and the checkpoint. Before they walked off the mountain, Doc Lee caught him and made him sit down so he could take care of wounds that he had received from a mortar round the week before. He re-bandaged the wounds and once more told him that he needed to get to the hospital. Scott promised he would. With his wounds bandaged, Bravo started moving off the Castle Hill under the command of the newest company commander in Vietnam.

When they made it to the day's objective, Scott was drawn to the spot where they had crested the mountain. He just sat and looked back to the place that he called The Castle Hill, it would forever be scratched into his memory.

He realized that no military commander had a grand plan to win the war. As a result, Bravo and every other infantry company in the field spent every day going from one map checkpoint to another. They were always looking for the enemy. If they did not start their own war, they would be picked up by choppers and taken to someplace where there was a war. If there was a coordinated movement between the companies in the battalion, that secret was kept at battalion.

There were months when Bravo did not see another unit in the field. There were no daily situation reports to tell the field commanders what was going on in their Area of Operation. Bravo did not know if there were any casualties or victories anywhere in the battalion. The only gauge to let them know how the war was going was when they reported their enemy body count. No geographical territories were ever taken and held.

Scott had read a lot about WWII and how the D Day plan was put in place. He knew that the plan did not go as they thought it would, but there was in fact a plan. The only plan that his battalion had was to tell the field commanders what check points they were to cover that day. They left it up to the commanders to handle getting to those checkpoints.

If combat broke out anywhere in their area, Bravo would

be told to stop and get ready for an extraction. They would move to a pick-up point and Huey slicks (supply helicopters) would come in and take them on a combat assault. With every CA, the men knew that they were going into a hot landing zone. They also knew that this ride could be their last.

When the choppers came into the pickup zone, the men would clamor aboard the incoming chopper. Six men would sit, three on a side, with their feet resting on the runners. The noise of the open chopper would not allow conversations to happen. As the chopper lifted off the deck, each man would go into what was known as a thousand-meter stare, an expressionless face, a cold stare that saw a thousand meters out, but not the man sitting next to them. They all knew that wherever they were headed that there would be a body count. That count would be of the dead enemy soldiers and that they could be a part of that body count, themselves.

When there is an insertion of a unit someplace in the jungle, the enemy would be firing AK-47's and rocket grenades at the incoming chopper. They wanted to bring it down before the troops got on the ground. These were known as "hot LZ's". There were damned few "cold LZ's."

Scott knew that tomorrow morning he would get a call from battalion with a list of check points and their grid coordinates. There would be no mention of yesterday's casualties or victories (if any). Bravo would head out for another day of slogging through jungles and rice paddies.

Killed as a Result of Hostile Activity
commonly called Killed in Action (KIA)

A field combat soldier stayed in the field for a year. The only time that he got out of the field early would be if he was wounded or killed, or he might get out of the field for a few days if he made it to his Rest and Relaxation time, R&R.

Each step an Infantryman took in the jungle brought him closer to a face-to-face meeting with war. When war broke out, men could be wounded. Someone who had just bummed a cigarette would die with the bummed cigarette still lit in his mouth.

The dead man's body would be laid into his poncho and lifted by the men in his squad and taken to a waiting Huey slick for extraction. Before his buddies could take off their helmet to show respect for their lost buddy, the slick would be fading away into the east. When the whop of the rotors could no longer be heard, that man was gone. His fight was done. His buddies would walk silently back to the platoon where they would silently saddle up. Their war would just go on and on.

The dead man would be choppered back to a fire base and kept in a refrigerated morgue tent where they would get a positive identification. Then the body would be flown to a funerary place in Da Nang that had refrigerated buildings filled with cold dead bodies and the smell of death. The man's body would be put into his military casket and taken to the air strip. There he would be put on a large refrigerated plane, filled with other KIA's. All of men would be given their final airplane ride across the ocean.

The man would receive military honors at his burial, and at the close of the burial ceremony, the mournful and respectful Taps would be played. The man's mom (or other loved one) would be presented with a beautifully folded American Flag, which she would keep on the mantle or on her son's favorite chair. It would stay there until grief made it impossible to keep it out in the open. Her mourning would only end when she, herself, was laid to rest.

The number of men killed or wounded in the past three weeks had taken its toll on Scott's mind. Last night's battle took more of a toll than ever before. As he sat with his feet dangling off the side of the mountain, he wanted what he could not have, to go home. Every combat soldier has that dream, but for Scott, that feeling was stronger than ever.

Remembering Last Night's Mortar Attack

Scott sat alone on Castle Hill. He had just finished a night of firing artillery. The night laager was covered with a smoky haze and the air was acrid with the taste of burned gunpowder. Hundreds of rounds of artillery had crashed into the earth a thousand meters away and every round was from Scott. With each new volley, he felt more and more buoyed. He had stopped the mortars and the force that would have overrun their small band of soldiers. No more incoming mortars and no more probes of his perimeter. All the rounds that he had fired was to pay back the sons of a bitches who had killed and wounded so many on the fucking hill.

Now, sitting on the ground in the dark there were no artillery rounds crashing into the ground, and Scott had nothing to do but think and wait for morning. He wondered how many NVA bodies had been quickly buried in shallow graves as all of those rounds crashed into one single grid, one thousand meters square.

He had been raised in a Christian family. He wondered which commandment he could use for tonight's artillery barrage. Artillery puts committing mass murder of an enemy out there somewhere. While his army training had him responding to an enemy attack, his moral compass was running counter to his hard-core military training. After twenty plus years of a Christian upbringing, the army had given him fourteen months of lethal training on how to kill people. In the late hours of a long night, it seemed that a war was raging inside of his head as Christianity was trying to reestablish itself in Scott's thinking.

He knew that the commandment Thou Shalt Not Kill did not have an asterisk for combat. He kept telling himself as he fired artillery that this was a fight for survival and a case of kill or be killed. The fact that he was questioning his actions told him that he needed to better understand the difference of the rules of commandments in Iowa and the rules of the commandments in combat.

He was vacillating between the calm of no more war tonight and the truth of the Naked Earth that he had inflicted on a determined enemy. He knew that in the last few hours he had achieved his military goal. With the absence of perimeter probes by the enemy and the absence of incoming mortar rounds, he had given his men the opportunity to walk off this hill under their own power. As he had been calling in artillery, his military heart was doing the army's bidding. Deep down in his soul, his moral compass had marked this day as time against his moral upbringing. He would have to deal with that mark for the rest of his life.

The night of artillery had been exhausting. His only experience with artillery had come a year earlier when he fired two rounds while he was in OCS. He knew that both rounds had hit the ground and he did not leave them hanging in the air. He did not know if he had hit his target. Last night he fired hundreds of rounds in a matter of hours, and the numbers were beyond his level of comprehension.

The Que Son Valley

With dark closing in, Scott shut the door on his thoughts and went to help Yancy, his radioman, set up their command post. As the last rays of sunlight disappeared into Laos, Scott told Yancy that he would take the first radio watch.

For hours, Scott sat and listened to the shush of the PRC 25 radio. His mind was filled with too much combat and too much killing and death in the past three weeks to consider sleep. Since the first week of May they had been in contact, almost daily. For the last four weeks, the NVA were pushing harder and harder on the US troops.

For Bravo, the war picked up the pace on the morning of May fifth. The company was instructed to go as quickly as possible and secure the area around two downed choppers in the Que Son Valley. They forced marched several kilometers to an area north and west of LZ Center. Scott knew that they were heading into an area where bad shit was happening.

As they reached the area, he discovered that the two choppers which had been literally blown out of the sky had been a Huey with a Long-Range Reconnaissance Patrol on board and a supporting Huey gun ship. Bravo had forced march most of the day to get there. Apparently, there was activity all over the Area of Operations and there were no Slicks to pick them up and bring them to this location. When they got to the area, they found both the choppers had gone down within a few hundred meters of each other.

Bravo was receiving incoming rounds from AK 47's. The company split and put two platoons around one chopper and the other platoon around the second chopper. Their job, along with securing the downed choppers, was to look for body parts of the men who were on the choppers.

The Que Son Valley was filled with enemy soldiers. With the strength of the enemy who were obviously still in the valley, Scott was seeing a change in the way the NVA were behaving. Normally they would have hit the birds and broke contact. Based on the amount of rifle fire and rocket propelled grenades that they were taking, the NVA were there for the long haul.

The two ships had blown up in the air and the bodies of the crewmen and LRRP team were scattered over a wide area. They put the men's body parts into a poncho and sent them back to the morgue via a Huey slick. Whenever a Huey came in for the extraction of the body parts, they came under heavy fire from a mountain (Hill 352), which sat to the north and west of LZ Center.

When Scott first saw the downed Hueys, he could not

believe how little was left of the ships. The motor and the ship's frames were gone. All that was left of either ship was a pile of burned ashes, the rotor blade, and shaft. The remains looked like the chopper had been built with an erector set.

They were told that Company D 1/20th Infantry had been temporarily assigned to the 1/6th Infantry and were on their way in to support them. When Delta company came in on Hueys, they came under heavy fire, but were fortunate to not have any casualties. They joined Bravo at the site of the downed choppers and started searching for body parts.

The two companies set up a night laager close to the downed choppers. Scott did not like the location as they had no high ground. The NVA kept mortar fire coming in on the perimeter. Fortunately, all the incoming was ineffective, however there was precious little sleep by either of the companies. During the night, Puff the Magic Dragon came in to hold down the fire from the base of Hill 352.

The next day the two companies worked together to locate and secure all the remains that they could find. On the second day, Delta Company would lose six men to an old French Bouncing Betty Bomb which had been left over from a war many years before. At first, they thought that they were being mortared and then realized that nothing had been fired.

On the third day, the two companies were told to move north from their night laager and secure Hill 352. At 352 meters tall, it was the tallest mountain in the area. It sat at the southern end of a mile-long ridgeline. The mortar fire that LZ Center and the two companies had been receiving was coming from Hill 352 or the ridgeline, north of the mountain. That was also the location of the anti-aircraft gun that knocked the choppers out of the sky.

LZ Center was one of the more important firebases in the center of Vietnam. That LZ had the large artillery pieces and supported a lot of territory. If this mountain was not secured, the valley below would not be safe for any American unit.

Hill 352

The plan was for both companies to hike north, up the Que Son Valley. At the northern end of the ridgeline, on the left, was a marked trail which would take the companies south along the ridgeline to Hill 352. As the companies headed north up the valley, the terrain was very steep. The trail, which was marked on the map, was mostly non-existent. Both companies had to work their way north. The valley between 352 and the mountains to its east was sometimes only twenty to forty meters wide.

Delta Company had moved out, well before Bravo. For some reason, Bravo was slow on the uptake on this day. Scott was frustrated with the company's inability to get moving and progress was slow. Everyone in the company could see the objective and no one was really anxious to get to the top of 352. They all knew that all of the fire power that had been coming down on them for the last three days was coming from that mountain.

The men knew that at the end of a long hard climb up the valley was going to be and even longer climb up to the top of 352. Both climbs were going to be a bonifide bitch. With the objective staring down on every grunt in the column, no one wanted to hurry. The men also knew that they were going to be fighting up hill, and when you are on the downhill side of any battle, you have virtually no advantage.

Delta company contacted battalion to let them know that they were at the trailhead and were turning south on the trail that would take them along the ridgeline to Hill 352. This information was relayed to Bravo as they struggled along. The afternoon was closing in on 1430 hours. To get to the trailhead would take Bravo another two hours and with daylight on the short side, Bravo would be stuck on the lower side of the mountain ridge with no way to make it to the top.

When they stopped to discuss the situation, Bravo was even with the top of 352. It was determined that Bravo would take a more direct route to the top of the mountain. Bravo turned ninety degrees and started to pack up the eastern face of the thirteen-hundred-foot mountain. There was no trail and the slopes were damned near straight up, this was going to be a double bitch.

Three hours later, the third platoon (the first platoon in the order of march) made it to the top of the mountain. They called on the radio to let everyone struggling below know that they had made it. They also let everyone know that there was a thirty-five-foot hill that sat on the mountain top, that small hill sat close to the eastern side of the mountain.

After a short radio discussion, it was decided that the third platoon would wait until the second platoon was on the mountain top before beginning to secure the perimeter. At that time, they would begin to move around the small hill to the right. When Scott's platoon made it to the top they would move to the left and come around to meet the third and second platoon. Until they could recon and find a better perimeter, the small hill would be inside the night laager.

It was coming onto 1730 hours when Scott set foot on top of the mountain. He watched as the last elements of the second platoon headed to the right. His first squad had already made it to the top and had begun to work their way around the base of the small hill to the left.

There was a dense patch of jungle to the left and the squad was working their way through the thick underbrush. By radio, Scott and his squad leader determined that they were only twenty-five feet apart, but no visual could be made. As he was talking with Sergeant Cross, the squad leader, a war broke out on the north side of the small hill.

Within minutes of that war, a bunker line that was apparently on the very south edge of the mountain started to fire thirty caliber machine guns and AK-47's at Scott's position. Sergeant Cross was able to get his M-60s into position and started to fire on the machine guns. The NVA had been firing blindly at Sergeant Cross's position, as none of his troops could be seen by the NVA who were in that bunker line.

Scott found a ditch that poured off the side of the small hill and used it for protection. He could feel the bullets fly by his position and occasionally the fire would dip down and hit the rocks at the top of the small ditch, blasting rock fragments on him and his radioman.

He could not move forward and was getting as much information as he could from Sergeant Cross on the radio. Scott told his last two squads to stay put on the side of the mountain as there simply was no room for anyone on top of the mountain. He instructed the two squad leaders to secure a defensible position where they were on the mountain side. He warned them to keep a watchful eye to the south as he was concerned that the NVA would try to flank their position.

At the same time that Scott stepped onto the mountain, the lead elements of the second and third platoon were turning the corner on the north side of the small hill. When they looked up and to the left, there was an NVA sitting out in the sun. He was just three meters above where Bravo was moving. The men killed the NVA soldier and then the war got deadly serious. That fire woke up the gun crew of the anti-aircraft gun. That gun set on the north side of the hill and had a 360° view of the valley's below.

The anti-aircraft gun started firing at the third and second platoon. The shells were swooshing out of the gun and that sound drove fear deep into everyone on the mountain. There were manned bunkers on either side of the large weapon and they were also firing at our men. The 12.7 mm Russian Zastava Russian anti-aircraft weapon was firing at ground troops.

On top of hill 352, there were two battles raging. The killing of the NVA soldier had the gun crews firing at the two platoons on that side of the hill. The gunfire woke up the troops who were in the bunker line two hundred meters to Scott's front. Scott realized that they had walked into the middle of an NVA base camp. While they had caught the NVA with their pants down, it was not to Bravo's advantage.

Until the M-60's and M-16s opened up on them, the NVA had no idea where Scott's platoon was located. They were just firing at the jungle, figuring to hit something. They were afraid to fire into the small hill because their troops were on the north side of that hill. The NVA never expected that an American unit would crawl up the side of 352 from the east.

Scott's platoon was in an indefensible position. The NVA were cutting down on them from the mountain crest to their south with thirty caliber machine guns and AK-47s. The M79 rounds that were being fired by the second and third platoon at the big gun on the hill were missing the large weapon's position. Those missed rounds were exploding in Scott's platoon area. Neither Scott nor his platoon could move to help anyone, because they were pinned down from both the north and south.

Scott could hear the anti-aircraft gun firing its massive caliber rounds at the ground soldiers. Sergeant Cross kept putting as much firepower on the enemy as was possible. The radio was alive with expletives as men were firing and scurrying out of the path of the massive anti-aircraft gun.

The NVA gun had been positioned to fire at aircraft, not at ground troops inside of their perimeter. It was estimated that some eight hundred NVA were on Scott's side of the hill. The fire from all those troops far outweighed the fire that Scott's platoon could cover. Because of the steepness of the mountain, the NVA had not put any bunkers or firing positions on the east side of the small hill.

Salvation

The salvation of Bravo came from three brave men in the third platoon. The three men moved off the mountain to the west where they found a large tree. One man climbed the tree and when he got even with the anti-aircraft gun the men on the ground tied a Light Anti-Tank Weapon to a rope. The man in the tree pulled the LAW up to his position. With one missile, the young soldier blew the 12.7 mm weapon and its crew into eternity. The second and third platoon took out the bunkers on either side of the large gun.

Strange things happen in combat

Under normal circumstances, the crew of the anti-aircraft gun would have seen the man climbing that tree. They were, however, focusing their attention on a young man who was pinned down by the large caliber weapon. Apparently he felt that there was no other option and he jumped up and ran at the anti-aircraft gun, throwing grenades as he ran.

He got far enough up the hill to take a direct hit in the front of his helmet from the 12.7 mm weapon. The round hit the helmet and tore a sizeable hole in the front of his helmet. As the round hit, it must have twisted the man's head to the right. As the man's head twisted, the round went around the inside of the helmet liner and fell onto the ground.

The young man had a burn on the right side of his head as the round traveled inside of his helmet. He had been hit in the arm with a round from an AK-47. He was also wounded from the shrapnel from his own hand grenades. Unbelievably, the man lived and was later medevaced.

His real contribution to the battle was an unplanned diversion. This was all happening at the same time the man was climbing the tree to the gun crew's left. The gun crew had paid so much attention to the crazy American soldier who was running towards them, heaving grenades, that they missed the man climbing the tree. As crazy as it sounds, this all happened simultaneously, as if it was planned. The result was that the anti-aircraft gun was taken out by an anti-tank weapon. A one-man assault made it possible for a large caliber gun to be knocked out and the surrounding bunkers taken out by the two platoons. Combat has few, if any, rules.

With the gun knocked out, Scott was no longer receiving M-79 grenades into his platoon. Now he could concentrate on returning fire on the bunker. The amount of fire from the bunker was now getting very serious and Scott was thinking that this could be the last firefight. At that time he got a call that gunships were on station.

The gunships that normally supported the 1/6th were supporting Alpha and Charlie companies up in the A-SHAU Valley. Their gunship support on Hill 352 was coming from gunships who normally supported the Eleventh Brigade. They were called the "Sharks."

The "Sharks" came on station and asked that the forward position of the unit be marked with a smoke grenade. Scott instructed Sergeant Cross to toss a can of smoke to mark his forward position. As soon as the gunships verified red, Scott heard the first rockets being fired. The explosion and amount of dust kicked up by those first rockets was painfully close to Sergeant Cross's squad.

Scott yelled into his mike, "Navigator 3 are you okay?" Sergeant Cross's reply was, "Y Ye Y Yes, damn that was close!" Scott yelled into the mike, "Sharks, move fire one hundred and fifty meters to the left of that last barrage, God Damnit man, what the fuck are you doing?" They gunships made their adjustment and the war went on.

The rockets started moving the length of the bunker system. Scott could not see the bunkers, nor could he pinpoint the gunships. Finally, he caught one rising up from a mountain that sat out in the valley to their east. The ships would set behind a mountain out in the Que Son Valley, rise up far enough above that mountain, fire their rockets and sink out of sight. The NVA would not know where the gunships were, so they could not return fire.

Scott knew that in a profession which was filled with bad assed and crazy sumbitches, pilots for the "Sharks" might just be at the highest level of crazy. When the last rockets were fired by the gunships, they seemed to evaporate. Scott thought that they had cut a choogie back to base. He was wrong. A few minutes later the Sharks came over the small hill from the north.

They were big, bad, and ugly. The cabins of the gunships were painted like the bombers from WWII. They had a huge row of sharks' teeth painted on the front of the ship. They looked scary. As they crested that small hill, they cut loose with mini guns firing thousands of rounds per minute from both sides of the cabin. From the nose of each ship came a stream of M-79 grenades being fired at a couple hundred rounds per minute. These ships did not have door gunners, their mini guns were being directed by the pilots and they were kicking ass.

With its mini guns firing and grenades pouring out the nose, one of the ships came by Scott's position, ten to twelve feet off the deck. Scott saw a sapling hit the rounded glass by the pilot's feet and knocked it out. Scott saw the pilot move his feet, but he did not stop firing those mini guns. When the "Sharks" made their last of several runs they were replaced by the A-4 Sky Raiders and Air Force F-4's. The jet jockeys were coming in hot and releasing their tonnage before they got to Scott's position, which meant that Scott was able to watch as hundreds of pounds of bombs were twisting through the air and he just hoped that they did not detonate early.

The concussion from the bombs blowing the bunkers away tore at his ears and shook his body to the core. When the bombs hit the ground, dirt chunks the size of basketballs were crashing down on Scott's platoon. The impact of the shock waves emanating from the blasts was unreal. The noise had Scott's mind reeling. The vibrations from the planes drove a wedge down his back and the explosions ripped at his face and ears. He shuddered as the smell of war tore at his nostrils and his Christian soul. This hell went on as four jets unloaded their tonnage on the NVA bunkers.

When their heavy ordinance was gone, the Sky Raider's unleashed their twenty-millimeter cannons. The shells were all high explosives and blew up on contact. These cannon rounds dug deep before blowing up. When the jet jockeys fire their cannons, it gives off a fearsome moan, as thousands of rounds pour out of the cannons. When combined with the noise of the jets, it is unfathomable. As the jets screamed by, they suck vast quantities of air and belched hellfire on a dug in enemy.

On the first run with his cannons, a pilot unleashed a torrent of 20 mm rounds. The burst of fire caught the top of a forty-foot tree standing a few meters from Scott's position and in the middle of where Sergeant Cross's squad was hunkered down. The high explosive rounds ate the tree from the top down. The tree was shaking so violently that Scott had to look away, as it was nauseating. It was as if a giant had grabbed the tree and shook it bare. When Scott looked back, the tree trunk was denuded from twenty feet above the ground. Not a branch was in place. All that he saw was a twenty-foot stump. The tree limbs were still falling to the ground. Sergeant Cross was on the radio to let everyone know that none of the limbs had hit his squad.

The first sortie of jets pounded the bunker on the edge of the mountain. The noise and the explosions would not let up. When the pilots unassed the area, mortar rounds started coming from some unseen spot on the long ridgeline that ran north of Hill 352. The mountain made it impossible to tell exactly where the mortars were being fired. Scott went from yelling, "G0 you son of bitches, go," to "son of a bitch, fucking mortars."

After fifteen rounds, the mortars stopped. Someone must have determined that they could be hitting their own bunker line. No one from Bravo had gotten wounded or killed. Night was on them and the war was, for the moment, stopped.

Scott was waiting for the small arms fire to start and it did not, he radio-checked his platoon and all were accounted for. They had not lost a person. Scott was able to get his last two squads up on the mountain top and in position before dark.

They were in the strangest perimeter of the war. They used as much of the jungle area as was possible. He had the men put out trip flares, even on the side of the mountain. With no enemy fire, he moved forward and made personal contact with Sergeant Cross. That was the first time that he had seen those men since getting to the top of the mountain.

When the last of two squads were in position he had more M-60's on the line. He felt that he had some possibility of defending this side of the small hill.

Delta Company had come up to join Bravo. They were positioned with Bravo's second and third platoon who were flanked out from the west side of the small hill. With communications with the other platoons, he felt better, but with the number of enemies so close, there was no thought of sleeping. The enemy could do an all-out attack, bring in more mortars, or wait out the night. Scott checked the jungle area for any possibility of a tunnel.

The night went without incident. The first thing in the morning the war started over again. There was small arms fire from the NVA. The US started and kept bringing in more planes, and gunships. M-60 machine gun fire along with M-16, and M 79 fire was keeping the machine gunners who were in the bunkers quiet.

In the afternoon, mortars were being fired by the NVA and Lt. Ron Adams was killed by a mortar round. He was sitting in his foxhole when the mortar apparently went off on the hillside above his position and killed him. Scott's foxhole was on the other side, in line with Ron's. If that round had hit just a few meters to the east, it would have been Scott that did not hear the last mortar round.

During the battle on that second day, Scott's radioman went down with heat stroke and was medevaced. Lt. Adam's body was extracted and taken back to LZ Baldy. As night closed in, the war got quiet. Scott found that he was able to move around in the jungle area. He found that on the south side of the small hill there was a line of good-sized rocks. The rocks were four to five feet tall and that gave him some additional perimeter.

During the late afternoon on the second day, Scott and Doc B had moved out of the jungle area using the rocks as protection. They made it to a position where Scott could see all the NVA perimeter. He found out that Bravo had been reinforced with troops from Delta 1/6th and they were positioned with the second and third platoon.

Delta Company began to advance on the bunker line and Scott and his platoon were giving support. As Scott and Doc B watched, Delta's men were moving forward. There was heavy firing from both sides. AK-47 fire was coming from the NVA and one of Delta's men went down in the heavy fire. The men who were moving forward with the man had all hit the ground and did not see him get hit. Scott alerted his platoon and he had them double down on their base of fire. Scott and Doc B ran close to the ground and zig zagged their way out to the man.

The man was hit in the left chest and they were trying figure out how to pick him up and protect the other lung. As they stood up, an AK-47 went off and Doc yelled, "I'm hit!" Scott gave him a once over and said, "You ain't fucking bleeding! Let's get the fuck out of the son-of-a-bitch's field of fire." Scott's could feel the intensity of the firing increase as they ran back to the rocks.

The NVA line was still cutting down on the two men as they made the safety of the rocks. Once behind the rocks, Scott was firing at the son of a bitches. He heard someone say, "Fuck you, you sonofabitches." That pretty much summed up the feelings of every Bravo company soldier on the hill. It also emphasized how close the enemy was to their position.

As the gunners were firing at them rock chips were flying onto their heads. Scott thought about the number of times he had seen bullets ricochet off a rock in a western movie. He knew that this was not a movie and those were real bullets flying by. The war was at full strength and he left the wounded man with Doc and moved behind the rocks to get back to his platoon.

The fighting broke off as night was once again on them. Scott sat with his new radioman in his foxhole and watched into the black night. All night he kept shaking off sleep. On the third morning, there was no sign of enemy activity. The NVA who had been in the tunnel complex were gone. They had boogied during the night and this battle was over, for today.

Hill 352 had cost Bravo and Charlie Companies 2 KIA, 25 WIAs, and 5 heat strokes. All been taken off the hill. The quiet on that mountain was surreal. As he walked the perimeter, Scott felt like he would be cut down at any time. He ran into Doc B. Doc who took his billfold out of his side pocket and opened it. There laying between pictures was a projectile from an armor piercing AK-47 round. Scott told Doc that billfolds could not get a Purple Heart.

Doc looked at Scott with a funny expression on his face, and asked, "Sir, what's wrong with your face?"

Scott said, "I am having a hard time seeing out of my left eye, but it does not hurt."

Doc took a mirror out of his pack and told Scott to look at himself. The left side of his face was completely swollen, from his hairline to his chin. He could not even see his left eye.

Doc said, "Sir, you need to go in and have that checked out!"

Scott told him, "It is alright and there is no one to take my place. I will stay in the field and it will probably go back down."

Doc had seen this in all infantrymen and went to Plan B. Doc said, "Sir, you could go blind!"

Scott thought for minute about the prospect of blindness, and relented, "Okay, Doc, get me off this fucking mountain."

The Morgue

Doc alerted him that a Huey slick and not a Medivac was coming in and taking him back to LZ Baldy. If the forward hospital at Baldy could not do anything, then he would need to go back to the Chu Lai hospital. Scott turned the platoon over to a squad leader and headed for LZ Baldy on a resupply chopper.

When the chopper sat down at LZ Baldy, Scott was

approached by an E4, who verified that he was Lt. Ledbetter. He then asked him to come with him to the morgue to give a positive identification on Lt. Adams.

Scott's heart was in his throat as he walked through the door of the morgue. It was little more than a squad tent stretched over a wooden frame. As he walked through the door, two things hit him simultaneously, refrigeration and the smell of death. The forty-watt bulbs which were strung across the top of the tent cast a dim shadowy countenance on the four bunk-like structures on the far wall. The corpsman walked to one of the bunks and pulled back a poncho curtain. There was Ron lying with his eyes closed in the sleep of the dead. Scott closed his eyes and said a prayer for the man's soul.

The corpsman asked, "Is this Lt. Ron Adams?"

Scott shook his head and weakly said, "Yes."

He signed the papers and tried to leave but could not move his feet. The corpsman clearly understood this reaction, as he did not move or interrupt. Both men stood and stared at the corpse for a long time. Finally, the memories of the dead man released Scott, and he was able to turn and go back out into the sunshine.

The driver took Scott to the medical facility on Baldy. The doctor looked at Scott's eye and swollen face. He gave him some medicine and put him on an IV. He was told to lie down and rest, an offer that was music to a man who had not slept in three nights. With the medicine, an IV, and two nights of sleep, the swelling went down.

His Last Patrol

Scott returned to the field after three days in the Baldy Aid Station. The swelling in his face was gone. They never figured out what was wrong, but three days of bed rest had been a welcome relief from the continuing onslaught of contact for now two weeks. In his absence, Bravo had been pulled onto LZ Center and was occupying an old night laager that sat just outside the fence. The Que Son Valley was spread out below.

When Scott arrived back in the field, he was told to report to the Tactical Operations Center. He was given the mission to retrieve the body of a soldier from Company D 1/20th.

After picking up the bodies from the downed helicopters, Delta had led them towards Hill 352.

Delta had made it to the trailhead on the north side of the ridge line to Hill 352. That trail head was three kilometers north of the mountain top. After making the turn and heading south, they came under heavy fire from dug in NVA positions. That battle was going on at the same time that Bravo was knocking out the anti-aircraft gun.

After two days and a lot of casualties, Delta had been pulled off the ridge line and they were directed to return to LZ Center. They were following a stream bed towards LZ Center when they were ambushed. Delta had lost five KIAs and had seven WIAs. Two of the KIAs were Missing in Action. One body had been located and Scott's platoon was to bring the man's body in so it could be sent home.

The news of the ambush shook Scott as he had met the platoon leader when they worked together at the sight of the two downed choppers. According to the operations sergeant on Center, the lieutenant had been hit three times and had lived. He had also killed the man who shot him. Scott checked with intelligence to find out what else had been going down, in the Que Son Valley. There had been contact by some unit every day.

On the way to find his platoon, he stopped at supply to pick up a body bag. Just the thought of having one in his backpack made his skin crawl. When he told the men of the mission and went over the map with his squad leaders, he knew that there was no need to sugar coat it. These were battle-hardened men with months of experience in the field. They had been with him in the Que Son Valley, when they had secured the choppers and policed up the bodies. They knew that they were going into a heavily contested area.

There were two trails heading towards the area where the ambush took place. Scott talked it over with his squad leaders and decided to take the trail that would keep them on a mountain ridge as long as possible. This would make the going slow, but it reduced the chance of being ambushed. There really was no reason to hurry as the man had been lying out there for five days.

The platoon plodded through some dense jungle as they moved down what was laughingly noted as a trail on the grid map. They had to pick their way through the heavy undergrowth to stay on or near the top of the ridgeline. When the platoon got even with the grid coordinates of the ambush, they turned left and headed down the mountain side. With so much activity and so much happening in the valley, Scott wanted a place to move back to, if and when they got hit. He positioned one squad on a natural crest of the mountain that they were moving down. That ridgeline was a hundred meters above where the ambush had taken place.

Because of the density of the jungle, the ambush squad would not be able to see them in the valley, but with the PRC 25's for radio communication they could stay in touch. If the platoon needed the support, the third squad could be there faster than anyone else. They could also provide fire if the platoon had to back out of the ambush sight because of heavy contact.

The two remaining squads moved down the mountain. When they got to the slew that ran towards the ambush sight, they turned to the right. Scott used everything that he had ever been taught about moving through a contested area. They moved very slowly and used every caution in the books. They rounded a bend in the slew and the valley opened up so that they could see several meters ahead.

They reached a spot where Scott could see that this was where the NVA had sprung the ambush. He had been told by the LZ Center Tactical Operations people that the Lt. was shot by someone hiding in a tunnel right where the platoon was when the ambush was sprung. That did not give Scott any good feeling about this mission.

They spotted the dead soldier several meters to their front. Scott doubled down on caution, as they kept to the right side of the opening. When they got close, the stench of a body left in one-hundred-and-twenty-degree heat and one hundred percent humidity was indescribable.

The man was sitting in a depression in the ditch, facing away from them. When they got to the body they saw that the man's rear end was down in a depression and that the NVA had covered his body from his knees to his chest with loose dirt. There was communication wire sticking out of the loose dirt.

When Scott saw the loose dirt, he knew that it had been dug up and shoveled over the body in the last few hours. The dirt was freshly dug, and this heightened his anxieties. He warned everyone to watch for tunnel openings as that is what got the lieutenant wounded. He felt like they were being watched and that they were walking into an ambush. The NVA knew that they would send a unit to police up the body. They had booby trapped that body to punish the unit sent.

Scott knew that he was dealing with a booby-trapped body and he had to come up with a plan to get the body out of the dirt without it blowing up. When he pulled the body bag out of his backpack, he found the eight-foot length of rope that he always carried. He determined that the best way to get the man out of the dirt was to pull him out. If they tried to dig him out with entrenching tools, they could set off a booby trap and get blown up in the process.

Scott tied the rope around the man's boots and had everyone get down, close to the ground. He wanted his squads away from the body, in case there was an explosive device tied to a tree nearby. Scott and two other men were lying on the ground behind the dirt that the NVA had shoveled onto the man. They were pulling on the rope as hard as possible and Scott was praying that nothing blew up or that the man did not come apart.

Scott had never dealt with death on such a personal, man to man basis. He did not know if the body could pull apart after five days. Slowly the body began to move. The men kept crawling away and pulling the rope as the man's body came over the mound of dirt. At last the head came over the mound.

Scott was still afraid that a communications wire was hooked to a secondary booby trap that was close to the body. He wanted to make sure that none of the communication wire had any connections with any explosive. After the man's body was clear of the hole, they just kept pulling it away from the depression.

The stench made everyone want to wretch. Scott kept telling everyone to choke back throwing up. He told them that it was impossible to defend themselves while they were upchucking from their heels. No one threw up, but lord it was close. After placing the body into the body bag, they cut down bamboo trees with a machete and used two bamboo shafts to carry the body up the hill. The stench for the four body carriers was unbearable. Every few hundred feet they would rotate the men carrying the body. They started moving back up the mountain towards the position of Scott's ambush squad. They used every tactic that gave them the best chance of survival should an ambush happen.

He contacted his ambush squad and found out that they had ambushed a squad of NVA who were on the way to the body's location. Scott's own ambush had cut down on the NVA. They did not know if any enemy was killed, but they had taken them by surprise. They turned and ran back from where they had come from. Everyone in the squad was okay.

Scott and the squad leader of that ambush sight had set up a place where they could safely meet. Radio communications can be misleading, and they had to ensure that the two units would not be shooting at one another. Everything went off as planned. When the body made it to the meeting point with the ambush squad, the men who had not been at the sight of the ambush started to gag. They could not believe what the rest of the platoon had been through.

Getting back up the mountain on the ridge trail took a long time, but Scott knew that this trail reduced the chance at being ambushed. Two hours after they left the ambush site, they reached LZ Center. They put the young man on a chopper and headed him toward home, wherever that was. As the chopper was flying out of sight, Scott realized that he did not know the young man's name. That made him feel bad as he should have taken the time to just look at the dog tags. He knew that the last patrol that the young man had been on was with his platoon. While he was a silent member, he had become a brother to the men who had risked their lives to bring him back from the jungle.

Combat Wounded

Scott sat there by his tent on radio watch, as he had been for hours. This was a repeat of the night of the mortars. The hours had slipped away, and he could hear Yancy snoozing away and wished that he could do the same. Scott was trying to recapture his commitment to the war effort, but that was not going to happen. Even though he was sitting in the middle of a combat zone, he was no longer committed to the war. The battles in the last four weeks, along with the dead and wounded, had taken away the purpose that he thought that he was fulfilling as a combat infantryman.

Just the week before, on May 25, his company was heading up a long and narrow valley that was completely overgrown. The trail stayed on the west side of the narrow valley and a mountain stream meandered down the valley between the two mountains. On this day, they had dodged the bullet as there had been no contact with the enemy. At 1330 hours, they stopped to take a break. Scott reminded the squad leaders to have everyone fill up canteens. In the next hour or two they would be heading up and away from the water to a night laager. Water in this stream was the clearest that he had ever seen. Normally the water in the jungle was brown and dirty.

The trail that they were hiking up was a few meters from the stream. When they stopped, four of his men went to get water from the stream. As they started to fill their canteens, an NVA officer and his radioman walked out on the far side of the stream some fifty meters from where they were getting water. The officer was looking downstream for the American unit that was coming up the valley. The men forgot about the water and cut down on the two men. When they did, the war broke out. Suddenly the valley was filled with gun fire. Neither side of the skirmish could see the other as the jungle was so thick.

While this had been an accidental contact, it was very serious. It got more so when the NVA started to drop 60 mm mortars down the tube from some place east of where they were positioned. The Company Commander called for air support. Before the O-1 spotter plane came on board, the NVA broke contact and disappeared. Scott believed that the

NVA knew that the jets were on the way and that is why they broke contact. He also figured that since the NVA had only seen four men, they had no idea the size of the force that they were up against.

The mortar fire had killed one of the Bravo soldiers. His squad brought his body to the Command Post wrapped in his own poncho. The man had been in country less than three weeks. Scott shook his head in disbelief when he saw that the man's fatigues were still green. The officers now had to figure out how to get this man extracted. There was no way they were going to leave someone in the jungle. Scott had just gone through the experience of bringing a corpse in after five days in the jungle and that was not going to happen.

The jungle trees were very high in the narrow valley and the ground cover was thick. There was no way to get the man's body extracted by chopper in this location. The Air Force 0-1 was by then on station. He was asked if there was a place for a body extraction. He had them pop smoke, so he would know where Bravo was located. Once identified, he told them that at the top of the mountain to the west there was a large banana grove. That might give them a place to extract the man's body.

They made the decision to move up the four-hundred-foot mountain to the west with the body. Once there they would try for an extraction. The move upward was at best daunting. They did not have a body bag. The man's body was wrapped in his poncho. They tied both ends of the poncho and used it to pull the man's body up the jungle covered mountain.

Everyone took their turn at this task. It was slow going

and heat exhaustion was taking its toll on everyone. There was no trail and they just had to make a path with a machete to get the body to the top of the mountain. They found the banana grove, but the trees were too tall to get a chopper close enough for an extraction. The company had two machetes and they used those knives to whack the banana trees off six feet above the ground. The extraction chopper had to be that low for the body to be passed up to the crew.

While the trees were being cut, the company set up a perimeter on the east side of the banana grove. A hole wide enough for a chopper to come down was cut into the banana grove. They called for an extraction. When the chopper came down to extract the body, they discovered that they had missed a couple of trees. The pilot used his rotors as a weed whacker.

He slowly lowered the blade while it was cutting off small chunks of banana tree. He managed to get close. They had hoped that the skids would be setting down in the cut off banana trees. The pilot could not get the bird down any further or they would not make it out of the opening. It took Herculean strength and a singleness of purpose to get one end of the poncho high enough for the crew to pull the body into the chopper. Everyone had to stretch and push until the crew could grab the end of the poncho and pull the man's body into the chopper.

As soon as the body was secured in the chopper, the pilot immediately started lifting up above the trees. When he had cleared the trees, he leaned the chopper into the south and got the hell away from there. When the whop of the blades was bleeding off into the east, that sound was replaced with mortars being dropped down the tubes. With mortars incoming, the entire company was sprinting across the banana grove towards the hard jungle to the west.

Banana trees do not stop mortar rounds. A mortar round will blow shrapnel through the tree and kill anyone on the far side. The only choice that the company had was to get everyone back into the hard jungle where the wood in the trees would hopefully stop a mortar round.

There were six men who had worked to get the man's body up to the chopper. With mortar rounds incoming, they were all scurrying back to where they had stacked their rifles and packs. All the men were running flat out towards the hard jungle to their west. Scott was the sixth man in the column.

He was ten feet away from the hard jungle when a mortar round hit the banana tree that he was running past. Shrapnel came ripping down onto his helmet, hitting his neck and shoulders. The impact of the mortar blast drove Scott towards the hard jungle and smashed him into a large and uncaring tree. The collision cold-cocked him. Two men who were running from the perimeter on the far side of the banana grove, saw Scott slam into the tree and get knocked out. They risked their lives to come back to pick up a fellow infantryman. They put Scott's arms over their shoulders and began running.

Scott was trying to come to his senses as they ran. He thought that he was running and later found out that his feet were just dragging on the ground. Scott tried to evaluate their situation, but his thoughts and his head were a mess.

They kept running through the hard jungle, until the mortars stopped. When they stopped, Doc Lee found them.

He got Scott's attention and then he started asking Scott questions about how he felt.

Scott asked him, "Why so many damned fool questions?"

Doc said, "Sir, you are hit!"

"Where?" Scott asked, confused.

Doc Lee said nothing. He took off Scott's helmet. The cover had a six-inch hole in the helmet camouflage cover. Doc had the men take off Scott's pack and he began to cut away his T shirt. He showed the bloody mess to Scott. That made him very woozy. The men helped him sit down while Doc took out fragments of mortar round. That hurt like hell. He then used water and hydrogen peroxide to clean out the wound. That got Scott's attention. At last the wounds were field dressed.

After treating the wounds, Doc asked, "Sir, do you want to be medevaced?"

Scott, who was starting to be able to reason, knew that the only place he could be medevaced was from that banana grove. He knew that that was not a good option. He opted to be left in the field and have Doc dress his wounds. He knew that there was no one to take his place and he did not want his platoon left in the hands of their company commander. He figured if the wound started to become infected that he could go in for treatment at that time.

Scott had a clean T shirt in his backpack and with some effort was able to get the shirt on over the wounds. His backpack looked like it had been in its own war. The top flap was shredded, and hot shrapnel had melted holes in the rest of the pack. The two men who had rescued Scott stayed with him as they walked. Scott was not very steady on his feet.

The company kept moving until they found a decent night laager. They settled in for the night. The next morning Scott was sore as hell. His face felt like he had collided with a tree. His shoulder and neck were hurting. Every day Doc would come and dress the wound and every day he would say that Scott needed to be medevaced and have the wounds cleaned out.

Promoted, But No Party

Scott thought about his promotion to Company Commander in the early light of this morning and came to the realization that he had been the CO since the mortar attack. The only thing that changed with the new responsibility was that battalion was sending him the daily checkpoints. Battalion did not mention that he was the new Commanding Officer.

He wished that being the commander of a field unit would have come by way of an actual promotion. That would have been a little bit formal, but in combat nothing is formal.

The field promotion was really not much different than when he made first lieutenant. A couple of months before, he had received a sheet of orders in a manila envelope. It simply listed his date of rank to first Lt. He was not able to go to the club and have a beer with his buddies and celebrate his promotion, so the biggest day of his military career passed without any recognition. Scott read and reread the orders. Just before the sun set, he folded up the typewritten document and stuck the sheet into the plastic pouch that he used to carry his writing material. That was the big celebration for his promotion.

Scott knew that he could handle the pressure of the position, but something inside of him had changed. He knew that it had been a pivotal point in his young life. He was not sure of all that that entailed, but he knew that he had mentally changed. He tried to think of all the things they taught him in OCS about being a field commander, but he could not get the images from last night to leave his mind. Overriding their impact was impossible.

He could not remember how long it had been since he laughed or was just happy about something. He could not remember the last time he smiled.

Fort Polk

He thought about when he was stationed at Fort Polk, LA with his friend Gordon.

It was Saturday evening and they were on the way to De Ridder, just to have a beer at the tavern. They were on a two-lane highway when the traffic came to a stop in the middle of the scrub pine timber. They were waiting for someone to turn left off the highway, into the timber. Three of four cars turned left off the two-lane highway and headed down a dirt road into the timber.

Scott and Gordon decided that that many people, going to the same place on a Louisiana Saturday night, meant that there was a party. They followed the three cars down through the timber. Gordon said he could hear the Banjo playing in the background. After a mile or so they came out into a clearing and there sat ten cars out in front of a house that had been turned into a true country bar. At the far end of the house they had built a metal building where a garage would normally sit.

There was no name on the bar. When they walked in through the front door, there was a bar in what used to be a kitchen, to the right. The living room and dining room had tables and chairs. Beyond the tables, there was that metal building. It had a dance floor and a stage had been built on the far end. On stage a woman was playing an accordion and singing. Her name was Zelda and Gordon named the place "Zelda's Cordine Club."

When they walked into the dance hall area, there was one table for eight with only six people sitting at the table. Gordon asked if the two empty chairs were open. They indicated that no one was sitting there, so Gordon and Scott sat down and joined their party. As others came in, the two men were sitting with locals. Consequently, the other locals welcomed them. It turned out to be one of the best nights that Scott and Gordon spent at Fort Polk. They danced with the ladies and drank beer with the men.

Scott had to go to the rest room, and they pointed back into the bar area. He was directed to a hallway off the old kitchen. When he opened the door to the latrine, he happened to look down before stepping into the room. When he looked down, he saw that the floor to the bathroom was a foot below the door. On the far side of the room the floor had sunk even further. It was at least six inches lower on that side of the room. The stool was balanced on top of a pipe that sat sixteen inches out of the floor.

Scott cautiously stepped down into the room. On the far wall, across from the door, he saw a strange outline. It was a ghostly looking face and there were handprints on either side of the ghostly figure. He realized that if he had opened the door and walked in, without stopping, that his face would have been planted on that wall. His handprints would have been next to his face. He would have done a full gainer into that wall.

He worked his way across the slanted floor to the stool and finished his business. He went to wash his hands and saw that someone had removed the gooseneck under the sink. The water to wash his hands was spilling out onto the floor and making a mad dash for the outside wall. He shook the water from his hands as there were no towels. Then as the Cajuns would say, "He unclimbed the restroom."

When he returned to the table, everyone knew about the rest room. They were all anxious to hear about Scott's adventure. They were disappointed that he had not fallen into the room.

Gordon decided to go to the restroom. Scott was considering not telling him about the drop in the floor but relented. He clued him in before he headed for the toilet.

Gordon came back to the table a few minutes later, laughing uncontrollably. He had climbed down into the rest room and was taking care of his business, at the stool. A man opened the door and walked in, which meant that he put a full-face print on the plywood. When that happened, Gordon started to laugh. The man must have needed to go badly, as he worked his way along the wall, past Gordon. He then used the sink as a urinal. With no gooseneck on the sink, he was peeing on his own shoes. The man kept looking at Gordon as he thought that he was peeing on him.

Gordon had a hard time climbing out of the bathroom, because he was laughing so hard. Scott remembered Gordon telling his bathroom story and holding onto the table to keep from falling off his chair. He had all their new-found friends laughing. The memory of that night made Scott smile, and that felt good.

The only other thing that made him happy, since coming to the field months earlier, had happened seven days earlier, in a jungle night laager. Captain Reeds, the company commander, told him that the company was going to be pulled out of the field for a stand down from combat. Reeds fenced his reply, when asked where they were going, but he did say that the choppers would be picking them up at 0800 the next morning.

Scott remembered telling his men that they were going in for a stand down. He did not remember laughing, but he was relieved that they would be out of the field and on some beach, somewhere. Scott knew that other companies had gone to Cam Ranh Bay, which was by the South China Sea. He was so looking forward to being out of the jungle and away from combat for a couple of days. Having no perimeter to watch or jungle patrols to go out looking for a war would be a blessing beyond measure.

Last Week's Stand Down

It seemed impossible but six days ago choppers were picking them up to go for a stand down. He remembered being happy as those choppers were on their way into the small opening in the jungle. They were going to take him someplace where he could just get drunk and chill out for a few days.

The choppers showed up right on time to police up their young asses and take them someplace where they could just unwind, drink a cold beer, and get to know each other as human beings. To make it through combat, men had to become "that other person". That person was on alert one hundred percent of the time. Laughing was seldom, if ever, heard in the jungle. By becoming that other person, the soldier was just trying to stay alive until tomorrow. Scott hoped to get to know his men's "other self".

When the Huey's took off, Scott expected them to turn right towards the South China Sea. Instead they turned left and started flying toward Laos. Twenty minutes later he could see that they were beginning to circle in preparation for landing. Looking down, Scott saw where they were going for their stand down. From the air, it was the sorriest location in the world. Their battalion commander and their captain had given them three days of rest and relaxation on a landing zone which was less than two kilometers from the Laotian border and the Ho Chi Minh Trail.

While the LZ looked bad from the air, it looked twice as bad when they got to the ground. The LZ, along with being completely misplaced, was totally understaffed. There was an artillery battery on the LZ. The battery set at the north end of the LZ. There was just enough crew to man the guns twenty-four hours a day. So, a third of the men on the LZ were asleep while a third of them manned the battery. No one carried a weapon inside the perimeter.

The landing zone was four hundred meters long and thirty meters across. At the north end where the artillery battery was set, the perimeter bellied out to give more room for the cannons. When a chopper landed, its prop came close to spinning over both sides of the perimeter fences.

While other infantry companies were taking a stand down from combat on the beaches in Cam Ranh Bay, Co B's stand down was a stone's throw from the Ho Chi Minh trail. That trail ran parallel with the Laotian border. The LZ was aptly named as it was forward of any landing zone in their area of operation. The NVA had been shuffling battalions down the trail for weeks and Scott figured that it would take a thirty second chopper ride to be in Laos.

Lt. Ledbetter stepped off the chopper and just looked around with his mouth hanging open. All the hills around this LZ were higher than the hill where the LZ was located. That meant that it was lower than any mountain in the area. It had been selected by an officer who had no experience in combat, was a moron, or some combination of both.

As soon as the men unassed the Huey's, the pilots quickly retreated towards Chu Lai. Once the whopping of those rotors bled off into the east, there was more than a small let down. Every man just stood there with their packs on their backs and rifles in hand. Nobody moved. This was the most miserable place that any of them had been since coming to Vietnam. It was even worse than a night laager in the jungle.

Captain Reeds, on the other hand, was acting like this was better than he expected. Scott had thought that Reeds was the stupidest son-of-a-bitch that ever wore a pair of combat fatigues. His actions at the LZ was making this fact even more obvious. Pathetic would have been giving this place an upgrade.

Scott had envisioned that they would be in a secure place on a beach and here they were assigned a section of a perimeter. Scott's platoon was given the side of the LZ that faced Laos. It appeared on his map that they were damned near "in" Laos as there was less than an inch of map between LZ Forward and the Laotian border.

After dropping his pack next to what was to become his "command bunker", Scott walked his side of the perimeter. The bunkers were filthy. Each one was filled with old ration boxes, cans, and paper. Most were infested with field mice. The platoon spent two hours of their "stand down" from combat cleaning the bunkers and making them livable.

The perimeter wire was mired in mud and no attempt had been made to make the perimeter secure. Even a short NVA would have no problem walking through the concertina wire, without catching anything. There was only twelve inches of wire above the mud. Scott brought his squad leaders together and told them that they would need to get the bunkers cleaned out and try to figure out something to keep the enemy from coming in and killing them. The men started emptying out months of old paper that had been chewed by mice.

In the middle of the clean-up, Reeds summoned Scott to the command bunker. His platoon had been picked to go out on a combat patrol. That is just what everyone on a stand-down wants: a fucking combat patrol. A very frustrated Scott and his radio man, Yancy, made their way to the tactical operations bunker for LZ Forward. Captain Reeds was using this bunker as his command bunker.

Militarily speaking, Scott's meeting with Reeds did not go well. Scott walked into the bunker and had to duck down as his head was touching the ceiling. Captain Reeds was talking to another captain, who was the tactical operations commander for Landing Zone Forward. Reeds ignored that Scott was standing three feet from him. The two men were talking about how important this stand down was for field troops. It would boost their morale and give them some down time. The men in Bravo needed time away from the field. Scott could not imagine that anyone with two licks of sense would think that this was a decent place for a stand down.

Scott had first met Reeds in Ft. Lewis, Washington. While at Fort Polk he had gotten orders to report to "A" packet at Fort Lewis. "A" Packet was made up of four hundred troops who were being shipped to Vietnam. Captain Reeds was the commander of "A" packet. A few hours after reporting into Ft. Lewis, Scott was summoned by Reeds to come to his office. Normally this was a time to sit down and get to know the commander and for the commander to get to know his officers. When Scott came into the office Reeds did not come out and greet him. He stood up behind his desk and waited for Scott to report to him as the company commander.

After saluting and reporting in, Scott was left standing

in front of the desk. Reeds sat down without offering Scott one of several chairs in the room. Reeds began talking in a low mumbling voice. Scott could not make out what he was saying and had to lean over the desk to hear. As Scott leaned forward, Reeds leaned forward until the two men's faces were a foot apart. Scott thought that they were going to kiss each other. Reeds had just won the "I am in command and you are my lackey" contest.

Scott stayed in the leaning position in order to hear what he was being told. Reeds blathered on about how important the "A" packet was to the war effort. Scott felt like he was being recruited to get behind the war effort. He knew that when the four hundred men got to Vietnam that the packet would be dissolved. All the men would be assigned anywhere that the army needed them. Reeds then told Scott that he was important to their mission. He winked at Scott as if to say, "This is just between us girls", or "I am your buddy and I will take care of you." Scott felt a little ill that he was standing there listening to this bullshit.

Scott was hopeful that no one had seen this meeting or the kowtowing that Reeds had gotten him to do. The wink was the topping on the cake as it was as phony as a nine-dollar bill. Scott took the wink to say that this meeting was over. He straightened up and said, "Thank You, Sir", he saluted and did an about face. He walked out of the office and thanked heaven that this was just a temporary assignment.

When "A" packet got to Chu Lai, Reeds and Scott were sent to the Infantry Combat Training Group. It was a training facility for incoming soldiers. They tell the guys who are new in-country what to expect when they got to the field.

After so many months in training, Scott was past the end of his learning curve. There was not enough room in his head to add one more training session, about anything. A week later he could not remember one thing of importance that he "learned" at the training center. Four days after arriving, Scott was assigned to Company B 1/6th Infantry, 198th Light Infantry Brigade. He left Reeds and sincerely hoped to never see him again.

His new commander was Capt. Ken who was an officer with an absolute feel for combat leadership. Scott learned so much from him. Unfortunately, he was pulled from the field two months after Scott arrived. He was given a new command with more responsibility. Capt. Ken left on a slick in the morning and Reeds arrived on a slick in the afternoon.

Scott had not seen or thought of Reeds since the Chu Lai combat training center. He could not believe his eyes when Reeds unassed the chopper. He felt that God was punishing him for something. Now, months later, he was standing in a hot bunker waiting for Captain Reeds to acknowledge his presence, so he could send his platoon from their stand down on a combat patrol. He could see nothing wrong with this picture.

Reeds continued to ignore Scott's arrival for some time and continued to talk with the other captain. Finally, he turned to Scott and without a, hi—yes, or go to hell, he told him to take his platoon on a patrol west and north of Landing Zone Forward. There had been enemy movement and battalion wanted to know more about that movement.

While Reeds was talking about the mission, Scott watched the other captain's face for verification of this "enemy movement." The look on the other captain's face told Scott that this patrol was so much bull shit. Battalion had not told Reeds that there was enemy movement. Reeds wanted to show everyone that he was the HMFIC (head muther fucker in charge). The best way to demonstrate that fact was to send one of his platoons out on patrol.

After being given his mission, Scott took out his map and plotted the checkpoints. The tactical operations center had to know their location as they moved out in the valley. As he was plotting his course, he listened to Reeds and the other captain talk about how great it was that the company got to come here for their stand down.

Finally, Scott asked, "Why this place for a stand down?" He waited and got no reply from either captain. He continued, "These men have been in the field since September without a break, and you bring them to a LZ that is a stone's throw from the Ho Chi Minh trail. Why would you take men, worn out from months in the field, and drag them to this fucking hellhole and act like it was the fucking Ritz Carlton in San Francisco?"

Reeds was immediately pissed. He let Scott know that he was not happy with him and his complete disregard for military discipline. Scott knew that this was done to show the other captain (and the lone radioman in the bunker) that he was in charge. He told Scott to take his men out on patrol "as ordered!"

Scott stood there and said nothing. The bunker, while insufferably hot, had suddenly turned frigid. Scott slowly and deliberately folded his map, so the current combat patrol mission was on the top section. He asked the radioman for the radio call signs and a frequency so he could call in his checkpoints. Other than the information requested, the bunker was stone cold silent. As Scott was on his way out, he stopped and looked at both captains for a long time. Then without saying another word he headed out into the sunshine.

His radioman, Yancy, who was standing outside. said, "That did not go all that well, sir."

That comment made Scott laugh. He was able to release the tension that must have been showing in his face. Scott had a lot of respect for Yancy as he shot straight.

He said, "Yancy, we are a part of a farce, that is being heralded as a command." He then asked, "Would you round up the platoon and have them come to our command bunker with radios, weapons, ammo, and water. Tell them to be prepared to move out on patrol at 1300 hours."

The men gathered around his command bunker, Scott told them that they were going to do a sweep of the area west and north of the LZ. He gave the squad leaders the checkpoints, so they could put the points on their maps. With practiced officer communications, he made it sound like business as usual. Only Yancy knew the back story. Scott could see him mentally shaking his head in disbelief.

When you have been on patrol for several months, it matters not how or why you are in the jungle. It only matters that you are in a combat unit and you must take all precautions. Once they crossed the wire (which made up the perimeter of the LZ), the stand-down became yesterday's news. Combat is dead serious, and you do not play or take anything for granted in combat.

When Scott's platoon was ready to leave the compound, instead of walking out the south gate, they walked through the concertina wire located in front of their bunkers. Scott concluded as they stepped through the concertina wire that this place was a military disaster.

The artillery battery on LZ Forward had more than one hundred and twenty men manning the 105-mm battery of three guns. Based on what he saw, the bunkers on his side of the perimeter were not being manned. For one they were filthy and no one could live in such squalor. As near as he could tell, the only protection that this base had was dumb luck.

There was a Quad Fifty machine gun which sat a few feet from the south exit gate. It could cover the end of the base and Scott's side of the perimeter. A Quad 50 is a long-distance support weapon. Its maximum effective range is thousands of meters. However, only one troop knew how to fire the Quad Fifty and when he was asleep, the gun and its power just sat empty.

That gun is normally part of a defensive perimeter that includes M-16s, M-79s, and M-60 machine guns. All those weapons were on LZ Forward, but since no one carried a weapon, he did not see any of the fire power. The artillery unit resembled a unit that was in some stateside base.

Scott's patrol made a sweep through all the check points. He called in to the tactical operations center as they went through each check point. One of the check points was in a village which had been deserted by the farmers. Even though it was deserted, someone had been sleeping in the hooch's. With the Ho Chi Minh trail less than a kilometer away,

Scott knew that the village was being used by the NVA at night. Scott marked the position of the village on the map for artillery to use as a target when the sun went down.

They returned to LZ Forward just before sundown. When he got back to the tactical operations center, the captain of the center was the only one there. Scott reported what he had found and suggested that the artillery use the village as a target after the sun set. Scott posted guards on his side of the landing zone. Someone needed to be awake at all times.

This place was more dangerous than being in a night laager in the jungle. A jungle night laager would only be their home for twelve hours. Come morning they would saddle up and move toward the next night laager. They would spend the day moving from checkpoint to checkpoint until combat broke out or they were picked up by Huey's and inserted into some hot or cold landing zone.

A jungle night laager was strictly a temporary position for Company B. The enemy would have to know exactly where the perimeter was in order to make an assault. It was possible that NVA or Viet Cong might accidentally walk in on the company. If that happened, they would hit the trip flares that had been placed several meters outside of the company perimeter. Those flares would bring the enemy into the light and the machine guns and M-16 rifle fire would make the intrusion less than desirable.

Each platoon carried claymore mines which would be set in the area between the perimeter and the trip flares. If there was a problem, those claymores would be detonated, and anything in the path of seven hundred square steel pellets would be exterminated.

LZ Forward, on the other hand, was right where it had been since it was selected years before. The enemy knew right where the LZ was located. Scott guessed that since the LZ never bothered the NVA, the NVA never bothered the LZ. While on the landing zone, Scott's platoon was in a known location with no protection from the concertina wire. They set out trip flares many meters out past the sunken wire fence. They also lined the sunken concertina wire with claymore mines.

The next morning, Scott was out early and found many rolls of rusty concertina wire on the far side of the battalion tactical operations bunker. All the years of working on his dad's Iowa farmstead came into play as he and his platoon worked until noon creating a concertina perimeter wire that gave the base some protection.

The area where the concertina wire was buried in the mud was forty feet long. They stretched three rolls of concertina wire the length of the opening. They put a three-wire pyramid on top of the two layers on the ground. It made for a wide and formidable barrier that was close to six feet tall. They hung "C" ration cans filled with rock on the inside of the concertina wire. If the wire was hit by anyone, those cans of rocks would make a sound like a baby's rattle. They also placed claymores on the bunker side of the wire. They left the trip flares wired and waiting outside of the wire.

The work was hot and miserable and was made more problematic because they had no real barbed wire tools. There were no gloves nor wire cutters on that hill. Soldiers from both the city and farm were learning what it was like to work with barbed wire. When they were done, the west side of LZ Forward was secure. While they were still in a combat zone, the addition of the perimeter wire made Scott feel a little less exposed. Scott still posted guards on his side. The wire would slow down anyone sent to take this miserable excuse for a landing zone.

The platoon settled into this garden paradise, as part of their "stand down from combat". As Scott stood and looked at their handiwork, he wished that the Sgts who trained him in OCS, could see what his platoon had built out of rusty wire, sweat, and Yankee ingenuity.

With two days down and one more to go, the men of the company had nothing to do, because there was nothing to do on Forward. The only entertainment was playing cards and drinking Carling Black Label beer.

The Wager

During the afternoon of the second day, Captain Reeds ordered his lieutenants to his command bunker. Scott figured that walking up and talking with his officers and men was way too civilized. Having a meeting was Reeds way to form a relationship with his officers. Scott hoped that this "meeting" would start to make this unit into a team that worked together. Reeds had not learned that the lieutenants and the men around him were going to keep his ass alive. He acted as if this was a stateside duty and he had no dependency on anyone, other than himself.

The company had three lieutenants and a captain in the field for most of the tour. Two weeks before, Ron the third platoon leader, had been killed by a mortar round on Hill

352. There had been no replacement assigned. When Scott arrived at the meeting he found Reeds talking with Lt. Fredericks, the second platoon leader. Scott attempted to join the conversation but was quickly cut off by Reeds.

He was on his favorite topic and that was how wonderful the Car-15 rifle was over the M-16. The entire company carried M-16s and Scott had his hanging on his shoulder, even in the landing zone. The M-16 was the rifle that he and the rest of the company depended on to keep them alive.

Scott guessed that Reeds did not know how to carry on a normal conversation with people. So, he talked about the one topic that was always on the top of his mind, the great CAR -15. The CAR-15 was the predecessor to the M-16 and that is what Reeds carried. Knowing it was Reeds who thought that it was a superior weapon caused Scott to doubt that it was worth a shit.

The conversation, which had quickly become a listen, was interrupted by the captain in command of the tactical operations center. He needed to talk with Reeds. As the two men headed into the TOC, Scott thought that he and Fredericks might be able to talk. Fredericks was from Tennessee. Scott always thought he was a good troop.

In the field, there is no time for anyone to sit and talk unless you are sitting in the same foxhole or sleeping in the same poncho tent. As a company, they moved all day and the last hours of sunlight were needed to prepare the perimeter, eat some chow, and get ready for the night. After months in the field, this was the first time that these two men had a chance to get to know one another. It was soon apparent that Fredericks did not care to talk to Scott.

Fredericks had been with the company since basic training and was part of the officer crew who was assigned to the unit at Fort Hood, Texas. This meant that he was one of the originals and if you were an original, then you were special. The officers in that group held themselves above any officer that was a replacement. Scott had been a replacement. Fredericks was doing his level best to ensure that Scott was not treated as one of the good guys.

After trying to start a conversation and getting no-where, Scott finally just shut up and said nothing. Reeds came back from his meeting and Scott hoped that they could just talk and get to know one another. However, as soon as Reeds walked back in, he started bragging about the prowess of his chosen weapon and how it was far superior to the sorry M-16.

Scott tried to change the subject, but to no avail. The Car-15 was brought up again and Scott jokingly said, "I think that the cyclic rate of fire on the M-16 is faster than the CAR-15". Instead of taking it as a good-natured ribbing, Reeds jumped to the defense of his rifle. He whipped out his billfold and pulled out a twenty-dollar military script note. He said, "I'll bet that the CAR-15 will out fire the M-16 on its worst day."

"Lord have mercy," Scott said to himself. Scott tried to fend off the bet, but Reeds was passionate that this had to be settled once and for all. Scott really had no idea which was faster, and quite frankly really did not give a shit. He just wanted to get back to his platoon and some sanity.

News of the wager hit the coconut highline. Within minutes every soldier who had nothing to do, which was everybody, readied for the contest. Reeds had two twenty-five round banana clips taped together on his Car-15. The only advantage of this double clip was the number of bullets you carried close to the weapon. Scott figured that Reeds thought it made him look like a bad ass.

Scott used a regular twenty round magazine for his M-16. He only carried eighteen rounds in a magazine. He was concerned that if the spring was fully compressed that it might jam the weapon in a firefight. The outcome of a jammed weapon in a firefight would not have been good.

The entire company and a lot of the artillery men gathered on the east side of the tactical operations center. To keep the contest fair, Scott and Reeds turned over an empty magazine to the men in the company. Those magazines were to be filled with the same number of rounds.

The magazines with fresh ammunition were handed to the two contestants. They put the clips into their weapons, and someone gave the order to commence firing. Bullet casings were flying out of both weapons. Scott was lowering his rifle to the ground as the last rounds were coming out of the Car-15.

Reeds would not even look at Scott. He saw nothing funny or even good natured about the whole event. He took a twenty-dollar military script note and slammed it in Scott's hand. He did not talk, and he just stomped off in the direction of the TOC. Scott knew that this was not good, but he doubted that he would hear about the CAR-15 superiority again.

As Scott was walking back to his bunker, one of the men who had loaded the two magazines, indicated that Scott's magazine was a little light on the number of rounds. Scott listened, smiled, and just kept on walking.

NVA in the open

The next morning Scott walked up the perimeter to the Quad Fifty machine gun position. He had fired a fifty-caliber single barrel but never a Quad fifty. He asked the young man if he could fire a few bursts. The man said yes and then took some time to fiddle with a setting on the gun. While he was working on the weapon, Scott picked up the 7 X 50 binoculars, which were hanging on the back of the gun stand and glassed the hills of Laos.

When he was scanning the rice paddies that ran along the Laos side of the valley, he saw NVA soldiers scurrying across an open rice paddy dike, as they moved down the Ho Chi Minh Trail. He immediately saw what the NVA commander was doing. He was short cutting his trip south. The immense rice paddy, which covered the valley, bellied inward toward the mountains. If he had taken his men around this huge rice paddy, they would have stayed hidden in the jungle. However, it would add two or more hours to his southern trek.

Since no one from LZ Forward had ever noticed this movement, the NVA commander had no reason to believe that this time would be any different. He took the short cut and was sending a few men at a time across the hundred-meter rice paddy dike. Unfortunately for that NVA commander, there *was* infantry on the LZ, and he was about to discover the difference between an Infantry unit and an artillery unit.

Jungle covered both sides of the rice paddy dike. Scott was not sure how many men had already run across the opening or how many were left on the north side. He called the

LZ artillery battery commander, who came on the hot foot. When he arrived, he determined that he needed to have artillery fire from LZ Center. He could not crank down his 105 mm howitzers to hit the position. He got on his radio and asked for support from faraway LZ Center.

LZ Center had a battery of large artillery pieces that could easily reach and eliminate this NVA troop. The artillery Lt. was on the radio and he suddenly got very excited. The Artillery coordinator told him that the Battleship New Jersey was going to fire on this enemy position. Scott found out that the New Jersey could fire a sixteen-inch shell over twenty-three miles. The part of Vietnam where they were was only twenty miles wide.

Within a couple of minutes, huge 16" shells started to fly over LZ Forward on the way to the jungle on both sides of the rice paddy dike. They sounded like a car flying by, two hundred feet in the air. The New Jersey blew the areas on both sides of the rice paddy into the next century. The areas on both sides of the rice paddy dike were gone and water from the paddies soon filled in the void.

While the big shells were hitting on both sides of the rice paddy, the quad fifty machine gunner was spraying both sides of the rice paddy dike. He went through a lot of ammunition. Scott had a feeling that the man would be testing the Ho Chi Minh Trail on occasions to ensure that no one else was moving down the trail.

This was one gamble that did not pay off for the NVA. Scott figured that he had changed the way the NVA would think about coming through this area in the future. While Scott never did get to fire the Quad Fifty, he did get a fire mission from a ship that had been commissioned in 1942, the year he was born. That was way beyond cool.

The End of the "Stand Down"

In the early afternoon of the third day, of their great "stand down", Reeds called a meeting of his lieutenants and told them to prepare to move off LZ Forward later in the afternoon. The meeting only took two minutes and he did not give them any check points or an indication of where they were to night laager that night. Given the relationship that had evolved over the past hours, a tormented Scott made his way back to his command post.

Scott sat and talked with Yancy, his radioman. He was a long tall drink of water from Mississippi. Like all radiomen, in combat, Yancy was far more than just the title. Scott depended on him to be his eyes and ears. The men in the platoon were his friends. They had all trained together at Ft. Hood, Texas and came over on the boat together. Yancy would let Scott know when issues in the platoon were causing or were about to cause problems. Scott would then take care of the issue without letting the soldier know how he found out that something needed correcting.

Yancy helped him keep the platoon running smoothly. During a day in combat, as a radioman, Yancy would receive calls from the commander regarding some situation. He knew what to pass on to Scott. If it did not need Scott's immediate attention, Yancy would often take care of the situation. When a directive came that he needed to pass on to

Scott, he was very good at relating all the details so that Scott could make an informed decision.

A good radioman does not have to repeat every word he hears on the radio. He must know the platoon leader and how he thinks. Yancy knew how Scott thought and kept the flow of communications moving without too much detail. In combat, communications are vital and it was Yancy's job to take in and pass along information as quickly as possible.

Yancy was an excellent counter to Scott because he saw everything from the soldier's side. Scott never forgot the fourteen months that he spent as an enlisted man, but he still needed someone to keep him grounded. Yancy would remind Scott that everyone put their pants on one leg at a time. Scott reminded him that he had not taken his pants off for a month or two.

Often the communications between Scott and Yancy were non-verbal or done with a paucity of words. The two men were literally with each other twenty-four hours a day. They slept in the same poncho tent and walked within a few feet of each other during the day. At night, they took two hour shifts on the radio, as someone always had to be awake. Scott was able to talk to Yancy about anything. He knew that whatever he said would stay between the two men. They trusted each other with their lives, and both had each other's back.

Yancy was with Scott when they got their marching orders to walk off the LZ and as they headed back to the platoon area, he quietly said, "This man is going to get us killed." Scott said nothing in reply, because there was nothing left to say.

Scott knew that if they had stayed in the LZ and left

early the next morning that they would be able to set up their next night laager out of range of M-16s and the Quad 50. Leaving in the late afternoon meant that they could not get out of the range of either of these weapons.

Reeds moved the company out through the south gate of the landing zone at 1500 hours. Three hundred meters from the south gate of Landing Zone Forward, Reeds called a halt and said that this was where the night laager was to be set. The company settled in for the night.

Scott was on radio watch shortly after midnight when he saw someone moving towards him, inside of the perimeter. Scott said softly, "Halt, who goes there?" The shadowy figure said, "It's Captain Reeds."

Scott was amazed and whispered, "Why are you moving about in the night?"

Reeds said, "We are going to pull out of this night laager and attack that mountain across the valley."

"When are you planning on attacking the mountain?" Scott asked.

Reeds leaned towards Scott and said, "Before dawn." Scott shook his head in disbelief as one stupidity was stacking on top of the other. All the stupid was coming from one man.

Scott whispered, "Why didn't we talk about this during our meeting this afternoon?"

Reeds cut him off and said, "Get your men ready to move out, Lieutenant!"

Now the company was going to move on a target that was not planned. Scott had no map points or check points on a jungle move at night. No planning had been done and the only person who knew where they were going, was Reeds. This move was a combat disaster. In combat, disaster can find you readily and you should never give it an open door. This move was an open door.

Scott and Yancy got the platoon up and ready to move without anyone getting shot. They took a count of each squad to ensure that everyone was ready to move out. Scott's platoon was going to be the last platoon in the order of march.

There was a feeling that this move was basically fucked up and was not going to end well. The company moved out while Scott's platoon sat and waited. As the last platoon, he knew that the movement down the mountain was going to go slow. The night move was done in ten-and twenty-meter increments as the column kept starting and stopping its forward motion.

Scott had looked over his map in the late afternoon to acquaint himself with the area around the landing zone. He saw a large ditch south of the mountain and hoped that when they left, that they would head in a different direction. The ditch appeared to be more of a ravine than a ditch. The company was now moving directly towards that deep ditch.

He knew that at night there was no way to reconnoiter the area to find a good place to cross the ditch. If men were sent in either direction to search out a location, there was a good chance that the men when they came back from looking for a good crossing place would be fired on by the company.

Two hours after leaving their night laager, Scott and his men were only halfway down the mountain. They were sitting on the side of the mountain when out of the jungle, on the far side of the ditch, came a man's scream of absolute terror. As that scream echoed out across the valley, every man felt the stark fear that had been torn from the man's vocal cords. They sat in nervous readiness. The scream was followed, seconds later, by a monstrous blast that rocketed up the mountainside. That blast was followed by silence. The only sound was the sound of the night jungle.

Everyone waited for the war to break out, but nothing more happened. No man who was in that jungle on that night will ever forget that scream. It was more powerful than the cry of the Banshee from Irish Folklore. It was a man's deep-throated terrorized scream. It left nothing and everything to the imagination.

The story filtered back that a python had come out of the trees and was wrapping itself around the man's arm. He had screamed in stark terror. The man behind him had an M-79 grenade launcher. He jacked a forty-mm shotgun shell into the launcher and blew off the snake's head. The blast also wounded the soldier. This was the first python that had gone after one of the men in his company.

The snake incident was just one more reason why a company did not move at night in the jungle. The jungle always has the advantage and at night that advantage is quadrupled. He was now even more concerned for the entire company. They had started this night trek without spending a second talking about the risks and how to minimize those risks.

One of the biggest unknown pieces of this night movement was the end goal and that was attacking a mountain that was a mile away. No one knew if there were NVA on that hilltop or what kind of firepower they had. As a company, they were hard charging into what could be a massive ambush. Certainly the NVA, if they were on that mountain, knew that an army unit was coming for them. If they did not know before the scream, they certainly knew after that unworldly sound.

While everyone had been trained in Advanced Infantry Training to attack a position, neither Reeds nor this company had ever attacked a known position. The company had been in a lot of firefights and the third platoon leader had been killed on top of Hill 352. The company had walked in on an unknown NVA base camp. They had to go into combat mode but they did not attack the hill, they had simply stumbled into the fire fight.

Military intelligence did not have a clue about the huge force of NVA who were on top of 352. If they did not know about that large force, the chances of any intelligence about how many were on top of tonight's target, was slim to none. Scott thought back to the patrol Reeds had dreamed up when they were on LZ Forward. Reeds had imagined enemy movement north of the LZ and sent a patrol out to find the enemy. Here they were two days later attacking an unknown position in the middle of the night. Scott thought back to Yancy's comment, "This man is going to get us killed."

In the three days that they had spent on top of Hill 352, he did not see Reeds once. In fact, he did not even know where the man and his CP was located. The men said that he found a cave in the side of the small hill and he pulled the command post into a cave, hunkered down and never came out. Reeds had not talked with anyone in his command, save by radio, the entire time they were on the mountain. In three days, he did not see one member of his command, other than his radio operators. Two weeks later the man is acting like he is John fucking Wayne or Audie Murphy and attacking something that he knew nothing about.

It took Scott's platoon four hours to make it to the ditch at the bottom of the hill. The ditch turned out to be a twelve-foot ravine. As each man reached the bank, they had no choice but to get down on the ground and lower their feet as far as they could and let go. There was nothing to hold onto as they went down. The first men, over the embankment, used the roots and rocks to break their fall. By the time Scott's platoon arrived, all the roots were gone. Each man in Scott's platoon had to do a free fall. The rocks on the face of bank smacked them in the chin as they fell.

When they hit the ground below each man would fall on their ass and roll to a stop in the water. The noise when they hit sounded like a base drum in the silence of the jungle night. As soon as a man stopped rolling, he had to immediately get up and run across the ditch and up a six-foot embankment in order to catch up with the man in front of him.

In the jungle, even during the day, it is often hard to see the man who is in front of you. He is your contact with the entire column and if you lose sight of him, then you and the column behind can get lost. The jungle is very thick and the direction of the column ahead of you was often a wild-assed guess. You cannot yell to the man in front of you as that can get a lot of people killed. At night with no light and the same thick jungle you do not want to lose contact with the column.

When it was Scott's turn to fall down the ravine, the rocks hit his chin twice on the way down and when he hit the bottom he too, fell and rolled into the water. Along with the noise, it hurt like hell. He crawled through the water so he would not be hit by his radioman when he came down. After his fall, Scott felt the bandages on the back of his neck. They had come loose in the fall. He did not want to chance having them come off, for fear of infection. Yancy hit the ground behind him. With all his gear and the PRC 25 radio, he made an awful crash. "Are you okay?" Scott whispered.

"No, I think I fucked up my ankle. Are you okay?" Yancy whispered.

"No, I think my bandages on my neck came loose," Scott replied.

Yancy said, "When we catch up with the column I will see if Doc can re-bandage them. I wonder where in this jug fuck I will find Doc?"

Scott and Yancy found the column. They were sitting down waiting to move forward. The company had come upon a massive vine that was literally growing across the entire side of the mountain. The first light of dawn was filtering into the jungle. Scott looked at the vine and it reminded him of Kudzu, which was becoming a problem in the south. This vine was three to four inches thick and the vegetation growing from the vine made it impossible to see through. To make forward progress, each man had to crawl through what turned out to be two hundred meters of vine and ground vegetation.

Scott's platoon was just sitting in the jungle waiting. Yancy was gone for a while and came back with Doc Lee, the platoon medic.

Doc said, "I was thinking about you this morning, wondering if your bandages had held up in that fall."

He was working on Scott's neck wounds. He cleaned them with water and a peroxide solution which stung like hell, but it would keep the infection down. Doc wrapped up the wound and headed back to where Yancy had found him. Before he left, he warned, "Sir, you need to get to a hospital and have your neck checked for shrapnel."

Scott agreed and indicated that when they got in a new Lt. for the third platoon, he would go in and have his neck checked.

The Vine

Yancy told him that according to what he was hearing on the radio that the men had to take off their packs and wiggle their way through the heavy vine. At long last Scott's platoon started the long crawl through the vines. Scott discovered that they were crawling up and through and over old rice paddies, built on the side of the mountain. Every twelve feet there was a rice paddy wall that each man had to crawl up and over to get to the other side. The vine was sometimes only six to eight inches above the wall and impossible to move. Scott hit his neck wounds on several of the vines and his neck was starting to hurt like hell. Each rice paddy was higher than the last, so the company was moving up the hill. one rice paddy at a time.

Scott had made it halfway through the vine covered mountainside and was waiting for the line to move forward.

He had crawled up on a rice paddy wall and was lying there waiting for Yancy to move forward. He examined the thick vine that was just above his head. The bark was stringy, and he realized where he had seen it before.

His mom had a grapevine that stretched the length of her garden. It shaded the ground and made it cool in the hot Iowa summer. As a small boy, Scott played under that grapevine with his tractors and toy farm equipment. He realized that this massive vine was in fact a grapevine. It was four inches thick and Scott figured that it may well have been growing over this vast area for thousands of years.

It took Scott's platoon two hours to make it through to the far side of the vine covered area of the mountain. They finally reached an open area where the rest of the company was waiting. They were still in the jungle but there were no more vines. The company had been moving for ten full hours, it was already 1200 hours, and they were a long way from the top of the mountain that Reeds wanted to attack at dawn.

As they got close to the top of the mountain, the NVA began pouring rifle and machine gun fire down on them. With no surprise advantage, Reeds made one of the few tactical decisions that made sense; he pulled the company back to an open area, close to the vines. Reeds ordered the artillery forward observer to put ample amounts of artillery on the hill, something that he should have done before the assault.

With a dog-tired company of men, he did not attack the hill that afternoon. The men had been up for fifteen hours in hundred plus degree heat, and it was still mid-afternoon. The next morning, jets started to drop bomb tonnage on top of the hill. At 1200 hours the company moved out to once more assault the mountain. Amazingly, the hill was devoid of any enemy.

The NVA left plenty of booby trap reminders that they had been there. One man detonated a Bouncing Betty mine that bounced up and exploded knee high. Scott watched as the medics and some of the man's buddies carried the man to a Medivac chopper, called a Dustoff. The NVA had been positioned on this mountaintop for some time. They had tunnels and positions which could not be seen from the air. This site was set up to keep an eye on LZ Forward.

A helicopter brought Doc B out from LZ Forward. When Reeds pulled the company out of the night laager he had left Doc, never checking to see if he had all four of his admin group. If anything is drubbed into an officer's head, it is to always take a head count.

When Doc woke up in the early morning hours, he could not hear any sounds of the company. He realized that he was all alone, three hundred meters from the LZ perimeter wire and that Quad 50. He told Scott that he had never been that scared in his life; he thankfully was able to make it to the perimeter.

That confirmed Scott's opinion that the LZ's only protection was dumb luck. They posted no guards at night or during the day. Scott was glad that Doc had lived through the ordeal. The two men had earned each other's respect on Hill 352, and that was something that never went away. Having a man of Doc's caliber as part of his company meant a lot to Scott. He shuddered to think what would have happened if his platoon had gone off and left him on that hill.

Doc told Scott that LZ Forward had been hit the night

before. The next morning seven NVA were hanging on the concertina wire. The trip flares and claymores had done their job. Apparently the NVA had not gotten the memo about the perimeter wire being rebuilt by an Iowa farm boy and his platoon.

The man who had left Doc on top of that hill was the one who was hell bent on getting to the top of this mountain. With the top of this mountain "cleared" Scott figured that they would head east on this long range of mountains, but discovered they were heading south off the mountain. Reeds already had a night laager all picked out.

Night laagers were normally selected once the commanding officer saw and determined which mountain top was more defensible. In this case, Reeds had picked out a night laager with the use of grid coordinates, something which made little or no sense.

Heading off the mountain, the company was almost at what would be called a quick step as they were going down a very steep slope as fast as they could. When they got to the valley floor, they picked up the pace. Instead of walking in a combat zone, they were moving like they had to meet some deadline in a stateside maneuver. Scott's platoon was the last platoon in the order of march and had to damned near run to keep up with the column.

The valley was one of the strangest places that Scott had ever seen in Vietnam. It was a large flat valley with short grassy fields and huge patches of ten-foot jungle grass. Each patch of the tall jungle grass was a perfect place for an ambush. Scott could taste the harm. There was death in the air. Reeds took no precautions to ensure that there was no enemy in the area. No scouting parties were sent out to secure the area. He just straight line pushed south.

The presence of danger clung to the air like the one hundred percent humidity. Scott's platoon had had no communications from Reed's command group. No plan of action had been revealed beyond traveling as fast as they could go. Suddenly the column came to a stop. Scott waited for someone to say something on the radio, but no communications were forthcoming. Scott and Yancy walked up ahead to see what caused "the whoa."

Mine Field

There, running from left to right, was a long slew with barbed wire on both sides. Scott guessed the wire stretched well over three hundred meters. Skull and cross bone figures and danger warnings had been scratched out on old cardboard and stuck onto the wire. This was the first time that Scott had seen a marked mine field in Vietnam. He felt like he was in an old German war movie.

Scott looked on his map for another hill they could use for a night laager and found a decent sized one off to the east. Then he saw the unthinkable happen: the lead platoon was going over the barbed wire into that marked mine field. Reeds was putting his men at the risk of being blown apart by walking them across a marked mine field!

When it was Scott's turn to step over that wire, he had never been so scared. He stepped over the wire and morbidly memorized where the soldier in front of him had stepped.

He would step in the exact same place with his footfall. It was one of the strangest things that he had ever done.

He had to be close enough to the man in front of him to see where he stepped and far enough back to keep from becoming collateral damage. It was the most grueling fifty meters that he had walked in his life. As he stepped across the wire on the far side, he gasped a huge sigh of relief.

1. The Castle Hill June 1, 1968

Scott's platoon made it across the mine field and then walked up on the hill to their new night laager. He did not dare talk to Reeds. This son of a bitch was going to get them killed. What they had gone through for the past two days was proof of that.

Scott's platoon slid into their side of the perimeter, which was facing due west toward Laos. Sergeant Bishop took charge and got the platoon into their defensive positions. Scott could only imagine how many of the NVA had walked down the Ho Chi Minh trail which was only two kilometers away. Scott and Yancy set up their poncho tent and discussed a way to dig a foxhole in the hard pan dirt. There was a ditch a few feet away and they decided to leave their entrenching tools in their scabbards.

For some reason a trench (three meters across and a meter high) had been dug from the river to their west and continued up and over the hill where they were laagered. The builders had cut limestone and made what would be considered a nice wall on either side of the trench. Nothing special had been done to the floor of the trench, which was hard pan dirt and stone. Over the centuries, clumps of trees had begun to encroach on the bottom of the trench. Those clumps had stopped sticks and rocks that had been washed down in past monsoons.

At the top of the hill, on the north side of the trench, the builders had left a ten-foot opening in the wall. They had dug out a large round circle five meters across. The same limestone rocks that walled both sides of the ditch were used around the circle. It looked like the beginning of a castle tower in Europe. What the builders were planning was anyone's guess. Its original purpose, at this late date, was of no consequence. Reeds used the circle of stone as his Command Post. Scott decided to call the place, the Castle Hill and Reed's CP, The Circle of Stone.

As Scott walked by the Circle on his way to his Command Post, he did not stop to talk. His thoughts went back to a class in OCS on combat tactics. The sergeant told them in combat, that if it looked too easy or pat, that they needed to reconsider their decision. Setting up a CP in that Circle of Stone looked too easy.

Incoming

With his platoon in position, Scott sat down to heat up a cup of Joe. Out of the valley to the southwest came the sound of mortars being dropped down multiple mortar tubes. Eighty-two-millimeter rounds were being dropped down the tube faster than he could count. It sounded as if it was an automatic mortar piece. For the enemy to have this number of mortar tubes and mortar rounds meant that they were being fired by the NVA, not Viet Cong guerillas.

Within a few seconds, explosions were spreading across the mountain like the wind and Scott could hear screams and cries of wounded men. In the first barrage of mortars they were coming down inside or close to the Circle of Stone. The onslaught of mortar rounds could only be described as a torrent of death. Men shrieked as shrapnel ripped through their bodies.

Scott had grabbed his helmet and rifle and jumped into the ditch and immediately realized that he should have dug a foxhole. A mortar round, going off anywhere in the three-meter-wide trench, would hit him. He looked down the ditch and saw a clump of junk trees, three meters away. The clump of trees was surrounded with stones and sticks that had washed down the ditch.

The Catch

Scott was turning to head to the clump of trees when he saw a young soldier running away from the murderous mortar barrage that was ripping through the Command Post. When he was a few feet from Scott, a mortar round went off behind him. The force of the mortar round picked him up off the ground and his momentum was carrying him towards the ditch.

Scott knew that if the soldier hit the bottom of the trench from that height, that he would be killed. He set his rifle on top of the wall and maneuvered himself into position to catch the young man. He caught the man full in the chest. He was completely off balance and started stumbling and falling down the ditch. At first, he was stumbling sideways and then backward. When he got close to the clump trees he tripped over the debris in the ditch and started to fall backwards into the clump of bamboo.

Both men crashed into the bamboo trees. The trees broke their fall. Scott's helmet separated two of the bamboo trees and as he fell, both trees popped over the edge of his helmet, and locked under his jaw. He could feel the bandages on his neck being ripped off as he continued to fall. When his body reached the bottom of his fall, his back and left kidney slammed into some rocks. A pain shot down his left leg and it started to get numb. He was lying on the rocks with his head locked by the bamboo trees and he began to panic. The soldier was lying unconscious on his chest and Scott's head was locked by the bamboo trees.

Scott could not move the man from his chest and he was screaming for someone to help, but with the mortars blowing up on the hill, no one could hear him. He wondered if his death certificate would read, "Death by Bamboo."

The man momentarily regained consciousness and let out a yell and pushed his body away from Scott. Scott pushed him off his chest and clung to the man's fatigue shirt as he slid toward the ground. Scott hung on to that shirt as if his life depended on the grasp. He used the man's momentum down and away from him to pull his head out of the bamboo head lock. He felt like his ears were being ripped off his head, but at last he was free of the bamboo. The weight of the young soldier pulled both men to the ground.

Blood from the man's wounds was running down the ditch. Scott pulled out his knife and cut the man's pants leg into strips to create a tourniquet. He knew that he could lose him if he did not get the bleeding stopped. As he was working feverishly to save the man, the man grew strangely quiet. Scott thought that he had lost him, but at last he took a full breath and kept on breathing. Scott was yelling for a medic and Doc Lee appeared and said, "I have this, sir!"

As soon as Doc took over, Scott tried to stand, but his left leg collapsed. His left kidney hurt like hell and his entire left side was numb. With mortars still pouring in and men screaming, a hurting kidney was of little consequence. He had to get to the Command Post to find out why no artillery was being fired. He attempted to stand again and again his left leg would not hold him up.

Doc left the young soldier and helped Scott get back to his feet. When Scott was standing, Doc held him up long enough for him to steady himself. He helped Scott take a few tentative steps. When able to stand on his own he started limping towards the Command Post. The more he moved, the easier it was to walk. The adrenaline of combat kicked in and he started moving faster.

Circle of Death

Scott was deathly afraid of mortars and here he was running directly into a pit filled with mortar fire. He gimp-legged the twenty plus meters up the ditch to the CP. As he turned the corner into the command post, the scene before him looked like the aftermath of a bad war movie. It was his worst nightmare. Men were lying on the ground. Some of them were writhing in pain and some already dead.

Scott came to a stop just inside the circle. He could hear or feel a mortar round coming in. He threw himself to the ground as a round hit on the far side of the circle. He heard and felt the explosion and buried his head deeper into the stone wall. Shrapnel whirred by him at a thousand miles per hour. He breathed a sigh of relief: he had just beaten death one more time.

Out of the corner of his right eye he saw something coming toward him, a body was twisting and turning in the air. Scott tried to get up and catch the man before he hit the ground, but he did not make it in time. The man smashed into the ground and rolled his back up against Scott's boots. Captain Reeds' radioman had been picked up by the 82mm mortar round and thrown three meters through the air.

Scott reached down and gently shook the man's shoulder and yelled his name three times. No response. Scott did not want to roll him over, because he knew that the other side would be shredded with shrapnel. With nothing to be done for the radioman, he moved to Reeds who was wounded and lying on the ground. His head was almost touching the radioman's boots. Scott bent over Reeds to check him out.

Reeds looked up at Scott and shouted, "I'm okay, just stop the fucking mortars!"

Scott knew that the mortars had to be stopped or they would all die. Worse than that, he knew that if the mortars stopped on their own, the NVA would be mounting an all-out attack on their position. He felt something move behind him and spun around. Doc B was holding the head of a man badly wounded. Scott looked at the man and knew he would be going home in a rectangular box. Scott's gaze locked on Doc's eyes and neither said a single word. Their exchanged looks, however, spoke volumes.

Do your fucking job!

The message exchanged was one of fear, caring, and being overwhelmed with real war shit. The message was more pragmatic: Do your fucking job! Scott nodded to Doc in agreement. He then turned his attention to the two men sitting with their backs to the wall. Both men had a wide-eyed death stare and their mouths were open from their last scream.

The artillery forward observer and his radioman were within two feet of each other. No doubt one mortar round had done in both men. The Lt. had the radio mic in his hand, apparently trying to call in artillery right up to the moment when shrapnel took his life.

Scott looked to his right and saw the company radio and its backpack, blown to smithereens. Scott rolled the artillery radioman away from the wall to get to the artillery radio. The man had not even released his backpack. Scott pulled the pack and radio and tried to set them on the wall, but was unable to do so, because the forward observer had the mic in his hand.

The forward observer had a virtual death grip on the mic. Scott had never really understood a death grip until that very second. With sweat burning his eyes and running down the crack of his ass, he went into a full out battle for the radio mic. Without it the company was going to be mortared to death, or overrun.

His hands were greasy with sweat as he wrestled with the grasp that was far beyond any human grip. Scott had gotten out his knife, but was reluctant to use it. Finger by finger Scott was able to pry the man's hands loose from that mic and at long last he had the mic in his hand. He set the radio and pack on the wall and started to climb out of the Circle of Death. Halfway over the wall, his Christian roots stopped him. The two men lying against the wall had given their life for the men of Bravo Company. He reached and closed their eyes and mouths so that they looked like they were in the hands of God. He asked the Lord to bless their souls. Their death stares were burned forever into his very soul.

Scott vaulted out of the Circle of Death. He walked forward trying to figure out where he could go to start calling in artillery. Fifteen feet from the Circle of Death, with mortars still coming in, he set the radio and pack down on the ground. Without thought he essentially drew a line in the rock and dirt. He knew he was going to live or die right here.

Blue Leg Six

He said two prayers as he set the radio down: that the forward observer had been able to call in his fire points before being killed, and that the frequency on this radio belonged to the forward observer for Bravo.

Dry mouthed, Scott keyed the mike and calmly announced

that he was Blue Leg Six for this infantry position and in serious need of artillery. He forced himself to keep any and all emotion out of his voice. If he started to lose it, then the company would be lost.

*Blue Leg Six: In military jargon a commander in the field is a Six. An Infantry commander is called a Blue Leg Six. An Artillery commander is a **Red Leg Six**.*

As soon as Scott identified himself, the Fire Base asked about their Red Leg Six.

In one of the calmest voices he could muster he replied, "I am the new Red Leg Six."

The Fire Base indicated that the frequency belonged to him and that the fire points were set. They were standing by with rounds locked and loaded, waiting for his fire point. Scott asked for three rounds at the fire point for the eight o'clock position. The artillery battery came back with, "Ready to fire at your command!"

With a lump in his throat, Scott gave the command, "FIRE". The word "Fire" was barely out of his mouth when he heard the report of the 105 mm howitzers on LZ Forward send three rounds on their way. Scott prayed that the eight o'clock fire point was where he thought it was located. He breathed a sigh of relief as three rounds came crashing down within twenty-five meters of what he thought was the eight o'clock fire point.

When the rounds hit, he immediately adjusted the artillery to get closer to the fucking mortar tubes. The sons of bitches were about to find out that you should not piss off an

Infantry lieutenant. Scott made his first adjustment and fired three more rounds. With the incoming artillery, the mortar fire paused and then started up again.

He made another adjustment and this time he told them, "To Fire for Effect." That meant that he wanted to put as much artillery on these muther fuckers as possible. The artillery rounds were screaming into the enemy position. On the Castle Hill, the mortars had stopped coming in and ripping the company apart. Scott kept adjusting fire and "firing for effect."

As the artillery was inbound, a few more mortar rounds were fired from a different NVA position. Scott changed his tactics. He started to spread his fire pattern to take in the entire grid. That meant that he was firing across a wider swath of map.

Scott kept firing and adjusting the artillery. He wanted to keep the NVA moving so they would not have time to reset their mortars or prepare for an all-out attack. This tactic seemed to be working, so Scott just kept firing. As the sun slowly sank into the west, a troop informed him that the Medivacs and Huey slicks were on their way in to pick up the wounded and the dead. With choppers on the way, Scott had the artillery battery cease fire, he asked them to have three rounds locked and loaded and to be ready to fire at a moment's notice.

Scott realized that the NVA would think that the choppers might be gunships, but that did not make him any more comfortable with leaving the radio. The holocaust they had lived through was hopefully behind them. The hill was eerily quiet.

Scott assumed that the second platoon leader, Fredericks, would be taking care of the company and helping evacuate the wounded and dead. Scott decided to stay close by the radio, concerned that the mortars would start up again. If one round was dropped down a tube, he was ready to commence firing. While he had reduced the threat of an attack by the NVA, they were only a thousand meters from their perimeter, and anything was possible.

Slicks and Medevacs

Waiting for the choppers to clear the area, Scott put himself in the mind of the NVA commander. He had to know that the American company had been hit hard, but he had no idea how hard. If he was that commander, Scott would attack in force. On another note, as the evacuation was happening, Scott had not seen Lt. Fredericks anywhere around the command post.

With the night rapidly closing the door on the day, the last chopper took off from the Castle Hill. It was a Huey slick loaded with the dead from the mortar barrage. Knowing this Scott just looked through the runners.

As the last slick passed, he thought he saw someone sitting up on the canvas bench seat. That seat was at the back of the chopper. No one, outside of the crew, should be sitting up in a Huey slick, as all the riders are dead. By the time he realized that there was someone sitting up in that chopper, the bird had made its turn and was booking east to Chu Lai. Scott dismissed this incident. He had bigger fish to fry.

With the choppers clear of the valley and the sun all but gone, Scott began to pour more artillery into the enemy base camp. He noticed that something had happened to his attitude. As he keyed the mic to call in more artillery, there was no lump in his throat. When he had gone on the offensive he had been scared to death. His mouth was dry and all he could think of was that this was way beyond deadly serious. He knew that everyone on that hill was depending on his ability to fire artillery.

Since starting his journey to becoming an artillery Forward Observer, Scott had gone from being scared to death to now being pissed at the NVA for causing death and misery. Now he just wanted to get even. The NVA had run up and down this valley and the Ho Chi Minh trail for too long and it was time for an important lesson from a farm kid from Iowa.

With night fully closed in, he fired a salvo of thirty rounds into the NVA perimeter. His hope was that these rounds would stave off any full-scale attack on his now depleted infantry line. The artillery salvos were starting to bring secondary explosions. This meant that the rounds were hitting ammunition dumps. He quickly let the artillery battery know that he was dealing with a very well-equipped force.

Scott knew that if he or the artillery failed in tonight's mission, they were in for a real ass whipping. At the close of the initial mortar barrage, the NVA had started to probe his side of the perimeter with small arms fire. He was determined to put all the power of the US Army on their sorry asses. What he really wanted to do was to walk the rest of the company off this hill tomorrow morning. He did not care what the cost. He once again moved the artillery around the grid where the NVA had fired their mortars.

The Big Hammers

Scott had just moved the artillery to another part of the grid when a new voice came on the radio. He identified himself as a Red Leg Six. Since no other person at the Fire Base had identified himself as a Six, Scott figured that this was a Lt. Colonel or maybe even a full Bull Colonel. The voice was heavy with command.

The artillery Six suggested that they use the big hammers on LZ Center to bring the kind of unholy firepower that Scott needed. LZ Center was positioned nine kilometers due east from Scott's position. The big hammers were what the artillery called the long guns. The battery at LZ Center had 155 mm, 175 mm, and 8-inch guns. Scott had never dealt with such large rounds. He was concerned with how far away the company had to be to escape the impact of the rounds from such big cannons.

Scott reminded the Red Leg Six that he was a Blue Leg Six, meaning that he was not trained to do this kind of firing. An oversight with these rounds would devastate what was left of the company. The voice of Red Leg Six assured him that everyone knew the situation and that he would keep Blue Leg Six straight. In fact, the Red Leg Six said that this was now his mission.

The voice said, "Blue Leg Six, I will coordinate the firing of my artillery."

Lt Scott Ledbetter just became a supporter of using the big guns. The radio went dead for a few seconds. When the radio came alive, the artillery Six announced, "Blue Leg Six, we are going to go with VT Rounds from all of our guns." [VT stands for Variable Timed Fuse: *The VT fuse is only used in large cannons. A fuse is inserted into the shell and causes the shell to blow up while some distance above the ground. The German soldiers in World War II labeled this round "Hell Fire" which was a very apt description*].

When the first of the large caliber cannon rounds reached the NVA stronghold, it sounded like a B-52 bomb run. The ground shook, and Scott could feel the impact of the explosion as the sound waves hit his chest. He could only imagine the hell that these rounds were creating a thousand meters away. He had seen and heard the rounds from the New Jersey as they hit the ground. These rounds were hitting with the same ferocity as those sixteen-inch rounds.

The New Jersey had fired six rounds and tonight the Big Hammers were firing that many rounds a minute. They just kept coming and Scott kept moving the rounds from one area to the next. Scott had never heard these big rounds explode anywhere near where he was standing. Now they were blowing up a thousand meters away and twenty-five meters above the ground.

The sound was at once awesome and awful. He knew that he was going to hurt a lot of people, but since those people had already hurt his people, it was payback time! Over the next six hours, Scott fired literally hundreds of rounds that ate the NVA camp and the valley alive.

On this night, on this hill, at some time during the six

or so hours, Scott entered what can only be described as an Artillery Zone. In that zone, he could see straight through the darkness to the targets. He had no idea how this worked or why it happened. Like any zone there was no rhyme or reason. It was just a zone. While he could not see the terrain, the terrain somehow was being displayed inside of his head. In a few short hours, he was disassembling a very large NVA force.

At one-point Scott asked, "Red Leg Six, are you concerned with the amount of artillery being expended?"

The voice replied, "I will worry about the logistics, Blue Leg Six." Scott just kept firing.

Scott thought that Chet Fredericks would come to his position, He could not understand where the man could be. Since starting his fire mission, he had not talked or seen anyone in his perimeter.

At some time after midnight, Scott was not getting any secondary explosions and no more contact from the enemy. It had been hours since he started, and it was time to stop firing artillery.

Cease Fire

The Artillery Six then heard new words coming from Blue Leg Six. "Cease Fire."

For the first time in hours, it was deadly still. He stood there afraid to move. His legs were like blocks of concrete and he suddenly was very hungry. He could not remember the last time he had had anything to eat. His neck felt like it was on fire and he was certain that the fall with that young man had opened his wounds.

Scott felt that he had certainly followed orders to "Stop the Fucking Mortars." Now, there was nothing but silence. No mortars, no rifle fire, and no one moaning or calling out for a medic. With no more artillery to call, Scott tried to sink to the ground. His on-the-job training as an artillery forward observer was over.

He just sat there trying to get his head around the past few hours. Shortly after he started to fire the shells, with the variable timed fuses, anxiety started to take over his mission. His insides were shaking and he needed some moral support. Since no support was coming, he went home to Millersburg, Iowa and touched his roots. His mental journey home helped him reduce his anxiety and complete his mission.

This had been real war shit. He wondered how many men had been wounded or killed on this freaking hill. He hoped that what he did was right. Killing was gruesome business. He knew that men had died in the jungle to the west and he really did not care. He was relieved that he had made it through the onslaught. The men who were left on this hill could walk off tomorrow morning.

As he sat there on the hard-packed ground, his legs hurt and his left side still felt numb with pain. It was then he realized that he did not have a rifle or a helmet. His helmet was still in the bamboo trees. When the soldier was blown into the air he had put his rifle on the stone wall. When Doc Lee got him to his feet, his only thought was the carnage in the CP and the men on this hill. His rifle and helmet were not on his mind. He could not remember a single time in the last many months when these two intimate parts of his life were not within arm's reach.

No moon filled the sky and Scott could not move from his position. He reached and pulled the artillery radio closer. He rationalized that it was still his only tool against the enemy, but it had become a security blanket that was dictated by the late hour and the now exhausted warrior.

The thought of sleep was far distant from his mind. He thought about the forward observer and his radioman. How death stares had replaced the prom king smiles, those stares were still right in front of him. Those men were taken in the prime of their lives, as were the lives of many other men. Losing the captain's radioman made him extremely sad. He was a good man with a sharp mind and a good sense of life.

He could not remember the name of the young man he had caught. He was from another platoon, but no name came to him. The fact that so many had been killed or wounded, because of a captain that was hell bent on setting up his night laager, on this hill made him cry.

The Castle Hill was the most traumatic night of his young life. The buoyancy that he had felt as he was firing artillery was gone. While not a rule person, he did live the ten commandments. He wondered which commandment served a combat soldier. He could see the page in the Baltimore Catechism that stated clearly: "Thou Shalt Not Kill." He did not recall seeing a, "Ya but" for combat.

The artillery firing had gone against everything that he had ever believed. His moral compass had fallen off the true north of Christianity. In his mind, he was having a battle royal with the military's white washing of "The Ten Commandments."

He shook his head and tried to think about his family and friends. He also thought about his responsibility to the men on this hill. That responsibility had pulled him through the long night. Try though he did, he could not think of anything that was not related to the past few hours.

There had been several times in his training where a month was added here and there. If he had gone straight through all his training in the correct amount of time, he would not have been with this unit, on this night. He felt that some higher power helped him get through OCS and ensured that he was here for this night. He even thought that having Reeds as his commander was a part of the fate that had put him in position to be there for the fire mission that he had just gone through.

Field Forward Observer Training

Three weeks before the Castle Hill battle and the mortar fire, he got a new Platoon Sgt, who was a joy to work with. He was infantry and had taken over Scott's job of setting the perimeter. For the first time since coming to the field, Scott had time to go over and talk with Lt. B (the artillery forward observer). Scott did not feel he knew enough about firing artillery, in case he ever needed to do that.

The classroom was a patch of dirt to sit on and a log to lean against. The teacher was a combat trained and experienced forward observer. The tests would be life and death experiences and the grades would be tallied by the number of men left to fight and go home standing up. The man walked Scott through a day as a forward observer. He went over what he did when they came into a new night laager. His first task was to set up fire points a hundred meters out from the perimeter. Using the face of a twelve-hour clock, he set fire points at each hour.

He explained that the direction the company was heading when they walked into their new night laager, became twelve o'clock. If the forward observer is killed in the field and an infantryman, like Scott, had to take over and start firing artillery, he needed to know where twelve o'clock was in this perimeter.

Lt B also covered the difference between the 105 MM artillery from LZ Forward and what he called the big hammers from LZ Center. The different guns were used for different needs. The effectiveness of the Big Hammers more than tripled the 105 mm Howitzer.

Along with the size of the shell, the big guns can fire what is called a VT or variable timed fuse. Scott had heard of these rounds but had never talked to anyone about how they worked in a serious firefight. The Lt. explained all about firing these guns. Scott had soaked up a lot of information about firing artillery that night, but his hope was that he never needed to use what he had just learned.

Sitting there on the Castle Hill, he thanked the good Lord for directing him to sit down with the forward observer on that night. The words that haunted him: "What would happen if the FO was dead and you had to start firing artillery? Pay attention to the direction the company is heading when it walks into the perimeter, and remember that artillery kills wherever it hits."

Scott realized that he had had the hand of God on his shoulder when he walked over to sit with the FO on that night, just weeks before. Scott knew that it was one of the most important things that he had done to prepare for tonight's artillery fire.

He hoped that he would be able to forget the scene with all the dead and wounded in the command post. He was especially hopeful that the open mouth and wide-eyed stare of the artillery FO and his radioman would not stay with him all his life.

Scott hoped that Doc had gotten there in time to save the young man he had caught, but he was not sure. To have saved someone's life without being able to say his name was a travesty. It was just another aspect of the toll war takes on its soldiers. For this Iowa farm kid, it was already impacting him in ways that he did not understand.

Scott was extremely tired but could not sleep. He wanted to walk off this hill and onto the rest of the war with everyone left in the company. He found a more comfortable place to sit and dangled his feet over the wall of the Circle of Death. When he came to, he realized that he was sitting right where the forward observer had been sitting. Somewhere in his meditation of the night's events, he had fallen asleep. With difficulty, he sat up in the predawn light and tried to comprehend what had taken place in the past few hours. No one was moving, and the only sounds were of the jungle night.

As light started to streak the sky, he limped down the ditch to his tent. He was able to make out the clump of trees that he had fallen into. His rifle was still laying where he had left it so many hours before. It was still too dark to try to retrieve his helmet. The cup of Joe he was brewing when the mortars started dropping down the tubes was setting cold on the dead heat tablet. His radioman, Yancy, was in the tent sleeping.

Scott was very anxious to find out who was wounded and dead. Even though he had not seen him, he knew that Lt. Fredericks was now in command. He hoped that Fredericks would realize that his actions had kept the company from a disastrous end. Even though he was not one of the originals, he was still an important part of the unit.

The new day was breaking in the eastern sky and more and more movement sounded good to Scott. Everyone wanted off this fucking hill. Everyone knew that while the mortars had been squelched, they could start up again. When the sun got above the horizon, what was left of the company was saddled up and ready to get the hell away from this hill.

The Second Morning After the Mortar Barrage

Scott had sat alone the entire night hashing and rehashing the events of the past few weeks. In the predawn light, he heard Yancy wake up. Yancy knew that he had not pulled watch for a long time. "Lt. are you up?" he asked.

Scott quietly replied, "Yes I am on radio watch."

"What time is it?"

"Sometime before 0500," Scott replied. "I think I need

a couple of hours rest. If you would take over radio watch, I would appreciate that."

"Have you been up all night?" Yancy asked.

"Near as I can tell," said Scott.

"Get some sleep, I will get everyone moving."

"Thanks, Yancy," said Scott. Scott crawled into the tent and went to sleep.

Battalion Calling

0830 hours Yancy was shaking Scott to life and saying, "Battalion called with our grid coordinates for the day. I have them written down for you. If you have questions, call them back. I told them that you and your sergeants were checking out the ammunition levels in the company."

Scott smiled, as he sat up and said, "Thanks, Yancy, the sleep was wonderful. All I did last night was go through all that we have been through for the last month."

NVA Base Camp

Scott took the grid coordinates for their checkpoints and posted them on his map. He saw that they were heading in the direction of the place where the mortars had been fired at them. That concerned him some, but he was still thinking that the NVA force was just moving down the Ho Chi Minh Trail.

Yancy was true to his word and had everyone ready to saddle up when Scott got up. He had even brewed Scott a cup of Joe, which was far and beyond anything that Scott expected from any of his men. Being treated as someone special was not part of Scott's upbringing.

He was very appreciative of Yancy's help as he put his pack together. Over the past three weeks, Scott's dedication to the war had all but disappeared. The night on the Castle Hill closed-down any path that would lead him back to be a dedicated field officer. His dedication was now to his men. Scott knew the army's daily objective would only lead to more men getting killed without gaining any ground on the NVA.

The NVA simply did not care how many bodies they sent to be killed. They kept sending more and more men to fight the US military. If they lost a hundred, they would send two hundred more. For the US, if the NVA lost a hundred and we only lost 25, that meant that we were winning.

Scott knew that the NVA had been trekking down the Ho Chi Minh trail for months and years and that they owned the area. He figured with the amount of artillery that he had poured onto their position that the force had moved on south. He sat with his squad leaders and Sergeant Bishop to go over the checkpoints for the day.

The company saddled up and headed south and east from their mountain top retreat. The path that they would take, once they got off the mountain, would keep them four hundred meters west of the swift flowing stream and the Castle Hill.

When they reached the valley, they were back into the jungle. Three hundred meters from the base of the mountain their path took them across a small stream. That stream fed the swift flowing river. As they crossed that small stream, the next checkpoint was three hundred meters to the south and east.

Scott's lead squad had reached a rice paddy and the squad leader reported that the rice paddy was dry. There were paddy walls but no water. Suddenly Scott was beginning to get the same feeling of fear that he had before they got to the marked mine field.

The Vietnamese waste nothing, yet a rice paddy with no water was ahead of them. On the top of the mountain where they had night laagered, there were three large patches of sugar cane that had gone unharvested. He was beginning to think that the NVA who had mortared them were not moving south, they were in a base camp.

The closer he got to the open rice paddy; the more alarms went off in his head. Every nerve in Scott's body was on edge. A smell hit his nostrils from years before, a smell that sent a shudder down into his soul. When he was younger he had gone with his parents to a wake of a family friend. He had been to funerals before, but this time his nose was above the edge of the casket. He experienced the smell of flowers and formaldehyde mixed together. Those two smells did not leave his nostrils for days.

With the dry rice paddy now meters away, he was hit with the smell of flowers and formaldehyde. He felt that he was being warned that they were walking into a kill zone from an NVA base camp. Half of Scott's small company was already walking on or just about to walk onto that dry rice paddy.

None of the men in his command had ever seen him excited. Now he was frantically running and passing his men and urging them to get into the jungle. He got all his men into the jungle and set up a defensive position. Once everyone was in the cover of the jungle, cautiously Scott started moving his men to the left. They stayed just inside of the jungle next to the dry rice paddy. Soon they came upon a position where a heavy machine gun had been setting for a long time. The ground was worn slick by men sitting behind the gun. The gun had a clear field of fire on the entire rice paddy. If that gun would have still been sitting there, manned, the company would have been cut down like winter wheat in a Kansas wheat field.

As they moved closer to the swift flowing river, they found three more positions where machine guns had been. When he saw all the machine gun nests, Scott shuddered to think of the withering fire that would have annihilated his company.

The trees were shredded, and the ground torn by the hundreds of rounds that Scott had poured onto this location. Bravo started moving cautiously south. This camp was for a very large force of NVA. Well-worn paths crisscrossed the area and tunnel openings had been well used.

There were tunnels, but Scott did not send anyone down the tunnels. He was pretty certain that they would be booby trapped. He thought that they should do a serious bombing run and sink the tunnels. That way no more American lives would be lost trying to figure out what else was below the ground.

They found an area, along a trail, that had been the kitchen. Three stoves had been cut into the side of a bank that was four foot high. The stoves were made to feed a large number of men. They were ingenious in their simplicity. He was dumbfounded by the way that they distributed smoke over a large area.

They NVA had cut each of the stoves into a dirt bank. The stoves were made in two sections. The bottom section was where the wood was burned. The top section had four chimney holes to pull the smoke away from the fire. The chimneys were made from rolled up banana leaves. The chimneys were laid into a six by six-inch trench. Those trenches ran for hundreds of feet.

The smoke from the fire was being pulled out into those chimneys. The smoke would then rise slowly across a wide area. So instead of having a column of smoke going into the sky, it would look like a fog lifting from the jungle floor. When a spotter plane flew over, he would just see the fog that rolls out of the jungle after a monsoon rain.

Along with the tunnels they found an anti-aircraft position. For that gun, the NVA had dug a round trench that was thirty plus inches deep. In the center, they left a chunk of earth that held a high caliber anti-aircraft gun. The gunner could walk three hundred and sixty degrees around the trench and fire in any direction.

They discovered where the mortars had been launched from four tubes that had been set on plates. The mortars and their plates were gone, but their memory made Scott cringe. He wanted to be the hell out of the place. This force, while not here, was very large and they had taken their mortar tubes with them. The NVA still had the coordinates of this place and could bring smoke on the unit if they knew that they had located the base camp.

Scott radioed battalion and told them what they had found. He was ordered to wait for an Americal intelligence team to examine the recently abandoned base camp. Scott was not expecting this turn of events, all he wanted to do was to unass the area.

Scott walked nervously around the camp trying to gain his own intelligence on an enemy that was no longer in the area. He found a twelve-foot mound of dirt in the middle of a small clearing. The mound had been built by the NVA. He walked to the top of the mound and could not believe what he saw. He was looking at the Castle hill and could see where Yancy and he had set up their poncho tent.

He imagined the commander of the NVA group had stood in this very spot and watched as the mortars flew from his base camp. Scott could not make out the command post from this position, but the commander would have seen the clouds of dust caused by exploding mortar rounds.

Why did he not attack? Scott stood and tried to figure out what had caused this man to stay put and not attack the American unit. He began to relive the horror of the night and had to shake himself to get back at the business at hand. As he was walking back down to the ground, he heard the whop of an incoming chopper.

Scott and Yancy positioned themselves close to the dry rice paddy and popped smoke for the incoming intelligence crew. Six men got off the chopper: a captain, E 7 sergeant, lieutenant, and three young men who looked like tunnel rats.

All the men, save the lieutenant, came over and introduced themselves. They asked about any intelligence that Bravo had picked up. Scott told them about the mortars, the tunnels, and the stoves for the mess. The Lt. did not come over to introduce himself. He had come to the jungle dressed for a f'n parade that would go past some headquarters. His boots were highly polished and every patch that he was authorized to wear was sewn onto the uniform. On his hip, he wore a .45 caliber pistol. The scabbard was also highly polished.

Scott's fatigues were old, faded, and dirty. His boots had never seen polish. His green army T shirt was sweat stained and filled with holes. Scott was not impressed with the young starched and polished son of a bitch.

The intelligence team spread out to look over the camp. The Lt. just kept walking back and forth like he was waiting to report to some four-star general. Scott wondered why the man had been sent to the field. Apparently, his job was to come out all starched-up so he could look down his fucking nose at the men who actually put their life on the line. Scott imagined that the Lt. had his Vietnam combat medals on the table next to his mosquito netted bunk.

The Lt. made a few attempts to walk over to where Scott was standing, without getting close enough to introduce himself. On one of his trips, Scott attempted to make conversation, but the shine on the man's boots were blinding. What Scott's men were seeing was the tale of two lieutenants. No one would imagine that they were in the same army.

The afternoon was growing late and Scott was anxious for the team to unass this area. The Lt. finally came back over to where Scott was standing, so Scott asked, "Why, with all of your military intelligence, would you send an undermanned infantry company into an area where there was a battalion sized NVA base camp?"

The man walked over to where Scott was standing and looked him right in the eye and said, "That is Infantry's job." The events of the past few weeks and especially the past two nights, rolled up Scott's back. He body slammed the son of a bitch. When he stopped moving forward his nose was less than an inch away from the man's nose.

"You sorry assed mother fucker. You may be one of the sorriest son of a bitches that has ever forked a pair of combat fatigues! Who in the fuck do you think you are to send a company of forty plus men into a battalion sized base camp and say that that is INFANTRY'S FUCKING JOB? I think it is time you get your fucking ass off a fucking chair and get to the fucking field and gain some understanding and respect for real soldiers!"

Scott's M-16 was resting on the man's helmet an inch from his left eye. The man's haughtiness had taken leave as did the color from his face. The two men stood nose to nose and the sopping wet situation could be cut with a knife. The intelligence sergeant pushed the two men apart. As he did, they could hear an incoming chopper.

The sergeant said, "Lieutenant, why don't you get onto the chopper?" The man took that piece of advice and ran towards the incoming slick. As he was running across the base camp, Scott could envision his tail tucked firmly between his cheeks.

The sergeant said, "Sir, I apologize for the lieutenant's behavior."

Scott said, "Sergeant, there is no apology that can be made for such a sorry assed son of a bitch."

The captain and his crew were heading towards the chopper when the sergeant beckoned to the captain. The captain and the sergeant walked off to talk. The rest of the intelligence crew kept moving towards the chopper, which was about to land.

The captain returned to Scott and said, "Lieutenant, I apologize for the lieutenant. We should have known that this large of a unit was in the area and a company that had been so depleted should not have been sent into this area. I am sorry my Lt. made an ass out of himself. I will speak to him about his attitude when we get back to base camp."

Scott said, "Sir, I believe it is time for that son of a bitch to be in the toolies and do real soldier work. I doubt if his shined boots and holster will let him last long in the real war that we are fighting."

With a nod of agreement, the captain turned and both he and his sergeant ran to get on the waiting chopper.

LZ BALDY

As the chopper was winding up to leave, Scott called battalion to get new checkpoints. They sent them north along the river and then east through two checkpoints. After checking his map coordinates, Scott stood up and realized that the entire company was standing there, packs on, ready to kiss off this god forsaken area.

Yancy who had been standing a few feet away from

Scott's collision with the lieutenant said, "Sir, you did not handle him very well."

Scott smiled and was able to take a deep breath and said, "I said what was needed to be said. Perhaps the next time he comes to the field he will look like he is infantry."

The company headed north out of the base camp and passed due west of the Castle Hill. Scott said a prayer for those who did not make it off that hill alive and for those who were wounded. As he watched that hill to his east slide by, he knew that Scott Ledbetter would never be the same.

When they came to a spot that looked like the best place to cross the swift flowing river, Scott made sure that everyone refreshed their canteens with the clear water. Soon after crossing the river, a torrential downpour hit them. When it started to rain, the temperature was close to one hundred and twenty degrees and it had immediately dropped by thirty degrees. Scott sat in the pouring rain as they waited out the deluge. It was getting colder and colder. Goosebumps ran up his arms and he was shaking as if it was wintertime. The rain stopped as quickly as it had begun.

Soon after saddling up and moving out, the temperature returned to normal, which was someplace north of a hundred degrees. As they walked, the steam rolled up out of the soggy ground and looked like fog on a wet Iowa day. This was Vietnam.

The company made it a few hundred meters from where they had waited out the storm when a two-man sniper team opened-up on them. No one was hit and almost on cue, Scott's men started a tactical process right out of Advanced

Infantry Training School. One squad fired, while the other moved up and then started to fire from their new position. The other squad then moved forward under the covering fire from the other squad. The company kept moving forward and the snipers kept falling back until they ran out of jungle. They found themselves in an opening and they "DeDe Maughed" (got out of there in a hurry) as fast as they could.

One of Scott's men saw them run into a dilapidated hooch, which sat just inside the jungle on the far side of the open area. The company opened-up on the hooch with rifle and machine gun fire, but when they got into the hooch it was empty. Scott thought that they had run in and out on the far side of the hooch, but there was just one door on his side of the hooch. Scott's men did a second search and found a well camouflaged tunnel entrance in the hooch. The entrance to the tunnel was covered with a straw mat which was covered with dust and dirt. He was not sure how they had accomplished that.

They tore down the hooch and put all of the material in and over the tunnel entrance and set it on fire. Scott saw smoke coming from the jungle behind the hooch. He knew that the snipers had lived to fight another day. After searching the area they moved out towards their next checkpoint.

On the way they located a good place to night lager. They called the position into battalion. After seeing his position on the Castle Hill from the NVA base camp, Scott and Yancy took particular care that their position was well hidden and secure. Scott blamed himself for becoming too lax with this very important part of jungle warfare.

The next morning, battalion gave them orders to move to

a check point where they would be picked up and brought to LZ Baldy. Long before 0800 hours, the company was standing in the jungle looking out at a small rice paddy with just enough room to bring in three Huey slicks at a time. The choppers would then ferry them to LZ Baldy.

Scott and Yancy got on the last chopper. It was so nice to have the prop wash air over his sweating body. Choppers were at once a blessing and curse. They were a blessing when they pulled you out of the jungle and a curse when they dropped you into another combat assault. Scott knew that before the day was over, another company of choppers was going to take them from Baldy to some other piece of jungle.

LZ Baldy sat fifty kilometers north and west of Chu Lai and about thirty kilometers south and west of Da Nang. It was never a garden spot, but after the last few days, it looked like heaven on earth to Scott and his men.

At the tactical operations center on Baldy, the Major gave Scott his new orders and their checkpoints for the day. The choppers would be in to pick them up at 1500 hours. They were going to serve as palace guard, which meant they were going to be in the area outside of Chu Lai, which was under constant threat of rockets. The palace guard companies were there to keep the NVA from torching a rocket from what was known as the Rocket Pocket, that was the name assigned to a part of the palace guard area.

Scott asked if there was any place where he could shave, shower, and sit in a chair. A captain on the TOC staff told him to use his hooch and his chair. When he left the tactical operations center, Scott went to talk with his men and let them know that hot chow was being served. At that time, a jeep showed up that was filled with clean fatigues, underwear, and socks.

The captain promised a warmish bucket of water would be setting just outside of the door. Scott used the bucket and wash pan to take a whore's bath and just be clean. This was the first real bath that he had had in quite a while. The captain also had a mirror and Scott had not seen himself in a large mirror for months. He shaved off his scruffy beard, put on his clean socks, underwear, and fatigues. He felt like a new man.

The heat and humidity would soon take its toll but for a few minutes, he was clean. He took the captain's invitation and got a Carling Black Label beer out of the apartment sized refrigerator. Then he sat down in a homemade plywood chair. Sitting on anything but the ground or on his haunches for weeks on end made this chair a joy.

Scott wrote a letter to his mom and dad back in Iowa and just sat there in the chair and rested. He thanked God for letting him and his men walk away from the Circle of Death. He thought back to all that had transpired that made him a part of that Castle Hill. His mind once again started to relive the experiences of the last three weeks but forced himself to go somewhere else in his thoughts.

Scott went outside and found some fresh water to refill the captain's wash bucket. He also found Doc Lee looking for him. "Sir," he said, "I need to look at your neck wounds." Scott took off his shirt and sat down on a bunker to have his wounds cleaned and looked after. "Ooh, this is not healing. It is infected, and you are going to have to go to Chu Lai to have this properly cared for by the hospital."

Scott knew that Doc was right. "Thanks, Doc, you have

been great, but with the fall into the bamboo trees and all that has happened, it is no wonder that the wound has not healed. Come with me up the TOC to let them know that this is medical and not my decision."

The Major was not happy that Bravo's only officer had to be pulled from the field. Doc was there to show him a wound that had become infected. The Major said, "Lt. find someplace where your men can bunk while on Baldy. We will try to figure out something. Maybe we can find someone to take your place."

Scott and Sergeant Bishop found a place for the company to stay at LZ Baldy and Doc made arrangements for Scott to be flown to Chu Lai Medical Center. Scott was pretty sure that since no officers had been sent to the field to re-place anyone, he doubted that they would find a captain or lieutenant to take his place. He figured that it would be four to five days to get the wound healed before he came back to the field.

Scott caught a slick back to the hospital at Chu Lai. The hospital staff was amazed when a soldier got off a Huey and walked into the hospital, carrying his weapon and a full pack. A young doctor looked at Scott's wounds and said, "Ohh, this is infected, you are going to need to be kept here for a few days."

After he was bandaged, he checked his weapon and kept his backpack. They gave him a bed with a real mattress and sheets. It had been months since that had been a part of his life. With time on his hands, Scott rested for the first time in months and was able to reflect how a farm boy from Iowa ended up as a field commander in Vietnam.

He thought back to a cold January day in 1966, in Peoria, Illinois.

2. In From the Cold

January 1966: Scott was headed home to one of the coldest houses in all of Peoria. He stopped to put a dollar's worth of eighteen cent gas into the 1960 white Ford. The ever-present wind cut through his trench coat and sent a chill down his spine. His fingertips were numb before he racked the gas nozzle into the side of the pump. He thought of the few dollars that he had in his wallet and about a life that had him in Peoria, Illinois. The dollars' worth of gas would bring the gas needle off dead empty. He figured that the five plus gallons of gas would get him through another week, maybe two.

In his billfold was a draft card with his "1A" draft status. That meant that he was draft eligible. No one would talk to him about a job because they knew he would soon get a letter from the draft board that would welcome him to the United States Army. It was like Vietnam was across the street instead of on the other side of the world.

On his way home, he drove past the Sacred Heart Church in downtown Peoria. He decided to stop and say a rosary. This church was often the only place where he could find comfort.

Only a few candles lit the darkened church, shone brightly above the altar. The quiet warm darkness let Scott focus on why he had come this way. He prayed that the good Lord would show him some way to get home to Millersburg, Iowa.

His brother had called a couple of days before and simply asked him to come home. Wanting to go home and getting there, were two different things. His old Ford had motor issues. He had limited travel funds and home was over two hundred miles away. In the dead of a Midwestern winter, that could be a forever trip in an old car.

Scott said his rosary prayers slowly. Each bead was deliberately prayed as Scott went decade by decade. Each Hail Mary and Our Father was full of meaning. He wanted to ensure that his thoughts and his prayers were in order. After quite a long time, he finished his rosary and reluctantly headed toward the door. He stopped and took one more look around the blessed sanctuary. The church to him was the timeless abode of Christ the Savior. With that thought on his mind, he pushed the large wooden doors and headed out into the cold.

This was Scott's twenty-third Midwestern winter, and he grimaced at the thought of the nasty cold and bitter wind that was beyond that second set of doors. As he shoved the outside door into the night, the wind smacked him so hard that it made him consider staying for one more rosary. He hurried toward the old Ford and hoped that it would once more grind to life.

As he got closer to the car, he stopped to look toward the light that was spilling out into the night from the church rectory. Then without considering why, he turned and headed back toward Sacred Heart's Rectory. Where, he hoped, a priest would be willing to see him at this late evening hour.

The rectory was made of the same stone that was used to build the church a hundred years before. It was a three-story building that took on the elements of being a house without really hitting that goal. It was kind of a cross between a dormitory and a building that accidentally became a residence.

Scott's footfalls caromed off the frozen granite steps as he walked up onto the porch. The front door had a large oval frosted glass with a beautifully etched cross. Scott could see a light from somewhere in the house and that light illuminated the glass oval. The oval invited anyone outside to come in.

In the middle of the door and just below the frosted glass was an old-time twist doorbell. As the bell groaned and clanged, it reminded him of a doorbell that might be found at St. Ambrose College. St. Ambrose, like this church and rectory, had been built in the 1800's. It is where Scott spent his college years.

Scott could hear the bell as it echoed and re-echoed inside the underslung mansion. He waited outside in the cold for some time and was just turning to head for his car when a porch light came on and the door was pulled opened. There stood a young priest who asked Scott to come in out of the cold.

As Scott entered the rectory he thought that the invitation, "Come in out of the cold" had more meaning than this young priest could know. Scott asked if he had a few minutes to talk and Father Shepler indicated that he did have some time.

He commented on how well-dressed Scott was,

considering most people at his door at this time of the night were looking for a handout. Scott replied, "Father I am not indigenous, but instead of a handout, I am looking for a hand-up. I would like to have a few minutes of your time to talk." He did not add that he was just a step or two away from being that other person.

As they walked down the hallway, the oak floors creaked and groaned with each step. Scott was pleasantly surprised to find a fairly new sofa and side chair in the priest's office. Father took a seat on the sofa and Scott settled into the side chair. After an awkward few minutes, they finally started to establish a newfound and friendly relationship.

The two men exchanged comments about the weather and the miserably cold winter. Father then asked why he was out and about on such a cold evening. Scott told him that life had not been as kind as he had hoped. He had ended up in Peoria working for the Encyclopedia Britannica Company. His sales were not paying the bills. He was slowly but surely reaching the end of his time in Peoria.

Scott told him that the one thing that kept him together was coming to Mass each Sunday and often for daily Mass. Father smiled and said, "That is where I have seen you before."

Scott went on to tell Father that along with mass he often stopped to say the rosary. Whenever life was attempting to drop kick him through some unseen goalpost, he took great comfort in the rosary. He told Father that when he stopped this evening that he had prayed for a way to move on to a better life.

Scott said, "Father, when you opened your door and invited me to come in from the cold, my prayers had been answered."

While he thought that his decision to come to the rectory was made on a wing and a prayer, it had really been done with a prayer. It could easily have been that Father would not have been there and his turning of that old twist bell would have fallen on a deaf or uncaring ear. Instead, his prayers were heard and were being answered.

The church had always been a place near and dear to his heart. He was a cradle Catholic who had attended St. Ambrose College in Davenport. When they suggested that he not return, he kind of lost his way. Today, after months of pushing against a life that appeared to be going nowhere, it seemed that he really needed to talk with someone. The ice that he was treading had gotten very thin and he was not certain if the surface was going to long sustain his weight.

In Scott's mind, this was a much-needed stay in the loving hand of God. As they talked, Scott started to feel whole again. Father did not condemn or denounce Scott's life or his decisions. Father asked him about where he had come from and about his years at St. Ambrose in Davenport.

Scott told him that he had been raised on a farm outside of Millersburg, Iowa which is in the southeastern corner of the state, not far from Iowa City. He told him about Father O'Brien who had been his parish priest for the first seventeen years of his life. Father had been transferred to Grand Mound, Iowa at the beginning of his senior year in high school.

His leaving had left a hole in his heart and in his life. Scott said it was like losing a part of his family. Father asked how he ended up at St. Ambrose. Scott told him that Father O'Brien's replacement, Father Rector had been an administrator at the Catholic high school in Iowa City.

Father had asked Scott what he planned to do after graduation. Scott told him that he was going to work on construction for the summer and then go into the Air Force. Father Rector fortunately had worked with a lot of seventeen-year-old students and knew that they had a hard time thinking things all the way through. Father asked, "Have you ever considered going to college?"

Scott admitted that he never had considered that as an option. Father Rector suggested that he should at least give it a try. If it did not work out, he could always go into the Air Force.

Father said, "I am going down to Davenport next week to visit with Bishop Hayes. If you want I can take you over to St. Ambrose College, where one of my seminary friends is the Dean of Admissions."

The Transcript

Scott talked with his Mom and Dad and they thought that he should go and at least check it out. Father told him to get his transcript from the school and bring it with him for his visit at St. Ambrose.

On Monday, Scott went to the school's office to get a copy of his transcript. Mr. Thompson was sitting at his desk writing. He glanced up at Scott and said, "Scott, what can I do for you?

Scott said, "I need to get my transcript to take to St. Ambrose College next Monday."

With that, Mr. Thompson raised his head from his

writing and stared in disbelief at the request. Millersburg was a farming community. Unfortunately, neither the school nor any of the teachers spent a single minute of their time counseling the students on things like a career path. In this part of Iowa, the boys went into the service, farmed, or worked for Amana Refrigeration. A lot of them ended up doing all three.

Mr. Thompson was smiling as he opened the file drawer and took out a paper. He slid that paper into an official school envelope. He sealed the envelope and gave it to Scott. He said, with a huge smile on his face, "Scott, I am happy to see that you are thinking about going to college."

The following Monday morning, when they got to St. Ambrose, Father took him into the admissions office and introduced him to an old classmate from their days in the seminary. He was the Dean of Student Admissions. After the introduction, Father Rector left to go meet with Bishop Hayes.

The dean smoked a pipe filled with cherry tobacco which simply smelled wonderful. Father had his pipe clenched in his teeth as he opened the official school envelope. As the transcript slid onto the desk, Scott stared in disbelief. Up until that time he thought that the transcript was some kind of form that said this student had graduated or would soon be graduating from school. Scott really did not know that a transcript was a listing of all his grades from high school. Until he heard the word from Father Rector, he had never heard the word "transcript" used.

Millersburg did not have a school secretary, so all administrative work was done by the superintendent or the principal. As the end of Scott's senior year approached, the superintendent, Mr. Hanson, brought a stack of paper and four grade books to study hall. He handed those papers to the class, all thirteen of them. He handed the books and the papers to a student on the other side of the room. He told them that they were to take an average of the four-year grade for each subject and list that grade on the grade sheets.

The grade books were just beginning to make their way down the first row, when a teacher came in to get Mr. Hanson. He told the class that he would be back at the end of the hour to collect the books and the grade sheets.

When Scott got the papers and grade books, the rest of the class was leaving the study hall and the next class was coming into the room. Scott needed to finish the assignment. Instead of trying to average letter grades, he decided to put down the best grade that he received in any subject. He quickly finished the assignment and waited in the hall for Mr. Hanson.

Standing in the Dean of Admissions office, he realized that his "Official Grade Sheet" was called a "transcript." He did not think it wise to let the dean know that the writing on that sheet was his. The dean had his "transcript" in his hand as he was studying Scott's grades and moving his head and his pipe up and down.

After a few puffs of smoke drifted toward the ceiling, the Dean put down the transcript and said, "Mr. Ledbetter, I do not see any reason that you would not be welcomed at St. Ambrose." He stood up and extended his hand. Scott gave him a firm handshake and Scott's smile got a whole lot wider.

The Dean of Admissions called his secretary to meet their newest student. She came in and congratulated Scott and took him to the outer office where she had him complete an application for St. Ambrose. He filled out the application and gave the lady a fifteen-dollar registration fee. With that, Scott was headed for the 1960 freshman class at St. Ambrose College in Davenport, Iowa.

Father Shepler shook his head as he listened to a story that was as simply true as it was simple. He laughed a hearty laugh and said, "So you created your own grade transcript without really knowing what it was. With that document, you were accepted at St. Ambrose?"

Britannica Books

In 1965, too many hours working and not enough time studying brought Scott's college days to a close. Ambrose did not think that he was holding up his end of the study requirement. They asked him not to return in the fall of 1965. He found himself in Davenport with no degree and no meaningful job. His college deferment from the military had expired. No one would hire him for a real job because of his 1A draft status. They knew that he would soon be heading for the military and Vietnam.

Scott told Father that while he did not believe in the Vietnam War, it was beginning to look like the military and the war was the only way out of his current crisis. Scott was neither a Hawk nor a Dove. All he really wanted was a job that would let him earn a living. Go to war? Well, he had not given that much thought.

Scott tried to find work for legitimate companies like

Alcoa or John Deere in the Quad Cities. Each time he would make an application at a legitimate company, the question would always come up about his draft status. As soon as they learned that he was 1A, the interview was over.

In the 1960's, the military had the right to draft anyone who was eligible. Scott had had a student draft deferment while in college, but that deferment was gone and his draft status was 1A, draft eligible.

When interviewing for a job or being pulled over by a traffic cop, a young man had to have his driver's license and his draft card. One of the things that the hippie generation did was to make a big display of burning their draft cards to protest the draft, and a lot of young men Scott's age had headed for Canada.

Scott had no desire to go into the military. One day he saw an ad for an Encyclopedia Britannica book salesman. Scott had not thought of sales as a career. When he was in high school, he had sold more magazine subscriptions than anyone in his class. That experience had taught him that it was fun to get someone to sign a contract for something that the customer wanted or thought they wanted. He was invited in for an interview and they did not ask about his draft status.

Scott needed a job, and they wanted someone who had a suit and was steadily breathing. Scott was hired and the experience gave him a place to go. As it turned out, he learned a lot about sales in the rough and tumble months while he was selling books.

In his first week, he sold a set of books and followed that one up with several more. There were moments when it all would come together and Scott would walk away with a contract and a check. Unfortunately, there were not enough of those moments to keep body and soul together.

Barney Standman

The guy who hired Scott was Barney Standman. Barney had been a pilot who flew the Burma Hump during World War II. He was 6'2", with curly hair, and horn-rimmed glasses. In the winter, along with a wool dress coat, he wore a white silk neck scarf that was eight feet long. The scarf went around his neck twice, leaving five feet of white silk hanging down in front.

He was the first real "character" that Scott was to meet. He was married more often than most and his current wife was a young redhead who was twenty years his junior. Barney lived on the outskirts of Peoria and Scott was certain that the rent was normally late.

Barney never had much money, but he always had a brand new hundred-dollar bill in his money clip. It was always the outside bill. There may have been two dollars inside of that bill, but that bill was always fresh and on the outside. When Barney was down to one hundred dollars, he was flat broke. While not a religious man, he did have rules. His first rule was to never screw the hired help. As far as Scott knew, that was his one and only rule in his life.

Barney treated Scott well and taught him how to sell. He told Scott that Britannica had given him Peoria, Illinois as his new territory. While they were doing well in Davenport, Barney thought that a move to Peoria would work out great. With nothing to really hold them in Davenport, Scott and the other salesperson, Mike Allison, headed for Peoria where Barney had set up an office in the basement of an insurance office.

Barney set up a bank of telephones with three women making calls for appointments. Barney taught Scott how to work the phones and make his own appointments. Scott worked the phone during the day and was out selling books at night. Scott sold several sets of books, but without a steady income it was difficult to have skittles (let alone beer) on the table.

Scott had scraped out an existence with the sales that he was making. Unfortunately, he was either too young or dumb to just go back home to Iowa. It was a mystery what kept him in Peoria. He was normally broke, and the weather was either too hot or too damned cold. Yet through it all he just kept charging on to the next sales call.

Scott told Father that the church had been his only respite in a sea that seemed to be drowning him. He could not imagine going through this time without the church. Over the years, Scott had realized that the Church was one of the Pillars of Life that kept a person anchored. Without such pillars, the waves of uncertainty would crush the life out of your soul.

Hitchhiking to NM

Father asked if he had been able to get out of Peoria since last summer. Scott told him that he did leave once, when his friend Dave Parkman from St. Ambrose got married in far off Portales, New Mexico. To get there, he had to hitchhike because he did not have enough money to buy a ticket.

He amassed all his funds ($50.00), packed a small traveling bag, put on his best JC Penney sports coat, and caught a ride to the edge of Peoria. From there, he hitch-hiked to Portales, NM, which was in the middle of no-where.

By the afternoon of his first day, Scott had made it to the east side of Tulsa where he was stuck. He had to get to the Will Roger's Turnpike or this trip was done. A cowboy in a red Chevy pickup truck stopped and said, "Throw your grip in the back of the truck and I will take you to the Turnpike."

As they drove across town, the man asked, "How do you meet girls when you are hitch-hiking?"

Scott said, "Right now I am more concerned with getting to New Mexico than I am meeting women."

He assumed that would take care of the topic. The questions kept getting stranger and Scott was beginning to feel trapped in the truck. He concluded that he had met a cowboy with a whole different persuasion.

Scott was watching their progress on his map of Tulsa and they were heading towards the turnpike. A sign announced that they were at the turnpike. At the next stoplight, he got out of the truck and grabbed his suitcase.

"Thanks for the ride, partner," he said. With that, he walked right past the toll booths, acting like he knew just what he was doing. He ignored the signs that said no hitch-hiking or horseback riding.

Will Roger's Turnpike

Within five minutes of sticking out his thumb, he was picked up by a guy in a large work truck packed with welding gear and acetylene tanks that clanged loudly when he came to a stop. He was headed for Oklahoma City to do a job for his construction firm.

Scott and the driver talked about life and what it was like hitchhiking across the country. Scott was beginning to think that he had a chance of getting to the west side of Oklahoma City before nightfall. The toll booths were a mile away, and Scott noticed that the man was checking and rechecking his rear-view mirror. After passing a large green sign that said End of Tollway, the man really started to act nervous.

He slowed down and pulled off the pavement onto the shoulder of the road. Without saying anything he got out and headed toward the back of the truck. Scott thought that he was checking on the load. Scott was looking into his rear-view mirror when he saw the man take off for the fence on their side of the turnpike.

The man climbed over the six-foot fence like it was not even there. Once on the other side, he took off running like a man who was running from the law. He had shimmied that fence and was gone in minutes. Scott sat there in absolute disbelief. He immediately realized that this truck was stolen. Any highway patrol person would assume that Scott had been the one who had done the stealing.

He was pretty certain that the sheriff or the highway patrol would have a hard time believing that he was just a passenger in this stolen vehicle. He had watched enough television to know that he needed to wipe off anyplace that he had touched, so that's what he did. When he had cleaned everywhere that he could think to clean, he grabbed his traveling bag and headed for the south side of the turnpike. He did not want to become tangled up with the guy who had just climbed over the fence.

Scott hoofed it across two lanes of traffic to the other side of the toll way. He knew that he had to climb a very serious six-foot fence. When he got to the chain link fence, he took off his sports jacket and tie. He dropped the coat and his bag on the far side of the fence and used every skill that seventeen years on his Dad's farm in Iowa had taught him. He, too, shimmied over the fence.

He managed to get over without ripping his clothing. He put his sports coat back on, shoved the tie into his travel bag, and headed for the outer road. He could see the truck sitting on the far side of the toll road and just shook his head at how ludicrous this trip had become. He shuddered to think what would have happened if they had been pulled over.

He had just started walking west when he heard a truck coming up behind him. A local rancher in an old Chevy pickup was nice enough to stop and take him to the end of the toll way. Scott was trying to come up with a likely story that would explain why a man dressed in sports coat and slacks would be walking on an outer road next to the Will Roger's Turnpike. Amazingly the rancher never asked.

The two men talked about the weather and the difference between farming in Iowa and ranching in Oklahoma. He dropped Scott off on a highway that went over the toll road, just past the tollgates. He was still on the east side of

Oklahoma City, and the day was moving into evening. Scott knew that he needed to find some shelter.

Up ahead there was an old Route Sixty-Six looking motel. The night's lodging was six dollars and change. Once inside of his "suite d'elegance" he drank a soda from the soda machine and ate the last of the sandwiches that he had packed in Peoria. With so many miles and the stress of what had happened out on the tollway, he collapsed into sleep.

A small diner and the interstate highway were a short walk from Scott's motel. He ate breakfast and got on the on ramp to the interstate. Most of the people on the highway were going to work and had no time for even a well-dressed hitch hiker. An hour went by and he was beginning to think that this might be at the end of the line and his return to Peoria seemed imminent.

Scott was seriously thinking about hitching east when a highway patrolman stopped and asked for Scott's driver's license and draft card. Scott had both. He asked where Scott was heading, and he told him about the wedding in New Mexico.

Highway Patrol to the Rescue

The officer left him standing outside of the patrol car and got back into his cruiser. Inside his car, Scott could see him talking to someone on his radio. No doubt he was doing a criminal check. Once he completed his check, he finished up some paperwork and got out and walked over to Scott and told him that he would take him to the other side of

Oklahoma City. On the way, Scott told him about his trip so far, with the exception of the stolen truck. He figured that the friendly attitude of the trooper would have changed drastically if he mentioned that part.

When he dropped Scott off at the entrance to Interstate 40, the officer told him to take care and to report to his draft board as soon as possible. With those words of wisdom firmly etched in Scott's head, he thanked the officer and got out of the cruiser and began to thumb his way west.

Snowbirds

A couple from Illinois calling themselves snowbirds took him to Amarillo, where they stopped at their favorite restaurant called Amarillo Slim. The sign outside the restaurant sported a twenty-five-foot cowboy waving his arm to the passerby's. The couple insisted on paying for Scott's chicken fried steak, which was the specialty of the house.

Highway 385 ran down the Texas and New Mexico border and it would take him south to where he could cut over to Clovis. 385 crossed Highway 40 in a little town called Vega, Texas. Vega was thirty miles north of Hereford, Texas which is where Scott would pick up Highway 60 to Clovis.

The couple dropped him at a gas station in Vega and wished him Godspeed. When Scott saw the town, he realized that he was in trouble. It was little more than a wide spot on the highway map, a town that was actually smaller than Millersburg, Iowa where he had spent his early years.

It was Saturday, the day of the wedding. Standing at the

little gas station with the day slipping away, Scott knew that the best that he could do was to make it to the wedding reception, wherever that was. It was beginning to look like he was going to have to go to Plan B, which unfortunately he did not have.

Vega, Texas

There was a lot of traffic coming South on 385 to Highway 40, but hardly anyone was going to Hereford, Texas. Everyone would turn left toward Amarillo or right to head to New Mexico. Night was beginning to fall and the two guys at the station were getting upset that this stranger, who had been there for too many hours, was still there. They wanted to close, and Scott wanted to leave. Neither they nor Scott were happy with the situation.

In 1967, Vega, Texas was made up of five stores and a gas station. The gas station's pay phone was one of the largest that Scott had ever seen. It looked like a regular home phone on steroids. Scott called the operator to ask which hotel in Clovis, NM was the nicest. Scott convinced her that she was not making a recommendation, just an observation. Finally, she said that the Holiday Inn was the nicest place in Clovis. Scott decided that that was where the reception was going to be held and that was now his destination. At this point, where the reception was made little difference. If he did not catch a ride from Vega, he would not be there.

The Old Semi

At dusk a semi-truck came down from the north and stopped on the far side of Highway 40. Scott stood and watched and figured that he was going east or west. He was dumbfounded when the old truck came across the highway. The following scene had to look like something out of a "C" movie script. Scott stood in the middle of the road with his suitcase and flagged down the driver. Scott was not sure what would have happened if he had not stopped.

The only reason the trucker stopped was to keep from running over Scott. The air brakes squealed when the big truck came to a halt. Scott climbed up on the running board on the driver's side to ask for a ride to anywhere that was not Vega, Texas. The driver told him that he was not allowed to have any riders.

Desperation must have been all over Scott's face as he pleaded with the man not to leave him in such a scary and unfriendly place. All he wanted to do was to get to Clovis just a few miles down the road. The driver looked at the shirt, tie, and sports jacket for a long time. Finally, the man told Scott to climb in the truck.

The next time he heard those air brakes, both Scott and his grip were settling down inside a truck cab. The passenger seat had exposed springs, but Scott and those exposed springs were all headed south, so that was okay. The old truck was so noisy that Scott could not hear what the driver was saying, so he climbed out of the seat and sat on top of the engine housing. Once there, the two men could hear each other and carry on perhaps the strangest conversation that either had had in their lives. Two men who knew nothing of each other were driving down a very narrow two-lane highway trying to act as if they were old friends. As they headed down the highway, the driver reached back under the mattress, right behind the seat, and pulled out a fifth of Vodka.

The driver took a pull of that Vodka and offered the bottle to Scott. While Scott was not a Vodka drinker, under the circumstances, he needed to at least act like a decent guest. Actually, it tasted pretty good. Each of them took two good pulls before the driver capped the bottle and slid it back under the mattress.

Lord have mercy, here they were, going down a narrow stretch of highway. The truck took all of one lane and some of the other and the driver was sharing a tope with some guy he did not know. The driver wheeled into Hereford and headed west towards Clovis, New Mexico. Scott could not believe that this was happening. They crossed the state line and the driver asked Scott where he could drop him off. Scott told him that he was meeting friends at the Holiday Inn in Clovis, please dear God.

When they reached the outskirts of Clovis, they came to a big intersection and the driver swung that rig down what appeared to be a main drag. A few blocks ahead sat a wonderful green sign, "Holiday Inn." The driver hit the air brakes and slowly rolled to the side of the road. Scott thanked the driver many times and climbed down the ladder to the street.

Wedding Party

As Scott was walking across the parking lot to the lobby, the Parkman wedding party pulled in under the awning. He had never been so happy to see anyone in his entire life. Sometimes the good Lord just takes over and protects really dumb people.

Mr. and Mrs. Parkman were surprised that Scott had made the trip, but neither Dave nor their old college roommate Jack Brechard were. They just figured that Scott had gotten lost. All told, there were fifteen people at the reception, which was in a semi-private room next to the bar and dance floor.

Scott had not met Marianne, the bride, before that evening. He asked her to dance, and when she stood up she was three inches taller than him. Scott figured that the look on his face must have given away what he was thinking, and she could not stop laughing. To be with old friends so far away from Peoria and the cold was just what he needed.

The next day, Dave and Marianne left for a honeymoon and Jack and Scott stayed for a couple of days at Dave's apartment. When it came time to head back to Peoria, Mr. and Mrs. Parkman bought Scott a train ticket to ride back to Illinois with them.

The ride through New Mexico and most of Texas was at night. Sitting in the touring car, Scott watched as the stars blossomed across the sky and the moon lit up the prairie as the train slid by at sixty miles an hour. Scott was not sure that he really wanted to leave the sunshine and beautiful weather to go back to Peoria.

The night was absolutely breathtaking as the train slid across the prairie. At long last Scott gave up his scenic view of the night and climbed down the stairs. This was about the best luck that he had had in a long time. He finally gave up and fell asleep. Some hours later he met the morning sun as its light played across his face. Late that afternoon he bid goodbye to the Parkman's and got off in Peoria.

Peoria Once More

When Scott returned to Peoria, he applied for jobs with real paychecks, but his draft status had reached a critical stage and he was now just days away from getting his invitation to join the US military.

Father Shepler had been fascinated with the story about Scott's trip to New Mexico. He had stopped Scott several times with questions and smiled as Scott warmed up to the telling of something that was obviously dear to his heart. With the evening growing late, Father had to finish his office and get ready for the next day.

He invited Scott to come by late the next afternoon so they could continue to talk over dinner. As he walked Scott toward the door, he excused himself and said that he would be right back. Scott put on his trench coat and thought how nice it was to be inside a warm house.

When Father returned, he handed Scott a small prayer book. He asked Scott to bow his head for a blessing. Scott felt like he had been given a ticket to rejoin the human race.

On the walk to the car, Scott found that the winter was

not as cold as it was when he walked out of the church hours before. He had spent time in the loving hand of God, and it rekindled the fire in his soul and rejuvenated his mind. While he was cold on the outside, he was warm on the inside. He had never thought of his religion in such a light.

His car had not gotten the same shot of adrenalin that Scott had gotten, and it was frozen. Scott was shaking with the cold as he ground on the starter several times until the motor finally climbed into life. He headed to a little downtown diner that had been his home away from home for several months, every time he walked in the waitress would call out, "Here's Up-town!"

She was always impressed that someone in a sports coat and tie would come into her little diner. She had coffee on the counter before Scott sat down. When he sat down he remembered the prayer book that the young priest had given him. As Scott opened the book a twenty-dollar bill slid out on the counter. It may as well have been a hundred dollars. He immediately changed his order from "the usual" to the cheeseburger lunch with French fries and a large glass of milk.

This was the most money that Scott had had in his hand in some time. He was certain that the waitress thought that he had must have stolen something because he never ordered the special. In all the months that he had been coming there, he had never eaten so "high on the hog".

As always, she stood close by to listen to Scott say his meal prayer. The meal prayer had been a part of his life since childhood. He always felt that it separated the haves and the don't haves. When he prayed, the diner always got quiet for a few moments. Perhaps other diners were reminded of home and said the meal prayer with their family.

Scott silently thanked the good Lord for directing him to the church and to the rectory on that bitter cold night. He never wanted to be like the nine who did not come back to thank Christ. He also said a silent prayer of thanks for Fr. Shepler for being such a gracious host. As he left the diner, he thanked everyone for their friendship for the last few months and told them that he was heading back to Iowa in the next couple of days.

This night, Scott pulled off the highway and onto the little outer road that ran next to the row of river houses. His lights played on his rental house as it sat dark and forlorn on the cold January night. He decided that after leaving the rectory tomorrow afternoon that he was ready to head home to Millersburg.

His roommate, Mike, was not home, which made three nights he had not shown up. While he left no note, Scott could tell that he had been there. He cranked the heater to full throttle and still the house was ice cold. It reminded him of the barn where they milked cows on the farm.

The old black and white TV pulled in a couple of stations. He turned it on just to have some noise in his life. He thought about his time at Sacred Heart and meeting Father Shepler. It had been so nice to be able to sit and talk with someone who cared.

Scott decided to get under the covers and try to get some sleep. He had had a lot of experience with cold bedrooms. The farmhouse at his family home was heated with wood stoves and oil burners. The stoves would all go out at night and would have to be restarted the next morning. He guessed that that was a precursor to his life in Peoria. It seemed like his whole life was a succession of making it through one damn cold winter after another.

The next morning Scott began loading a few months' worth of stuff into the old Ford. When he was done, there was only enough room for him to sit in the car and drive. All told he had fifteen dollars left out of the twenty and in combination with his small stash, thirty dollars. The car was filled with gas and he could make it through the day without spending any money.

He headed for the YMCA which was another of the places he frequented in Peoria. He got into a game of pickup basketball and remembered dribbling to his right. When he came to, he was lying on his left side with his left arm twisted under his body. He could not remember exactly what happened, but he did have a very sore shoulder.

The YMCA manager had a trainer look at his shoulder. He found a sling and suggested that Scott keep his arm against his body to give his shoulder time to heal. The manager told him to lie down on a couch in one of the offices and Scott was able to fall asleep in the warmth of a friendly place.

When the manager woke Scott up he told him that there had been some sandwiches left over from a banquet meal and that he was welcome to them. Scott realized that he had slept for over four hours. It was time to head back to the rectory to meet with Father. He told everyone at the YMCA goodbye and thanked them for their hospitality over the past few months.

Scott did not want to look any more pathetic than what

he already did, so he left the sling off when he went to the rectory. Scott thanked Father for the gift of the prayer book and the special bookmark that was inside.

Father asked Scott, "Now that you have had some time to consider your life is in front of you, have you made any new plans?"

Scott answered, "Father I have decided to go ahead and join the army and get past this draft card thing. The military will give me two things that seem to be missing, direction and discipline. I am not sure of the direction thing, but I do know that the military knows all about discipline."

A few weeks before his visit to the rectory, Scott had gone to visit military recruiting offices. The recruiters were not used to having a twenty-three-year-old come in to talk with them. Normally someone who was that old would be somewhere in San Francisco or Canada.

Scott had investigated the Coast Guard and went through a battery of tests only to be told that he was not made of the "right stuff." Next, he contacted the Army recruiters and told them that he would join the Army if they got him into training that he could use later in life. The recruiters set Scott up with an interview in Chicago with the Army Intelligence group.

With the recruiters working to get him into the Army and Father giving him a hand up, Scott was ready to go on into the military. Father was very happy that Scott had made that decision. Scott told him that his car was packed, and he would be on the road first thing tomorrow morning. He told Father, "With your generosity my car is full of gas and I still have a couple of dollars left over to buy food on the way home."

Going Home from Peoria

Father got a call and had to head to see a parishioner who was critically ill. He told Scott to stay until he came back to eat dinner. Scott spent the next two hours sitting in a warm house reading books from a well-stocked library. When Father returned, he was pretty well exhausted from his time at the hospital. Scott did not ask, but he could tell that Father was having a hard time dealing with whatever situation he had just left at the hospital.

Scott said, "While the situation that you left at the hospital may not be a good one, the situation you came back to is thankful and prayer-filled."

Such Good Men

Early the next morning, Scott threw his shaving kit in the car and headed north to the new Interstate 80, by way of Kewanee, Illinois. The day was turning into late afternoon when he noticed that the red oil light had come on. He stopped at a small gas station on the outskirts of Kewanee.

Scott knew that the car was internally hemorrhaging, so he did not shut the engine off. He poured the oil in and returned the glass oil jars back into the rack. On his way back, he could see a very large pool of wet and shiny oil under the blown engine.

The engine was making an awful racket as Scott headed down the main street of town. He pulled into a spot in front of the police station, left the car running and ran into the station to see where he could leave the car until he could junk it out. The desk sergeant was just coming out the front door to see what was making the terrible noise.

The sergeant suggested that Scott leave the car in the impound lot. That would get it off the street and Scott's belongings would be safe behind the chain link fence. Scott headed the old girl around the building to the impound gate and shut down the engine, which was more like a mercy killing. The policeman led Scott into the station and into the break room. There he poured him a hot cup of coffee. "Where are you headed for on this cold night?" he asked.

Scott replied, "I am heading for Millersburg, Iowa and waiting on my orders to go into the Army."

When two policemen came in from patrol, the sergeant briefed them on why Scott was their guest for a couple of hours. The officers insisted that he come back to the station after going to buy his bus ticket home. The officers were in the little lunchroom when Scott got back to the station. The patrolmen were complaining that their wives had packed way too much dinner and shared their sandwiches with the young stranger. When it was time to head for the bus station, Scott was on a first name basis with everyone. They told Scott not to worry as the car would not be in the way, take as long as needed. Scott had filled a suitcase with his clothes and one of the officers gave him a ride to the bus depot.

As the police car dropped him off, Scott figured that the people on the bus must have thought he was a criminal that was being escorted out of town. The highway sounds and the warmth of the bus let Scott drift away. The bus finally got to Scott's hometown at eleven thirty that night.

When his mom heard the front door open, she was up and making Scott dinner. Within a few minutes she had pork chops, creamed corn, and mashed potatoes reheated, and setting on the little drop-leafed table. That was one of the best meals of his life.

In all his years of coming home, this was the finest homecoming of all. Scott and his Mom sat at the little drop-leafed kitchen table and talked. This was a ritual that they followed each time he would come home. Finally, Scott's Dad called down from upstairs saying that "you'se" should get to bed. As they said their good nights and as he went to his room, Scott knew that his life was looking a whole lot better.

Chicago

By the time the Army recruiters got around to scheduling him to go Chicago to take tests for the military, Scott's brother had gotten him a construction job in Iowa City, very possibly one of the coldest jobs that Scott had in his life.

Twice the recruiters sent train tickets for Scott to go to Chicago for testing and twice his Mom and Dad took him to the train station in Marengo, Iowa. Though the station had been closed for years the engineer somehow knew that someone was waiting at the station to be picked up.

The trip to Chicago took five hours with short stops at the small towns and a little longer wait at Iowa City and Davenport. When Scott arrived in Chicago, he reported in at the Army's Induction Center, where Scott had been twice and had taken more tests than he could remember.

This time they were testing him to be a part of the Army's Intelligence community. At the end of the testing, he found himself in a room with two hundred desks filled with military staff. As he took his number from the little red number machine, he had the feeling that this was not going to be a good news event.

Scott sat there for a few minutes before an E-6, Sergeant Murphy, came to get him. The sergeant sat down at his desk. There was a brownish green folder in front of him. Without saying anything, he reviewed each page of the folder. When he looked up he told Scott that it had been determined that Military Intelligence was not the place for him.

Scott wasn't surprised. This was the way his life had been going for several months. He had heard the same thing when he talked to the Coast Guard. Now he was apparently not smart enough for Military Intelligence. Scott stood up, thanked the man, and began to leave.

Someone who cared

The sergeant looked at the expression on Scott's face and held up his hand for him to stop. He asked Scott to sit down while he went through his file one more time. Scott really needed to get some cooler air, but he decided to listen to what the man had to say. The sergeant reopened the folder and spent some time going through a fair stack of papers.

"I see you have some college," he said.

Scott said, "Yes, I have three years at St. Ambrose College in Davenport."

"Have you ever considered going to Officer Candidate's School?"

"I do not even know an Army officer and I have no idea about such a school," Scott replied.

The sergeant said, "I think that you might be a good fit for the Army, as an officer."

That said, he took a form out of a drawer and rolled the form into his old Royal typewriter. Using the information from Scott's folder, he began filling out an application. Scott thought that it was odd that he could not make it as an enlisted man in Army intelligence yet somehow be an officer. The logic escaped him, but for the first time in months there was something new and exciting on the horizon. That something was called hope. He readily answered questions and was amazed that someone had taken time to give a damn about the young man sitting by his desk.

This simple act of caring took Scott from rejection to elation. While he did not have the foggiest idea what Officer Candidate School really was, he signed the form. He wondered out loud what would happen if he did not make it through OCS. The sergeant told him that he had to be positive and put his mind and body into making it through OCS. Scott had never even talked to an Army officer in his life and now there was a possibility that he could become one.

This was one of the best days that Scott had had in a year. For the first time, since forever, he had a direction. He did not know what life was going to hold for him as he headed back to the LaSalle Street Train Station, but for the first time in a long time he was ready to try a new path.

As Scott thought back to that day in Chicago from far

off Vietnam, he realized that this was one of the events that had him on that hill in Vietnam, June 1, 1968. Without this man suggesting the OCS application, so much of Scott's life would have been totally different.

When he got back home he continued to work in the cold that surrounded Iowa City as he waited for his Army paperwork to arrive. The packet came in late February with orders to return to the Army's Induction Center in Chicago on April 14, 1966.

3. The Army

The Induction Center was large enough to put all of Millersburg on one floor. Thousands of men processed through this enormous structure. Scott was part of a hundred and twenty men who would be together all day for testing. An array of different colored strips led to every testing station. Scott's group followed the yellow tape on the floor to each testing station. With no one in charge of the men, the group got through all sixteen test stations.

Analogies

During the day, it was one battery of tests after another. Scott answered such questions as:

Metal is to a car as a Wood Board is to:

- An Automobile
- A Rock Cliff
- A Wooden building

All the tests included such brain queries. Each test was twenty minutes long with fifty questions. One of the tests took Scott five minutes and he had to sit and wait for the rest of his group to finish. Based on facial expressions, Scott figured that the tests these men were taking was on Einstein's Theory of Relativity. It was kind of scary as the questions were about as simple as a question could get.

At the end of the first day, Scott returned to his tiny room at the YMCA and was happy that his belongings were still there. As the night wore on, Scott could not sleep and the only way to stay in this room you had to be asleep, drugged, drunk or all three. After several laps around the huge building, he came back to his room and was able to fall asleep.

The next morning, he reported to the Induction Center with his small suitcase. This was the real deal. He would not be going back to the YMCA or to Iowa. At the close of this day he would be a part of the military. He had signed paperwork to be sent to a company clerk school if Officer Candidate School should fall through. He was sworn in, but that was just a formality. When the papers were signed, the US Army had him by the gonads.

As Scott had trucked through his second day at the induction center, he found himself in the company of one young man by the name of Pinard. He was wearing the oldest pair of pants that Scott had ever seen. They were a couple of sizes too big, as was the belt that kept the pants hanging on his ass. The end of the belt hung down six inches below his waist. He had a shock of hair that had not seen any shampoo in a long time.

The young man turned out to be like the truck that you

decided against passing as you were nearing your exit. That truck always gets off at your exit and turns the same way that you are going. So it was with Pinard, no matter where Scott turned, there stood Pinard. Since there were several hundred men being sworn in on this day, Scott figured he would soon lose his sorry ass. A hundred and six men were "picked" to head for Basic Training and the Army induction center at Fort Polk, LA. Included in those one hundred and six-men, Ledbetter and Pinard.

As soon as the swearing in was finished, the Army ran the new recruits through the mess hall. With induction center mentality, eating was just a task to be gotten out of the way. When the meal was over, they put one hundred and six men onto two buses, and they went to Chicago's O'Hare airport.

They were scheduled to fly out on two airplanes from Butler Airlines, but the planes only held fifty passengers. With one hundred and six inductees, this posed a logistical problem. There was momentary panic amongst the military types. Scott felt right at home as this was just more of how crazy his life had been over the past few months.

Scott was one of the six names called to come to the front of the group. The six men would be flying commercially on a Braniff jet to Houston. They would be staying in Houston overnight and flying commercially to Fort Polk the next morning. Scott assumed that he was picked because of his advanced age of twenty-three. In reality, a sergeant picked up the list and called out six names. That is military logic!

Thirty minutes later, the six were sitting in Braniff Airline's waiting area, fifty of the recruits came walking by them. One of the planes could only get one propeller to spin, so they had to take a different plane. Scott was very happy that he was one of the six going on Braniff.

Scott's first jet experience on the flight to Houston was wonderful. Scott's only airplane ride had been on a DC-3, when he flew from Rock Island to St. Louis for a wedding. He remembered sitting in the cabin while the pilot revved the engine up at the end of the runway. Before the brakes were released the plane was literally shuddering on the tarmac. When the pilot released the brakes, they lurched into the sky. This Braniff jet was off the ground in a whisper, very cool.

The flight was empty of paying passengers, so each of the men had his own row of seats. Scott was the only one who was old enough to drink liquor, so he ordered a Budweiser. The rest had to settle for a can of soda.

They arrived in Houston's Hobby airport at nine o'clock PM and stayed at a Route 66 kind of motel. It sat two hundred feet from the Quonset hut which was the Houston Hobby Airport. The group checked in with their "we are in the military, approval code". They stayed in three little houses with two single beds per house. The room was very similar to the one that Scott had stayed in when he was hitchhiking through Oklahoma City.

The men flew to Fort Polk on the Trans Texas Airline. Its logo had two T's stacked on top of one another. The regulars called it Tree Top Airlines, as the airplanes barely got above the scrub pines in LA and TX.

No Welcome Party at
Fort Polk Induction Center

At one o'clock in the afternoon, the Trans Texas plane dropped down onto a single runway in the middle of what they were told was Fort Polk, LA. The plane stopped next to a two-story tower. The men got off the tail dragger and the crew threw down their luggage and closed the exit door. The plane immediately travelled down to the end of the runway, spun around, revved up the engines until the plane was shaking. As the plane got even with the men standing by the tower, it lurched into the sky.

In a matter of moments, the DC-3 disappeared into the east, leaving the men standing in silence. Scott went into the tower to find out what they were supposed to do next. A quick search of the single room downstairs and upstairs found no one at home. A few feet away from the tower they found a tree with ample shade for them to wait.

When the young troop in charge said that they should call someone, Scott asked, "Who?" Since the leader had no idea who to call, they just sat on their luggage and waited. Soon everyone was asleep under the large pine tree. At four in the afternoon, Scott woke up to the sound of a jeep grinding up through the woods. The soldier driving the jeep stopped by the tower and asked who they were, as if six civilians would just be sitting out in the "comfortable" Louisiana weather. Scott told him that they were recruits reporting for duty.

The soldier went into the tower and called the induction center. That must have been quite a conversation. Scott was certain that someone got reamed for leaving new recruits out in the wilds to suffer without food or water.

A small army truck was sent to pick up the recruits, in a truck that was a little bigger than a pickup, called a 6 X 6. That was the size of the box on the back of the cab. Scott loved that the military called something exactly what it was, with little or no fanfare. They climbed aboard what was to be the first of many military truck type vehicles they would climb into during their military career.

The first problem was that there should have only been one hundred recruits sent to O'Hare from the induction center in Chicago. That was the beginning of the screw up. This situation best explained the military. In the military, there is only one way to do something. Once you stepped out of the mainstream, the less than flexible minds had a hard time reacting and adjusting to a new situation. A civilian would just make an adjustment and move on.

When they had arrived at O'Hare Airport, the soldier in charge of the inductees had no authority to call out six names and put them on a commercial airline. To make matters worse, no one had told the induction center at Fort Polk that they were short six people. If someone had told them that recruits were coming on a private carrier, a truck would have been at the airport to police them up. In the Army, this was a catastrophe.

Induction Center

When Scott and his five cohorts got to the Induction Center, no one knew what to do. Sergeants yelled at each other as the recruits stood sort of at ease, or as at ease as you can be when you are lost between being in the army and still looking like a civilian. They were civilians in a military situation.

When the six recruits walked into the barracks, the other one hundred inductees, whom they had just seen yesterday, looked like people from another planet. Just twenty-four hours ago they were at the airport with civilian clothes, long hair, and beards. Now they were all shorn, shaved, and smelling of army green dye. All of them just stood and stared at the six civilians.

Clothing Issue Point

The military clothing issue point is a massive building with large doors on each end of the building. A counter runs the entire length of the building. The counter is sectioned off by the type of clothing that is being issued to each recruit. In the first section, the recruit is handed a new and stiff duffle bag. The next section is where boots are issued. There are sections where the recruit picks up five T shirts, five pairs of shorts, 2 pairs of black socks, five pairs of green work socks, combat boots, dress shoes (called low quarters), five fatigue shirts, five fatigue trousers, one fatigue jacket, one fatigue overcoat, one dress green jacket and slacks.

A recruit runs in one door and is immediately hit with a

brand-new duffle bag. He carries the duffle bag on the bottom of the pile of clothing, that he is about to receive. As the troop goes from one section to another he shouts out his clothing size or boot size. Someone on the other side of the counter throws the clothing at the troop. There is no time to look and see if it is small or extra-large. The recruit would get what he got.

To ensure complete misery in this process, the Drill Sergeants are all yelling to move the line along. The men going through the line, are yelling out their sizes, while the soldiers on the other side of the counter are yelling out the clothing size they are throwing to the inductee. No clothing or footwear is tried on. When the recruit reaches the far end of the building, they run out with a huge pile of clothes.

All those clothes have to be pushed and shoved into a that brand-new duffle bag that is a stiff as new leather. The Drill Sergeants are all yelling for the recruits to hurry up. The Louisiana sun and humidity makes every recruit sweat and pray that this will come to an end. The trip through the issue point for a hundred men normally takes ten minutes. Stuffing the clothes into the bag takes fifteen minutes. The troops and all the gear are soon back on the troop carrier and heading for their next processing station.

When the six recruits arrived, there was just the six men. No sergeants were yelling to hurry up. The clothing issue people had no idea how to handle six men who were quietly walking through with a Specialist Fourth Class. The men were actually able to get clothing and footwear that fit. All of them sat down and tried on their boots and shoes. At the end of the counter they all stayed inside the barn and took time to put all their new clothes into the duffle bag.

"Shave and a haircut, two bits"

Next stop was at the barbershop. As soon as the truck stopped on the parking lot, two men jumped off the deuce and a half and ran to the barbershop. Scott and the others unclimbed the truck slowly and stepped down on the asphalt. When Scott got into the shop the first two were in the chair getting a buzz cut. When it was Scott's turn, he told the barber that he wanted a flat top, not a buzz cut.

The first men to get a haircut asked, "You mean that we could have asked for a flat top?"

The barber explained, "We only give buzz cuts if no one asks us to do anything different."

After hours of being trucked to all the different buildings to get shots and other official military things, the six were dropped off right in front of their barracks. With the addition of army green clothes and black combat boots, they now looked like the troops that they saw last evening. When all the troops came back from some kind of detail, Scott saw his new friend Pinard.

That afternoon Scott went on his first detail, to rake pine needles which in Louisiana were as plentiful as hot humid air. They raked up twenty-bushel baskets of needles and carried them thirty feet to dump them on the ground. In Scott's mind, this was busy work and he decided that he was not a candidate for details. Over the next few days he planned ways to exclude himself from as many details as possible. Sometimes he was successful, sometimes not, but always, he did try.

The next day they fell out into the company area along with at least a thousand other recruits. Everyone was sent to briefings about everything Army. They learned about syphilis and how to protect themselves. In the only air-conditioned room in all of Ft Polk, a young Specialist was explaining the life insurance policies. When he got to the page about beneficiaries on their insurance policy, he stopped talking. After the silence had everyone's attention he said,

"Gentlemen, I am here to tell you that there is a high mortality rate in the military… on sweethearts! I want you to list your parents, uncle, aunt, or cousin as your beneficiary. Do not put the little girl who is waiting (not) until you get out of the service.

Have any of you heard a Jody Song? Jody has been with us through every war that has ever been fought and is still with us. After all these years, he is still not in the service, he is out there dating all of those young ladies "waiting" for their soldier boy to come home." Scott wondered how many honeys were in fact the benefactors of a young troop going to Vietnam.

The testing and endless meetings went on during each day until it was time for some useless detail. On their fourth morning, the induction center cadre came in and rousted their sorry asses out of bed at "4 dark thirty in the morning." They were instructed to fall out into the company area with their entire issue of sierra, including duffle bags, laundry bags, and AWOL bags. The induction center was finally going to be left behind. They would be assigned to their basic training company.

This was the first of many times when Scott and his unit at the time would have the opportunity to see the world hours before the sun rose in the sky. They created four lines of men and equipment that stretched the entire length of the induction center street. Even in the darkness, you could see the lines of men as they disappeared over the hill.

When a man's name along with his new Basic Training Company was called out, he would grab all his stuff, fall across piles of gear on the ground, and disappear into the night. Hopefully he could find the army truck that was calling his name.

Scott was excited to start his military career in basic training. When the roll call concluded, the sun was at last stretching across Ft. Polk's Louisiana pines. Unfortunately, Scott and a lot of other men were still standing in the formation. No explanation. The silence was deafening.

The cadre brought all the troops not assigned to Scott's end of the line. A specialist did a roll call and the seventy-nine men were present and accounted for. They led them down a sandy path, past barracks where they had been for four days. They came to another barracks where they were told to wait. There was no "Hi, yes, or Go to Hell" as to why they were not assigned to a unit. They selected a bunk, put their belongings in the locker and footlocker, and just waited. Two hours later another E-4 Specialist showed up and told them that they were being sent to Ft. Riley, Kansas for their Basic Training.

No Unit Assignment

The group made themselves at home in the new barracks. Scott met a young man named Jim Coleman from Chicago and they hit it off. With nothing to do, they lounged around for most of the morning until another E-4 showed up and marched them to the mess hall for lunch. After chow, more E-4's showed up and selected everyone for some kind of a detail.

Scott's detail was marched back to the induction center. There an army cattle truck (semi-trailer, open top) was parked next to the supply room. The truck was filled with army blankets stacked four feet deep from front to back. Their detail was to take all these blankets into the supply room and stack them on shelves. Jim and Scott were assigned to the truck. They got in and started handing armloads of oily army blankets over the side to the fourteen other men in the detail.

The afternoon sun was up in the high nineties, and the Louisiana humidity was pushing one hundred percent. Scott and Jim passed armload after armload to the inductees carrying them into the supply room. As soon as the men would stack their pile of blankets in the supply room, they would come back for Scott and Jim to load them up again.

I'd Rather Watch

Two hours later, Scott and Jim had made it a couple of feet past the back wheels. Their hands had become so oily and sweaty that it was almost impossible to pick up the damned blankets. With no apparent path to take them away from this detail, the two decided to make themselves disappear.

When the E-4 walked the detail back into the supply room, both men climbed down on the far side of the truck and walked back into the timber. Scott knew that the E-4 had no idea who used to be in the cattle truck, because he did not know one person on this detail. He would not be able to recognize anyone's face because inductees were faceless people.

Scott and Jim stood well back in the scrub pines and watched as the detail reappeared from the supply room. The E-4 did not miss a beat as he ordered two new recruits into the truck and the detail continued hauling the blankets into the supply room. Scott and Jim found a comfortable pile of pine needles and watched the day go by.

If this would have been a real army outfit the E-4 would know the names of the men in his detail. In a regular company this bold adoption of Beetle Bailey would not have worked. However, this was an induction center where no one knew anyone.

It took two more hours for the detail to unload the cattle truck. As they were reaching the front of the truck, Scott and Jim walked around the supply room and simply got in line to get a stack of blankets. Fifteen minutes later, the detail was done. No one had any idea where they had been or noticed that they had not been there.

After evening chow, Jim and Scott went for a walk and found an Enlisted Men's club a block away from their back-water barracks. They went in for a beer and some country music. After taking a break from the rigorous life they were leading, they headed back to the barracks where they slept well.

Pizza Oven Detail

The next day after returning from morning chow another E-4 showed-up to take a detail of twenty recruits to the mess hall. They were there to clean ten pizza ovens. The inductees were issued steel mesh gloves and a three-pound block of some kind of abrasive that crumbled and got beneath the mesh gloves. This detail was a "bitch."

Scott and Jim were given the first oven on both sides of the mess hall. They cleaned ovens for most of an hour. The E-4 finally left to get a glass of iced tea. When he did, Jim and Scott left for the woods. They simply walked out the doors on either side and headed into the woods.

There they found some comfortable pine needles and rested. They watched the men clean the ovens. As they were getting done with all the ovens, the two men walked back into the mess hall and were the first in line for chow.

Scott realized that there was a pattern to this detail thing. Within fifteen minutes of getting back from eating breakfast or lunch, many E-4's would show up and grab whoever was in the barracks. The barracks had become a treasure trove of trained detail people. They did not have to be taught how to do a detail. Scott figured out that the E-4's had no idea how many inductees were in the barracks. They would just take everyone standing there.

The next day, when Scott and Jim got back from breakfast,

they walked into the barracks with everyone else and then walked back out and went behind the barracks. When all the recruits were taken for some detail, the two would go back inside and relax.

AWOL Inductees

For three days, Scott and Jim missed all the details the same way. The two got bored with nothing to do so they decided that they would go to the post exchange (PX), even though neither knew where the PX was located. This was to be an adventure.

They left the induction center and headed for what appeared to be the main post, some ten blocks away. This meant that both Scott and Jim would be "Absent without Leave" (AWOL). As civilians in military clothing, neither of them knew about this "minor military law". They headed out without telling anyone that they were going.

They asked a soldier along the way and found the PX. They picked up some playing cards, a checkerboard game, cigarettes, and toiletries. On the trip back to the induction center, it started to rain, and it was getting colder. They were walking with their hands in their pockets. They did not know that this was a horrendous breech in the code of military conduct. You do not walk with your hands in your pockets — ever.

They were walking along fairly briskly as the rain had started to fall harder. A captain stopped them and reprimanded them for having their hands in their pockets and for not saluting him. They managed to get their hands out of their pockets and gave the worst salute in military history.

The captain returned the salute and just shook his head and walked away. Scott could not imagine why he had picked on them. The encounter did give them something to talk about on the trip back. They had learned a lesson: Keep your hands out of your pockets. They also knew that they had to keep a watchful eye out for anyone they should salute.

When they got to the induction center, they walked down the sidewalk that took them past the Orderly Room. Neither Scott nor Jim knew about the orderly room or the fact that it was command central in any military unit. If you are AWOL from your assigned duty station, it was considered taboo (stupid) to walk in front of an Orderly Room. That rule was doubled down if you are carrying bags from the PX, where you should not have been in the first place. The only thing that Scott and Jim could have done to draw more attention to themselves was to have been buck naked.

As they sauntered by the window of the Orderly Room, Scott saw one of the sergeants spew his coffee out his nose and he knew that they had seriously screwed up. That sergeant immediately started for the door. Scott said to Jim, "Run as fast as you can."

By the time the sergeant made it out of the door and yelled at them to stop, the two men were three buildings away.

The luck that had been keeping them out of trouble for most of the week held out. A couple hundred inductees were policing the grounds in the company area (This meant that they were walking aimlessly, looking for anything on the ground that should not be on the ground). With the exception of the PX bags, Scott and Jim fit right in.

The sergeant yelled for them to stop a second time. By that time, they were past the mess hall. They turned and ran to their hiding place in the woods. They knew that there was a large flat rock at the edge of the timber. They lifted the far end of that rock and shoved in the PX bags under that rock. They ran back to join the other inductees who were policing between the buildings. They walked slowly as if they were on the police call.

Two sergeants came running around the building in search of the PX renegades. Scott and Jim put on their "best new inductee on a police call," walk. As one of the sergeants was hurrying by them, he asked Scott, "Did you see two guys running down between these buildings?"

Amazingly they had not seen anyone running. The sergeant moved on and both the men just kept searching the ground for an errant piece of anything to police off the ground.

The sergeants finally gave up and headed back to the Orderly Room. Scott and Jim wandered away from the police call detail and headed for the barracks. When they got to the barracks, the two wayward soldiers walked in with their fellow inductees as they came back from a detail. It looked like they had been with them all day.

That evening they went back to the rock, took their stuff out of the PX bags, and carried it to the barracks. For the next two days, Scott and Jim missed every detail. With the checkers and cards they bought at the PX, they had something to pass the time.

Early Morning Wake Up

On the fourth day of this Induction Limbo, all the recruits were rousted out of bed at 0430 hours. Scott wondered if they had decided to start a detail so early that both Ledbetter and Coleman would actually join the group.

They were rousted out of bed and told to fall out with their Duffle bags and AWOL bags. In the formation, they were introduced to Sergeant English from Fort Riley, Kansas. They would be traveling by train to Riley for their basic training. The inductees were run through the mess hall and hurriedly loaded onto army buses. They arrived at the train station in Leesville, LA, two hours early. "Hurry up and wait" was the key.

Seventy-nine recruits and one sergeant boarded a regular train headed north to Kansas City. Along the way, they stopped, and sleeper cars were coupled onto the train. Jim and Scott were put into one of the sleeper units with two bunks. Scott thought that was one of the most fun trips he had ever been on in his life.

The two men were like little kids, intrigued with all the gadgets on a sleeper car. They played some checkers before pulling down the drop-down bunks and climbing into bed. They were laughing about the orderly room episode and the great week they spent in the barracks waiting for chow. Soon the rails rocked them both to sleep.

Fort Riley Kansas For Basic Training

A barracks bathroom gave a whole new meaning to "Not Personal." Eight stools lined up against one wall with no wall between. On the opposite side of the room twenty sinks lined the wall. The metal mirrors which were mounted above the sinks reflected a blurry image at best.

Let Basic Begin

The next afternoon the train pulled into Kansas City and recruits were put on charter buses for the three-hour trip to Ft. Riley. There they were greeted by normal Sergeants (not Army Drill Sergeants). These men would be their trainers for the next eight weeks. They found out that these sergeants would be going with them to Vietnam as part of the 9th Infantry Division. Scott did not think that having a whole division go from training to Vietnam was the brightest idea, but no one had asked him for his opinion.

At Ft. Polk when the troops made their way to the trucks from the induction center, the amount of yelling was unbelievable. So Scott and Jim were expecting the same treatment. Instead they were welcomed and asked if anyone was sick or needed any special attention. This was a stark contrast to their earlier experience, but they weren't complaining.

As it turned out, there were too many recruits assigned to the company and they split Scott's platoon in half. Half of the platoon was housed over the company Day Room. The other half was quartered in the day room across the battalion area. Scott's half of the platoon was across the battalion area.

Each half of the platoon had thirty guys. Pinard (of course) was in Scott's half of the platoon and in the same fifteen-man squad. It was hard to imagine that he had been with this guy all the way from Chicago. Pinard volunteered to be the trainee sergeant for the platoon and that lasted less than a day.

GI Bath

For the first two weeks, Pinard did not take a bath. He was given repeated warnings about cleaning up his act, but those warnings fell on deaf ears. One evening, seven men grabbed him from his bunk and took him into the shower for a "GI Bath."

Soldiers lived in a confined area and when someone is not bathing, the men in the barracks will take care of the stinky-assed person. On this night, they grabbed Pinard and drug him into the shower, stripped him buck assed naked. They used the long-handled brushes, which are used to clean latrines, on his bare ass. The brush is made with three-inch wooden bristles and they will wear the skin off. Pinard seemed to have gotten the message. After his "GI Bath" he started to take a shower morning and night. He also started to launder his under clothes and uniforms, which he had not done. After a couple of weeks of bathing and laundering clothes, he began to be a real human being.

Scott's boot camp experience was connected with the

smells and sounds of the barracks. At night, he would lie and listen as twenty-nine other men slept in his bedroom. The snoring and breathing sounds were at times comical. Scott had never been around that many men and certainly not men who walked around the barracks in shorts or a towel to the latrine and while they worked on boots, or squared away their uniforms.

A barrack's bathroom gave a whole new meaning to "Not Personal." Eight stools lined up against one wall without any wall between them. On the opposite side of the room twenty sinks lined the wall. The metal mirrors mounted above the sinks reflected a blurry image, at best.

The shower room bristled with ten shower heads and there were no interior shower stalls; just ten shower heads aiming out from the wall. If you wanted bathroom privacy, then you had to get up in the middle of the night and use the bathroom or shower. Even then there would always be someone coming or going. The lack of privacy kept thoughts inside, as there was no place to let them out.

A normal day started at 0430 hours with a sergeant yelling everyone out of bed or shaking a can of rocks over your sleepy head or sorry ass. This was followed by a flurry of activity as the latrine filled up with people who had two minutes to do what used to take thirty minutes in civilian life. Within ten minutes of being shouted out of bed, all the recruits were up and dressed and headed out the door for morning formation.

At roll call, each name was called out and that man had to holler out, "Here, Sergeant." The first roll call in a new company was always fun as the sergeant would butcher the hard to pronounce names. Whatever came out of their mouths during that first roll call would often become the man's name for the rest of Basic Training—and sometimes their entire military career.

Then the sergeant, who was standing in near darkness, would give them the training schedule for the day. That same information was posted on the barracks bulletin board. Scott believed that the Army started the saying, "Tell 'em what you are going to tell 'em, tell 'em what you told em, and tell 'em again."

When the formation was over, it was off to the mess hall. A military mess hall line was steeped in tradition. Everyone lines up an arm's length from the man in front of him. The mess sergeant, or one of his henchmen, stood in the doorway and yelled, "Next." With that command, everyone in line would come to attention and the first five men in line would run into the mess hall. The rest of the line would close on the steps and go back to parade rest.

The Shot

In his second week of boot camp, Scott and his company came back from training in the heat of the Kansas plains. After chow, they were told to line up outside the supply room. Inside were two Corpsmen with a pneumatic needle who shot each recruit in the ass with Bi-Cillin. While Scott had no idea what malady the shot was supposed to cure or prevent, like a good soldier he dropped his trousers. The pain of the shot was excruciating, and Scott struggled to button up as he slowly limped away.

During the night, the pain in his backside became unbearable. He could not lie on his side or roll over to get out of bed. He had to drop one knee to the floor and push himself into a standing position from the floor. He took a hot shower and walked off the pain in his leg and backside.

The sergeant's call at 0430 hours came long after Scott was up and dressed. He had read the training schedule, and it looked like they were going to the theatre to watch a training film. There was a change in plans and instead they sat on their ponchos in a shade-less parade field, field stripping an M14 rifle. Scott had to balance himself on one leg and put the M14 together. The sun was beating down and the reflected heat from the poncho made this onerous task totally miserable.

Once his rifle was assembled, there were more demonstrations by the cadre on handling a rifle in parades and in formations. After what seemed like forever, they left the parade field and checked in their rifles. From there they went to noon chow. As Scott was trying to choke down the mess on his plate, a troop passed out as he walked by Scott's table. When he went down, the tray of food slid out in front of him and both the man and the tray just lay there.

As the sergeants picked this young man up to carry him outside, Scott weakly asked the sergeant, "How do I go on sick call in mid-day?"

They took one look at Scott and saw that he looked like a ghost. They took the two men outside and put ice packs on their necks and called an ambulance to take the men to the hospital. Scott had only been to a hospital one time and that was with his folks a long time ago. He asked the lady at the front desk how he was supposed to pay for his hospital stay. She jokingly told him that he would be "billed," so Scott said okay and gave her his ID card. The clerk realized that Scott was not kidding and was just too sick to catch the humor. She was very apologetic and told Scott that his medical was taken care of by the military.

After his exam, the doctor checked Scott into the hospital. It was a real treat when they put him into an air-conditioned room, especially during the summer in Kansas. Four days later, he returned to the full load of basic training.

Kitchen Police (KP)

Scott saw on the daily bulletin that he had been "picked" for KP duty, another sacred ritual in any Army. The cadre took a special delight in coming into a dark barracks at 0400 to wake the chosen ones for Kitchen Police. When Scott arrived, three other KPs were already there and had taken the best jobs. Scott could pick between washing pots and pans or take the outside job which was to take care of the garbage. He opted to take the garbage job.

Scott had done every kind of clean up job at St. Ambrose, where he worked in the cafeteria. None of those jobs could have prepared him for the amount of slop that one hundred and thirty basic trainee soldiers could create in any one meal. Take that times three meals and the waste was enormous. Scott thought that feeding pigs was bad, but that could not hold a candle to basic trainee troops.

His day was spent dumping large heavy trash cans into a

dumpster. Then he would clean the trash can and dump the next trash can into the dumpster. The clean-up after breakfast took well over an hour. When the mess sergeant came out to check his progress, he saw that Scott was falling behind. The mess sergeant brought all the KP's out to help him catch up. That is how Scott developed his "KP Theory."

He knew that if he looked busy and fell behind, the mess sergeant would order all the other KP's to come out and do his job. He knew from experience that no one bothered a troop who is cleaning a garbage can. Scott would take a clean garbage can, sit down on the concrete deck and scrub that can with a long-handled brush. He could sit for twenty minutes and clean one garbage can and no one would question him. At some point, the mess sergeant would once again have all the KP's out to help the outside man. It was like the best of all worlds for a basic trainee on KP.

On his first day on KP he learned that as the outside man you never go into the mess hall. He made that mistake. He went into the mess hall to get a cup of coffee. He was just turning to go back outside when the mess sergeant saw a soldier who had nothing to do and assigned him to clean the grease traps. The grease traps caught every piece of garbage that is in the massive arrangement of sinks in a mess hall.

Scott had never seen these traps; he had cleaned much smaller grease traps when he was working at his college kitchen. Scott got under the sinks and looked at the traps. "Disgusting" would have been a gross understatement. He knew that his being assigned to this task had nothing to do with the job he was supposed to be doing. He was merely a target of opportunity.

Scott filled two buckets with water, crawled under the sinks and sort of hammered around on the top of the traps. He never actually cleaned up that ungodly mess. When he crawled out from under the sinks with buckets filled with water, it looked like he had cleaned the traps. He quickly threw the water away and went back outside to his real job.

Physical Training

Scott kept a low profile and made good friends because he could out work or out pack any person, regardless of his physical attributes. While he could outwork anyone, he would only apply his shoulder when it made sense for him to do so. If there was no reason to apply his skills, he would let someone else apply theirs.

Most of the men in the Basic Training unit were younger and in better shape, but Scott knew something that most did not, muscles do not finish the race. The race is finished by someone with the inner strength to carry on, regardless. He had learned that muscles are on the outside, the real strength comes from an inner strength. Inner strength was the ability to stand and work when others failed. That was the strength he developed as he worked alongside his brothers and his dad on their Iowa farm.

PCPT

Each Saturday morning, Basic Trainees had to take a **P**hys-ical **C**ombat **P**roficiency **T**est (PCPT). A recruit could earn one hundred points per event. To pass Basic Training, recruits had to score at least three hundred points. The first time that Scott took the test he scored three hundred and fifty points.

There was one event that Scott could not do because of the shoulder injury at the Peoria YMCA, the parallel ladder. The ladder was eight feet off the ground and had fourteen rungs on the ladder. The trainee had to go hand over hand down the ladder, turn at the far end, and come back to the starting place. If Scott attempted this event he would dislocate his shoulder, so he wisely skipped it.

Another nemesis in the PCPT test was the low crawl. To properly low crawl you used your elbows and knees to pull and drive the body forward. Scott learned to tuck his hurt shoulder close to his body and drive his body forward with just his legs. Using this technique, he was able to make it through this part of the proficiency test. While his score was a little off in the low crawl and he got no points for the ladder, he maxed the other events and was able to pass the proficiency test.

Details forever

Details were a standard in the military. If you were standing around in a training area, you could expect that you will be doing some detail. If they "fell" you out into a formation at an odd time, you would be picked for a detail. The cadre in a training company all know who you are, so you cannot walk away like Scott and Jim did at Fort Polk. The only control that a trainee has is to try to improve on your situation.

One Saturday morning Scott, along with six others, were "picked" for a typing detail. Getting a detail that did not involve sweating or getting dirty was a good thing. They were sent to battalion HQ where they typed a lot of training bulletins on blue-waxed mimeograph paper. While they were typing, the rest of the company was running and preparing for the Post Physical Proficiency Test at the end of the training cycle. They had finished typing the pieces they were supposed to do before the company started the mile run. Scott had everyone wait inside of battalion until the run was done so they avoided having to run with the company.

On the following Saturday morning, the company was in another formation and the cadre was assigning work details. They were working their way from the far end of the company to Scott's platoon. As they reached Scott's platoon, he held up his hand to tell them that they were supposed to go back to battalion and type.

The sergeant said, "Well get your butts over there and type."

The six men who had finished up typing last week were all heading towards battalion.

One of the men said, "Ledbetter, we finished that last week." Everyone on the detail said in unison. "Close your Pie Hole." They showed up at battalion headquarters and went back to their typewriters and no one said a word to them.

There really was nothing to type so everyone sat around

and had coffee and talked. Scott typed an 18" paper on the care and cleaning of the P-38, a small two piece can opener that folds in the middle. It is used to open "C" ration cans in the field. Scott typed the directive and registered it just like he had with the documents they had typed last week. When they saw that the PCPT training was done, the detail wrapped up and went back to the barracks.

Detail gone wrong

The next Saturday they wanted a detail to work on the Vietnam village that had been built at Ft. Riley. Scott wanted to see the Vietnam village and ignored his own volunteer code which was to never volunteer. Jim and Scott both went on this detail. Instead of seeing the village, they found themselves in a field of long tall grass a half mile from the village. They could barely see it off in the distance, but they never got close to the structures.

Scott knew that he had picked a bad detail, but he just kept cutting and hoping for the best. They were four miles from the main post with no hope of rescue. Scott had just brought his bundle of grass up to the road when a jeep pulled up. The Specialist E-4 driving the jeep said, "I need two men to clean the Chaplain's recreation room." Scott said, "We are your huckleberries." Scott and Jim handed their machetes to the E-4 who was in charge of the detail and got into the jeep.

At the Chaplain's office, they dry mopped the recreation room and watched television. The Chaplain came in with fresh donuts to go along with a pot of fresh coffee. This was really a "tough" way to end the day. For the life of him, Scott could not believe that the E-4 drove from Camp Forsythe to the Vietnam village to find two people to clean the Rec Room. Perhaps he heard him praying for a way out of that crummy detail.

The Firing Range

"Ready on the right, Ready on the left, Ready on the firing line! GENTLEMEN Lock and load three rounds ball ammunition" Ready on the right—Ready on the left—Ready on the firing line—Fire.

The company walked everywhere the entire eight weeks of training. There had been no real basic training at Riley since WWII. Consequently, there were no vehicles available for transportation to or from the ranges. The ranges were built for Ft. Riley proper. Camp Forsythe was a mile away from the main post. Every day they covered that mile plus several more.

Their unit was the only unit being trained on post, so they were an anomaly. When they walked through the main post on the way to the rifle range, all the old troops would stand and watch. Some made snide remarks while others just watched and tried to remember when they were that young.

When they walked past the NCO Academy, the men out in front of the classrooms never made any catcalls. They knew that someone in this group was going to be their ticket back from Vietnam, standing up. The NCO's, new and old, just stood and watched and showed their respect for these men being trained to be ground pounding sons of bitches.

Learning to fire a rifle was driven into every troop from the moment he arrived at Basic Training. In the first week, M-14 rifles were issued each troop. By the morning of the second day, every basic trainee had to memorize the rifle's serial number. The M-14 rifle weighed in at thirteen pounds with a maximum effective range of 460 meters; total range was just over a mile. That meant that a bullet from an M-14 could bring down an enemy over a mile away. It had a pretty serious impact.

The M-14 was the replacement for the carbine, which was popular at the end of WWII and the staple in Korea. Its mate was a forever heavy Browning automatic rifle. Scott lifted one of those things once and had to ask for help. It fired a 30.06 bullet and must have been brutal at close range. The M-14 was being replaced with the M-16. It was used in Vietnam but had not made it into Basic Training.

In the military, especially in Basic Training, a rifle became a part of your entire being. You carried it from the time you left for the field until you got back. You fired it with and without ammunition; you fire it with blanks and a flash suppressor when you are taking part in mock battles. A blank had powder and the flash suppressor was mounted on the end of the barrel to keep the powder from hitting someone in the face. Unfortunately, firing a blank round made the barrel dirty and the weapon had to be cleaned every time blanks were fired.

On the rifle range, there was not one Army private (from the Vietnam era) who did not hear, "Ready on the right,

Ready on the left, Ready on the firing line! GENTLEMEN Lock and load three rounds ball ammunition — Ready on the right — Ready on the left — Ready on the firing line — Fire." This rifle training went on non-stop for eight weeks straight. Out of the eight weeks of training they spent four weeks on the firing range.

The Night Fire Range

The day started at 0500 hours. After breakfast, the company walked to the firing range, five miles away. They fired the M-14 as many times as they could during the day. After evening chow, they sat around and waited for dark so they could fire their rifles at night. At 2200 hours, the last platoon fired their last rounds and the company saddled up for the five-mile hike back to Forsythe.

The night had grown very tired and Scott's twenty-three-year-old body was showing wear and tear. The first part of the trip was on an old dirt road that was high crowned. Scott fell asleep walking. His friend Carl Toban was right behind him and grabbed him by the back pack as Scott started coasting toward the ditch. Carl kept his hand on Scott's pack for the rest of the hike.

They made it to the company area at 2400 hours. They checked in their rifle which had fired a lot of rounds that day. The trainee armorer was no other than Pinard. After his failure as a trainee platoon sergeant, this was his role. Scott was standing in line when he saw that Pinard was judiciously checking each rifle barrel to ensure that it was ready for combat the next morning.

Trainee after trainee had their rifle rejected by Pinard. Before they could turn in their rifle, they had to break it down and clean it. Once it was clean and shiny, Pinard would accept the weapon and rack it in the arm's room. When Scott handed Pinard his rifle, he started to hold the weapon up to the light to check the barrel. If he had, he would have seen that there were boulders of dirt on the rifling of the barrel.

As Pinard went to raise the rifle so he could look down the barrel, Scott said, "Pinard, if you raise that rifle to the light I will jam that son of a bitch up your ass and you can check it from the inside." Pinard remembered the "GI Bath" and decided, with no eminent military threats, to rack the rifle. While others were bitching about having to clean their rifles, Scott took a shower and went to bed.

A Good Friend

Carl looked over to Scott and said, "Ledbetter, you are the first white man that I have ever talked with in all of my life. Now I have been yelled at by white folks, but I have never talked with one. Not one of them ever sat down and talked like we are doing now."

Carl was a young black man from Texas in the same half of the platoon as Scott. Their bunks were directly across from each other. On Friday night, before the first Saturday inspection, Scott was laboriously shoving piles of polish onto his low quarters. Carl sat across the aisle on his footlocker, watching Scott and shaking his head. Finally, he got up and came over and said,

"White people can't shine shoes!"

Scott looked up and said, "Well then sit your black ass down and show me how to polish my shoes!" He did, and from that time on, the two men never shut up. Over the next seven weeks, they polished shoes, boots, and barracks' floors. Together they cleaned showers and latrine floors. No job was hard when the two of them worked together.

One day Carl and Scott were sitting out on the back stairs trying to catch some breeze when Carl looked over to Scott and said, "Ledbetter, you are the first white man that I have ever talked with in all of my life. Now I have been yelled at by white folks but never talked with one. Not one of them ever sat down and talked like we are doing now."

He went on to explain that he did not know that white people sat down and talked to each other, he thought that they just yelled at each other. Scott told Carl that he was the first black man that he had ever known or talked to in his life. He said that the only blacks that he had seen was at the Drake Relays in Des Moines. Carl found that hard to believe.

Scott told Carl about a night during the riots down in Selma. He was at home with his mom watching the news broadcast when she turned and said, "Why can't everybody just get along like we did when I was a little girl?" Scott did not know what she was talking about, as he had no idea that she was ever in an area where black and white folks lived together.

His mom explained, "When I was a little girl my folks moved to Frankfurt, Kansas. My folks rented a small house on the edge of the town. The place had just over an acre and my dad could plant a garden. The house sat in a long row of houses and some people were black and some were white. All of us were poor. When mom and dad walked into Frankfort to buy staples or cloth, they would leave us with a neighbor. That neighbor was either black or white. It made no difference because we were all poor and needed each other. The color of skin made no difference to my folks, and the same was true of our neighbors."

Both Carl and Scott took something away from their Basic Training. Something that could not be found in the military manuals. Carl found out that white people do have normal conversations and Scott found out that there is really no difference between them, they were both just folks trying to make it through life.

The Smashed Window

On that same afternoon, while sitting out on the back steps of the barracks, an E-5 sergeant named Williams came back from the club and started to climb the stairs. Sergeant Williams lived in a cadre room on the second floor. He had been in the military for twenty years and spent most of his off-duty hours drinking. During his on-duty time he had a hangover and hated everyone in the military. On this day, when he started up the stairs he drunk-cussed Carl and Scott for sitting on his steps. Both Carl and Scott stepped inside the barracks and treated the SOB like an Alpha Dog. His breath made them drunk.

The barracks had windows that opened out. When Williams got into his room he tried to push his window open and slipped. He rammed his right arm through the glass pane and fell on the jagged glass. He sliced the under-arm part of his arm muscle wide open. Scott heard the glass shatter and the scream of pain.

Scott kicked open the door and found the sergeant on the floor. Blood was spurting about a foot up and out of his arm. Scott applied pressure to the wound while Carl was trying to cut strips of a towel for a tourniquet. He was able to get two strips cut and Scott tied those tourniquets on the wound. He continued to hold the bloody arm and keep pressure on the bleeding while Carl ran to the orderly room for help.

The cut was three to four inches down from the armpit, and it was very deep. The only time Scott had seen that much blood was when they butchered hogs or cattle on his Iowa farm. Fortunately, they had had a lot of combat first-aid training. He applied all the techniques that he had learned about stopping someone from bleeding to death.

The medics managed to get the bleeding stopped before they took him by ambulance to the hospital. The sergeant lived, but Scott did not see him again. The next morning the company commander, Captain Stemsley, called both Scott and Carl to the orderly room to thank them for saving the man's life.

If Scott and Carl had not been there, Williams would have died from the huge amount of blood that he lost. Scott thought it strange that no one said anything about the incident to any of the troops. No investigation by CID, just like it never happened. Scott knew that Williams was as unpopular among the cadre as he was among the troops. Even though he was not a stellar person, Scott was grateful the he was there to help.

At the end of Basic Training, Scott passed his proficiency test and graduated from Basic Training. This graduation was step one of his self-building program. With a few minor hitches, everything had gone as he had wanted. Unfortunately, at the end of the eight-week course, Scott did not receive orders for Officer Candidate School. Without those orders, he was sent to a company clerk school at Fort Riley.

Company Clerk School

The building where Scott's company clerk class was held looked the same as when George Custer came through Fort Riley. Each of the two stories was twelve feet high. There was a wide walkway on the front of the building on both floors. When you walked on the porch, on the second floor, you walked by nine-foot windows which were a part of the classroom. The purpose of these large windows was to provide some breeze to the un-air-conditioned classrooms.

After two weeks of going to class, Scott decided that he had not qualified for OCS and had put that thought out of his mind. He was learning how to use a manual typewriter to create a morning report for a company. He was also taught how to run a military orderly room that would make the First Sergeant proud. Scott knew that being a company clerk was not really his thing, but it beat going through infantry training.

Each day he watched his fellow soldiers leave early and come back late. He determined to just ride the wave to the shore.

Each day Scott would get up when his platoon got up and would fall out with them for the early morning formation. He would eat breakfast with his friends before they headed for whatever infantry training that they were doing on that day. Scott would watch them march down the street and then go back to the Day Room to watch television until his class started at 0800.

At the end of the second week, the class was preparing to take their first test. Scott was sitting at the back of the room, close to the windows. Scott heard someone walking on the porch behind him. He looked and saw his company clerk pass by the windows. He immediately started to pray that his orders for OCS had come through. The sergeant had just passed out their first test, minutes before.

The clerk appeared in the doorway of the classroom. The training sergeant went to the door and the two men talked quietly for a few minutes. The sergeant stepped back into the room and yelled, "Ledbetter!"

"Here, Sergeant," Scott responded.

"Ledbetter, your orders for Fort Ord have come through. From there you will be going on to Ft. Benning, Georgia for Infantry Officer Candidate School, Lord Have Mercy on us all!"

Everyone screamed and whistled as Scott jumped up. He damned near took the desk with him. Scott yelled something unintelligible, shook the sergeant's hand and headed down the stairs to the jeep. In his joy, he left his books laying on the desk. He was going to Officer Candidate School and blowing this pop stand.

The company clerk was all smiles. He told Scott that his orders were the result of Captain Stemsley's running interference with the OCS people. The captain had met Scott and Carl when Carl and he saved the sergeant's life. During that meeting, he found out that Scott was supposed to go to OCS. When he discovered that Scott's orders had not come through, he took it upon himself to get those orders cut.

Having graduated from OCS at Benning, he knew who to call. Scott immediately realized that if they had not saved the sergeant's life that the company commander would not have met him. He would not have known that he was supposed to go to OCS. The results of that meeting had Scott heading for Fort Ord, California and OCS. He wondered if this was part of some grand plan or it was like a lot of things in his life: Serendipity.

Regardless of how or why it had happened, Scott was beginning to feel that OCS was part of his destiny, though not sure why. When he got to the company area, Captain Stemsley called him into his office. Scott thanked Captain Stemsley for getting his orders issued and saving him from being a company clerk. The captain wished him much luck and good wishes. He shook Scott's hand with a very sincere handshake. After shaking the man's hand, Scott took a full step back and gave the man the sharpest salute that he could muster. The salute was returned with a nod. Scott did an about face and marched out of the office.

As he headed for his barracks, he could not wait to tell his friends the good news. Suddenly he was going to OCS.

The guys he had been training with for the past three months were very proud of their friend. They, like Scott, had no idea what OCS really meant, but it meant that he was getting out of Fort Riley and escaping to California for Advanced Infantry Training.

That night a bunch of Scott's friends took him for a round of beer at the enlisted club. Jim Coleman from Chicago and Carl were both drinking to the success of their friend. Even though they knew that they would never see him again, Scott prayed that both of them would be able to make it through Vietnam.

It was a good night to spend with friends. These men had each other's backs. The men often referred to Scott as the old man as he was twenty-three years old. Most of the trainees were eighteen and nineteen years old.

When they returned from the EM club, Carl and Scott sat and shined his shoes and boots three times. They packed and repacked his "sierra" twice before everything fit into the duffle bag, AWOL bag, and a laundry bag. At long last they reluctantly turned in for the night, knowing that tomorrow was going to be a goodbye.

Before the company left for training the next morning, Scott said good-bye to everyone in his half of the platoon. He even said goodbye to Pinard who had become a decent young man. No longer dorky and certainly "not dirty." It was hard saying goodbye to Carl. Scott knew now that at the very least Carl knew that he could sit and have a beer and talk with him as a friend.

Scott's bus to Kansas City was leaving at 0900 hours. He rechecked his already checked "stuff" and waited for the clock to move. Scott had just gotten into the company jeep for a ride to the bus station when the company came walking into the company area.

The company clerk drove slowly by the line of soldiers as they walked towards them. Scott put his hand out and high fived each one of them. He saw that the straps on their backpack were encrusted with salt from that day's march. When the clerk asked, "Are you going to miss these guys?" Scott could not answer.

Fort Ord Bound

The air brakes on the Continental bus shrieked with a blast that signaled to Scott that a new part of his life had just begun. For the first time since leaving for Ft. Polk, Scott felt free. Nothing was holding him back. He was heading off to see a world that he had only read about.

The bus arrived at the KC bus depot at 1230 hours. Scott put his bags in a fifty-cent locker at the bus station and headed for downtown Kansas City. This was the first time that he had ever been to this city. He wanted to at least experience its flavor before flying to California. He walked to the Macy's department store. On the way down the hill to Macy's, he passed a very nice family-run deli filled with people having lunch. He decided that this would be a good place to have a sandwich before heading to the airport.

As he walked back to the bus station, he saw that the deli crowd was gone, Scott went in to have a sandwich. The owner introduced himself and said that his son was in the Air Force.

When he found out that Scott was planning on going on a commercial flight to San Francisco, he suggested that Scott take a military hop out of the local Air Force Base, Richards Gebaur. Scott knew nothing about the air force base or that a military hop was possible. The man called Richards Gebaur and got someone to pick Scott up at the bus depot and take him to the Air Force base. A flight was leaving at 1800 hours for Travis Air Force base in California.

Going on a military hop meant that the three hundred and fifty dollars that Scott had in his wallet for a flight to California could stay in his pocket. Scott thanked the man and tried to pay for his lunch, but the man would take no money from a soldier. Fate had taken a hand to get Scott to his next post with money in his pocket.

An Air Force pick-up truck arrived at the bus depot right on time. The driver drove Scott several miles to the air base where the driver dropped him off in front of a large hangar. He told Scott that he had to get his name on the roster for the flight. After getting his name on the roster, he lugged his three bags over to a cafeteria, a block away. He bought two cheeseburgers, fries, a Coke and had just sat down to eat when they announced that the plane for Travis was preparing to leave. He stuffed the cheeseburgers and fries into his laundry bag and ran to the terminal. He ran across the terminal and out the back door and saw his plane (four engines running) at least two blocks away.

There was only concrete and air between him and that plane. Scott ran as fast as his legs would carry him. As he hustled up the inclined ramp of the tail section, the load master was just starting to close the door. When the last piece of light disappeared above the door, the pilot started to spin the plane around and head toward the runway.

The sergeant helped him secure his bags and aimed him towards a "seat" which was a canvas sling. There were no seat belts, but they were so packed in, he doubted if it would have mattered.

Scott was certain that the TWA flight that he was scheduled to take, would have been much more comfortable, but taking a military hop would give him money to spend in San Francisco. Counting the flights to Houston and Fort Polk, this was his fourth time in an airplane, but this was his first military flight. If the rest of the flight was as event filled as the start, this was going to be an odyssey. Fate and circumstances seemed to be playing a large part in this latest episode of his life. If he had not stopped by that deli, this flight would have gone to Travis without him and he would never have known.

The sling seats were strictly for sitting, not for comfort. At eye level a three-inch pipe ran the full length of the plane on both sides. The Sling seat was attached to the top pipe. There was another three-inch pipe at knee level. Between these two were a lot of crisscrossed nylon straps that served as the back rest and seat. The lower pipe hit right where the knees were supposed to bend. Unfortunately, the nylon made the passenger sink lower than the pipe and made it impossible for the passenger's feet to make it to the floor. After a couple of hours in the air, the backs of Scott's knees were throbbing.

There were a lot of duffle bags stacked on the drop-down tail section where the sergeant had lashed his bags on top. The rest of the duffle bags were stacked four high between two poles in the middle of the plane. As the hours went along,

Scott needed to get some sleep and the sitting position made that impossible. He decided to lie down on his bags lashed to the drop-down tail section.

He tried to lie on his bags, but the angle was too steep. He kept sliding down toward the end of the plane. After several hours of misery, Scott crawled on top of the stack of duffle bags in the middle of the airplane. Once there he did his impression of an old sow making a nest amongst the shoes and multifarious things that soldiers carry in their duffle bags. He did manage to get some sleep until a boot heel in one of the bags dug into his back.

At 0100 hours, they landed in a concrete field in the middle of absolutely nowhere. Supposedly another Air Force plane was forced to land in what they said was Wyoming. His plane was going to pick up the passengers and crew from that plane and continue to Travis. It was during this stop that Scott climbed up the stairs to the cockpit and noticed that there was no one sitting in the flight engineer's seat. He asked if that seat was open and the pilot told him that they no longer needed a navigator, so yes that seat was open. The pilot told him that once they got airborne that that seat was open for him to use.

The other plane crew never showed up. Scott had no idea what had happened, but they closed the hatch and took off for Travis. Once they were airborne, Scott went up to the cockpit and sat down in a regular seat with springs and cushion. He sank down into this very comfortable seat and slept the next three hours.

The pilots woke him as they were getting ready to land. He sat down next to a Navy type and the man found out that

Scott had never flown a military hop. He took the Army guy under his wing. He told him to stay with him when the plane landed. When they dropped the tail section of the plane, Scott grabbed his bags and stayed right behind the Navy guy.

The Navy guy had told Scott that a Continental bus would take them to San Francisco. When they got off the plane, instead of getting in line to go into the hangar, the Navy man took them to a small gate and they walked between two buildings. There was a bus waiting and they were the first two on that bus. The driver sold them tickets and Scott fell back to sleep on the long drive to San Francisco.

San Francisco

Up ahead he could see someone moving in a plastic cage. That cage was ten feet off the sidewalk. That cage was four-foot square and six feet tall. Inside of that plastic cage, was a woman who was dancing to the beat of the music, that was coming from across the street."

They arrived in San Francisco at 0600 hours and the sailor guy said good-bye and wished him good luck. He told Scott that there were some cheap hotels just around the corner from the bus station. He suggested that he take the third one on the right, as it was the "best." Scott gathered his luggage and headed for the street. He realized that he had been moving for twenty-six hours since getting up at Fort Riley. He felt as tired as he was the night that they walked back five miles from the night fire range. He could barely keep his duffle bag on his shoulder.

Scott was surprised how cold it was in the city. The sun

was not up as he half-carried, and half- dragged his bags down the street. He went to the third hotel on the right and tried to check-in. The charge for a night's room was four dollars. The clerk told him that he would need to wait until 0700 hours to check in, or she would have to charge him for last night. Rather than pay for the night that he had just had, Scott dragged his bags to a small diner that he had just passed. The crumpled-up cheeseburger and fries that he ate hours after they were cooked had worn off. After a full breakfast, he checked into the hotel at 0701 hours.

The elevator was old and shaky. The door of the elevator was one of those that have the cross pieces of metal. They first appeared in department stores in the 30's and 40's. When the door was closed, the doors on each floor were still visible as they slid by the elevator. The elevator took off with the flick of a switch on the wall and it shuddered to the third floor.

Scott slid the iron door out of the way and walked out into the dimly lit hallway. The doors to the rooms were old and dark, each with four inset wood panels. The doorknobs were heavy porcelain knobs set in the middle of a large brass plate that had not seen any Brasso for a lot of years. A faded flowery carpet lined the hallway.

Inside his room he found clean sheets and a pillowcase. The bed was actually turned down. It was a nice touch for four-dollar-a-night hotel. The bathroom was down the hall four doors. The door had three chain locks. After taking a shower and getting back into his room, he locked all three of them.

This place reminded him of the lovely YMCA in Chicago, except here he could not touch both walls at the same time. At this early hour it was very chilly, but he figured that once the sun came up it would be warm. After all, this was sunny California. He opened the window and found out that he could touch the brown brick building next door.

It seemed like a hundred hours since yesterday. The city by the bay would have to wait as he was just too tired to care. When he came to, at 1500 hours, his room was colder than hell on a frosty night. After shutting the window, he unpacked his bags, trying to find some warm gear. His only long-sleeved civilian shirt was pretty well mangled and the only jacket he could find was his military fatigue jacket. He was not going to wear that in San Francisco.

Dressed in the mangled long-sleeved shirt and a pair of tan Chino's, he returned to the "lobby". He asked directions to a clothing store and had to spend some of his flight money for a nylon blast jacket and a warm San Francisco sweater. The nylon jacket by itself was not warm, but when worn over a sweater and a long-sleeved shirt, it cut the wind and kept the body warm.

For the next two days, he traveled the city. On Fisherman's Wharf he found an old wooden ferry that used to ply the waters to Sausalito before the Golden Gate Bridge was built. When he walked on board, he could feel what it was like to live during a simpler time. The seats were made of long oak slats which were beautifully crafted. They were more comfortable than an upholstered chair. You could sit for hours in total comfort.

Inside the ferry, he could stand behind the glass and just stare at the Golden Gate Bridge and the bay, out of the wind. He had never seen the ocean except in the movies. Now here it was just a boat railing away. He spent a long time watching the waves which kept the boat moving up and down just like the movies.

He could not take his eyes away from the Golden Gate Bridge. Too often a national treasure or great monument will be disappointing when at last you get to see it for yourself. This was the most magnificent structure that he could have ever imagined. It lived up to every boyhood expectation with its sweeping grandeur and beauty.

The late start on this first day had him scurrying to find something to eat and grab a cable car back to his luxury suite. Pier 39 gave him a lot of choices with all kinds of wonderful seafood that he would never have imagined existed. He ended up eating a couple of crab cake sandwiches and his first bowl of fresh clam chowder. It was so filled with morsels of clams that it was simply a joy to eat.

He headed back to Woolworth's Turnaround and got there just in time for what was a San Francisco tradition. He was able to help push the car around and head it back up the hill. As he rode the cable car through the hill covered area, he was certain that this was one of the most fun days in his entire life. Having been raised on a farm meant that there was never a time when there were no chores to do. There was no time off from milking cows or feeding animals. Here he was, with no chores to do and two full days before heading for Fort Ord, California.

He got back to the hotel and dropped his many treasures and went out to search for a place to have a beer. He found a small tavern two blocks away from the hotel. Beer was a dollar and thirty-five cents which was, for the big city, a bargain.

Scott found a booth in the tavern that had some light and he was able to sit and read and wet nurse a bottle of some kind of beer.

The bartender learned that Scott was heading for Ft. Ord. Of course he had gone through Ft. Ord when he was in the Army some years ago. He told Scott that Ft. Ord was in Monterey, California, a city that was a little over an hour away from San Francisco.

Golden Gate

As he started out on his second day in San Francisco, he decided to go on a tour boat over to Sausalito. He easily found the cable car to Fisherman's Wharf and while the unusual sunny day looked warm, it was anything but warm on the bay. The wind had waves beating against the boat and any attempt to stand outside of the cabin was met with a fine spray of salt water. Cold or no cold, it was so wonderful to pass under the Golden Gate as it stood outlined against the azure blue sky.

The thirty-minute ride brought them into an old dock in Sausalito. His best description of the town was quaint. It was a lovely little town. He wondered about the impact that the Golden Gate Bridge had on the sleepy fishing village. One day when the bridge opened several thousand people were flying by their little village on the way to somewhere.

The boat docked in Sausalito, where the vestiges of the past were valiantly holding on while the city was being dragged into the modern era. The dock had seen its better days, but it safely carried the passengers into a beautiful little park that covered two city blocks. Flowers, trees, and a lovely lawn just beckoned you to sit and watch the sea. Across the street there was a row of boutique type shops where Scott bought a loaf of sourdough bread, some cheese, and a small bottle of Chardonnay. He went back to the park to eat and to defend his bread from the seagulls.

The sunlight warmed his face as he sat and enjoyed being someplace that no one in his family had ever been. For the first time in years he had no place to be and no one to give a care if he was not there. He knew that in a couple of days that would change measurably, for now he was free.

As other tourists came into the park they assumed that the young man sitting on the grass, with his wine and bread, was a local. They would come up and ask about the best places to eat in the city. A couple from Ohio were Scott's first visitors. He invited them to sit down and enjoy the day. He offered them some bread and cheese, which they took. They talked for a while and moved on, never noticing that Scott had not answered their question about a decent restaurant.

Scott went and bought a package of ten plastic wine glasses and another bottle of wine. He sat for a couple of hours offering travelers a glass of wine and a chance to talk to someone who looked local. He did take a walk around the downtown to see what restaurants were in the area. While he could not afford them, the tourists could.

When Scott left Sausalito he headed for Golden Gate park. The park was a different world. Along with just the beauty of the city by the bay, there were artists who were taking in the beauty and putting it on canvas. While most artists would not take the time to talk, those who would were fascinating. One artist told him that he was retired and was just painting for the pure joy of putting brush to canvas.

Originally from Southside Chicago, he stayed in the city when discharged from the Navy after WW II. He had lots of stories to tell and an eager set of young ears to listen to those stories.

He had been a mechanic for the cable cars for years. He used to live just off Broadway. He said while he had not visited that area in years he heard that it was a good place for young fellows like Scott. When Scott left the man and the park, he was off to find Broadway.

Girl in a Plastic Cage

As Scott walked down Broadway he saw signs about The Kingston Trio playing tonight as he passed a lot of bars and small restaurants. Up ahead he could see someone moving in a plastic cage that was ten feet off the sidewalk. The plastic cage was four-foot square and six feet tall. Inside was a scantily dressed woman dancing to the beat of the music, blasting from a bar across the street. "Big Al's." Neither the scantily clad woman in the booth or the flashing sign in front the bar, left much to the imagination.

Scott was intrigued but continued down Broadway. He saw the "Hungry "i"" and was sad that he could not afford the posted admission fees. Finally, he came to a place that fit his lifestyle and pocketbook. It was a tavern called, "Your

Father's Mustache." It was a piano and banjo bar that played sing along Dixieland music. It offered three-dollar pitchers of beer and free peanuts. This was his kind of place.

Scott took a seat on a long harvest bench. At the other end of the table was a group from Wisconsin who were valiantly trying to sing along with the banjo and the piano player. Scott was singing every song and enjoying his mug of beer. It was not long before one of the Wisconsin revelers carried a full beer down to him: a bribe to get him to join their group. Scott joined the group as they started to play, "My Wild Irish Rose." He sang all the words with just a "wee bit of an Irish accent."

People from two or three tables joined in, and the party was in full swing. The only thing that these people had in common was that they were looking to have a good time. Soon they were toasting each other and acting as if they knew the words of the songs. Scott's glass stayed full of good cold beer and his heart full of joy.

Scott realized that the last cable car would be passing the Broadway stop in thirty minutes, so he reluctantly left his new friends. As he was heading out the door, they were singing another verse of Michael Rowing His Boat Ashore and waving him goodbye. This young man from Iowa, the folks from Wisconsin, and all the customers at Your Father's Mustache had had a great night in San Francisco.

He smiled as he thought about a wonderful evening spent with wonderful people. The singing had made everyone happy. This was what he believed to be the best part of traveling to new places: people being people and letting a perfect stranger join them in song.

On his final day in San Francisco, he put his gear into the bus station lockers and bought his ticket to Monterey. He decided to go back to the Golden Gate City Park to look for his artist friend. He traveled the park and was just getting ready to leave when he spotted him. Scott told him about his old neighborhood and the artist just shook his head when he learned about the woman in the plastic booth above Broadway. He left the man with a smile.

He found a real art gallery with paintings that sold for more than his Iowa farm was worth. The fellow that ran the place was way past "kinda spooky." He acted like Scott was going to grab one of his art pieces and run out the door. He followed Scott the whole time. Scott stayed for a while, just to piss him off.

Scott made it to the bus station in time to catch a 1400-hour bus to Monterey. He was amazed at the change of scenery as the bus headed south. At first it seemed like the city went on forever and then the bus spilled out into what was the northern part of the Monterey Valley. As soon as they left the city and its suburbs, there were miles and miles of farm country. No corn or oats, just cabbages, lettuce, tomatoes, and some of the other "vegetalbly looking" things. He arrived at the bus station in Monterey in the late afternoon and it was a pleasant seventy plus degrees. It was hard to imagine that San Francisco, some ninety miles away, was so cold and overcast.

Fort Ord, California
Advanced Infantry Training—let it begin

With so many soldiers moving to or away from post, a military bus made regular trips to Fort Ord from Monterey. It was with great trepidation that Scott got on the Fort Ord bus. He was not worried about going to AIT training, he was sad to leave the freedom of his first few days in California. As they left the Monterey city limits they drove into a fog bank as thick as any that he had seen in San Francisco.

The bus driver knew that everyone was checking into AIT. But when they got to the bus stop, they were told that the AIT check in building was five blocks away. The driver had driven right past where he could have let them off. Each of the men shouldered his bags and headed back up the street.

After check-in, the men were taken by another bus to their assigned companies. The clerk at H-2-2 sent him to the supply room to pick up his sheets, pillowcases, and blankets. In the middle of summer in California, they were issued two blankets. That should have been a clue to the weather at Fort Ord.

The difference between starting Basic Training and Advanced Infantry Training was the knowledge that there was nothing you could not handle. AIT was sort of a military thumbs-up as each of the men had had their trial by fire in Basic Training. Here they did not need to prove themselves like they did in Basic Training. This new level of training would simply make them better skilled.

His bay mate was Danny Phips, just seventeen years old and grew up an army brat. Scott met all kinds of people from every part of the country. A lot of men in his platoon were slated to go to Officer Candidate School.

Scott went back to the supply room and signed out his M-14 rifle. The weapons were cared for by a trainee armorer, a young man who had the bluest eyes he had ever seen: Bob Simons, from Los Angeles.

The first time Scott met Bob he was wearing a flannel shirt, which seemed out of place for a true Californian. Scott and Bob hit it off and were friends throughout the eight weeks of training. Like all friendships, there was neither rhyme nor reason for it, it just happened.

H-2-2 sat next to a highway fence. Someone said that they were across the road from the Pacific. Scott could hear the ocean but with the fog that shrouded Ft. Ord during the day, he had no idea how far it was from the company area. On his third day in the company, he walked to the top of the hill and finally saw the Pacific, literally across the Interstate highway.

PCPT: Scott knew that the inevitable Physical Combat Proficiency Tests and Saturday morning inspections would begin on the first Saturday of the cycle. Given that neither of these rituals was high on his list, he started searching for ways to miss them. A bulletin board announcement caught his eye. They were looking for troops who wanted to get a military driver's license.

For the next two Saturday mornings, while the rest of the company was taking the Physical Proficiency test, Bob and Scott were at the driver's training course at the motor pool, where they learned how to change the oil and make small repairs. *On the third Saturday, they were to go and take the military driver's test.*

After the second Saturday of class, Scott was "picked" for guard duty. A long time after dark he was taken out to a parking lot filled with Armored Personnel Carriers. He was taken to his guard post in an army jeep, driven by a private from an AIT company. He realized that Bob and he would be delivering troops if they got their driver's license. As advertised, they would not be on guard duty, but they would be delivering troops all over post, even on weekends.

As Scott was guarding twenty-five armored personal carriers, he realized that it was time to go to plan B. He was not sure how to extract themselves from this self-inflicted fate. This was much like the detail at Fort Riley when Scott wanted to see the Vietnam Village and ended up cutting long grass a half a mile from the village. Here he was not sure how to undo what had been done.

The next morning the two men talked about what to do. They decided the best path was to not take the license test. They skipped going to the motor pool the next Saturday and went with the company to the PCPT course. It soon became apparent that no one cared if they had driver's licenses or not. On Saturday night while their buddies were delivering troops to guard a row of tanks, Bob and Scott were someplace far from Fort Ord.

Yosemite

It was just like an old Ma and Pa Kettle movie.

Scott had never seen a redwood tree so one weekend Bob told him that they would go to see these giant trees. Scott did not question where they were going, as they set out hitchhiking on Saturday morning. They were headed towards Yosemite, which was close to the California and Nevada border.

They soon learned that east was not a very "California" direction. Californians went north, south, and west. East does not work for them. They did not head east, out of state. A lieutenant from the post gave them a ride for the first fifty miles and the next ride dropped them off at the intersection of no place and someplace. A closed motel sat at the intersection and there was a house a half a mile away. They stood for a long period of time, watching people pick tomatoes on a truck farm across the road.

Finally, a farmer with a truckload of chickens stopped and gave them a lift to where they stood a better chance of catching a ride. It was just like an old Ma and Pa Kettle movie. They were sitting with their feet hanging over the back of the truck bed while four hundred cluckers cackled and shit in the cages at their back.

The farmer dropped them off at an intersection several miles away where two fellows from Los Angeles gave them a ride all the way to the park. Soon after they arrived at Yosemite, they discovered that the Redwood trees were north of San Francisco. At this point they would just have to stay where they were and enjoy the park and the hundreds of people there. A group of Hell's Angel's motored by on their Harley's, each rider accompanied by a woman dressed in an obnoxious and revealing outfit. Leopard skin seemed to be the outfit of the day.

They walked the grounds and found the campgrounds and a virtual sea of campers. Scott did not know that there were that many kinds of campers in the world. An old friend who had hitchhiked all over the US told Scott how to get a meal in a campground. Find a place close to a large family or group of people camping together. They always have more food than they could possibly eat. He told Scott to sit close to one of these groups and chew on a sorry piece of bread. It was important to look forlorn, not poor.

Bob and Scott tried this tactic with a group of five campers. They sat down and looked pathetic and soon they were invited to eat the leftover burgers, chips, and of course drink a beer. Using this method, they earned their Saturday night meal.

Before the end of the evening, the campgrounds were alive with strumming guitars and running rangers and the late 60's rock and roll and folk music. Anybody who thought that they could carry a tune was singing. A 1960's Hootenanny could break out at any time.

For some reason, the park rangers lived in fear that the crowd would rise up in rebellion if they heard one more chorus of "Michael Rowed the Boat Ashore". The rangers would hear the sounds of strumming guitars and picking banjos and would immediately run to break up the songsters.

Soon after dark, this "Play until we have to run away" became a game. Different groups of banjo boys and girls would start to play and as soon as the park gendarmes arrived, they would split and start to play in two different places. Before the end of the evening, the campground was alive with strumming guitars and running rangers. It was in good fun just to watch the rangers and rangerettes run around like idiots.

One of the most memorable experiences on this trip was watching the fire fall from the top of El Capitan. When the sun disappeared from the sky, the rangers who were not chasing the hootenanny kids would light dead evergreens on top of El Capitan and push them over the shear face of the cliff. The many thousand-foot drop of burning brush would have everyone oohing and aahing. It was very cool.

Later that evening, Scott and Bob were at a campfire with their folk singing friends when Bob recognized the guys who had given them their last ride to the park. He went to say hello. He found out that they had decided to head back to Los Angeles that night to skip paying for a motel. Somehow Bob talked them into giving him and Scott a ride back to Fort Ord.

The pair drove two hundred and fifty miles out of their way to get to Fort Ord. They pulled into Fort Ord at 0600 hours, dropped Bob and Scott off in front of their barracks, and headed south. Just another day in the life of Scott Ledbetter. At 1000 hours their buddies woke them up to see if they wanted to go on a USO trip south of Fort Ord. Reluctantly, the two weary travelers said yes and got ready to go.

They drove through the Seventeen Mile Drive and stopped at the Pebble Beach Golf Club. The thirty-minute stop at Pebble Beach turned into two hours as the bus driver left to see his girlfriend who worked at the club.

This weekend was the last of a five-weekend month, so everyone's hundred dollars had run out. None of the men had money with them. They killed time roaming the grounds and watching people with a lot of money spend it on themselves.

Visiting Pebble Beach was like watching a rich man eat steak when you were both hungry and broke. The driver finally showed up and they headed back to Monterey and the old Spanish Mission. When they got to the mission, Bob, Scott, and a soldier named Buck were at the far end of the mission grounds when they heard their names being called. The driver decided that they needed to get back to the motor pool and was leaving. The three of them burst through the front door and saw the bus hit the street. The bus driver looked right at them and smiled as he sped off, the son of a bitch.

They were many miles from post and not three dollars between the three of them, but they were infantry trained and knew how to walk. They headed north on Hwy 1 and Scott used all the hitchhiking tricks he learned when he hitchhiked to New Mexico. The chance of someone picking up three men was pretty slim, but he gave it a try.

Soon two young ladies in a white convertible stopped and gave them a ride to the post. Schoolteachers visiting California for the first time, talked all the way to Ft. Ord. When they pulled up in front of the barracks, the windows were soon filled with men. They were all hollering and hooting that three of their own were being dropped off after what had to have been a great weekend. It made no difference what did or did not happen: the men in barracks saw what they saw and the three soldiers were the talk of the barracks.

The weekend had been an unbelievable journey. Two soldiers traveling from the coast to the Nevada border and back on one weekend pass. They had visited an expensive golf club, smelled Seal Island, and caught a ride with two pretty women in a convertible. For a couple of slick sleeved privates, it didn't get any better.

The Hike

Two things at Fort Ord will be remembered by every trainee who has gone through AIT. One was the night air. The wind blew in off the ocean dropping the forty-degree night close to freezing. This was an everyday occurrence.

The second thing was the hike to and from a rifle range. Fort Ord had hosted literally thousands of troops in its long run as a training facility. Each troop walked along the same paths as Scott's company did as they walked to and from the firing ranges. The boots pounding on the sand over the last fifty plus years created what could only be called micro-dust.

The micro dust was kicked up by the first platoon in the order of march. It hung ten to fifteen feet in the air for the rest of the company. Every troop breathed this dust into their lungs, and it settled on everyone's clothing and faces. When a company returned from hiking anywhere from three to five miles they looked like statues. The only thing that brought the micro dust back down to earth was time and gravity. It would lay on the ground and wait for the next ground pounders to head to the range.

Going for a long hike in an Army formation was an experience. On a long march through the back trails, no one was trying to stay in step. The men were in a single file as they hiked the many miles to a rifle range. When they walked through a flat terrain, the pace stayed constant. At the first hill, the lead platoon slowly reduced its pace as everyone worked their way to the top. When the lead platoon crested the first hill to start down the other side, that platoon started to pick up speed.

By the time the last man of the first platoon reached the top of the hill he had to run to catch up. The second platoon had to run up the hill and run even faster down the hill. The last platoon in the order of march had to run most of the way to the rifle range, just to keep pace.

On a normal day of training, by 0900 hours an Advanced Infantry Company would have run for at least two to three miles. They would have sucked in a pound of dust and dirt, all before the training even began.

When they left their barracks at 0700 hours it was fifty-two degrees, with the wind pushing off the ocean the wind chill would be forty degrees, the post was shrouded in fog. As the company neared the ranges, the sun would burn off the fog and the thermometer would rise to the mid to late seventy degrees. Trainees would ditch their fatigue jackets and would be soaked to the skin with sweat. All day they lived in sweat soaked uniforms. When the sun went down, the training continued as the mercury plunged back down to forty degrees and the fatigue jackets went back on.

Night Firing

"Scott was crushed when Bob actually had the audacity to say, "Why am I not surprised that you would be in the only heated place in all of Ft. Ord?"

During a night firing session, Bob and Scott had gotten separated. Scott looked all over for him, but it is almost impossible to find someone in the dark when everyone was dressed alike. Scott finally gave up his search. A stiff wind was blowing off the ocean and the temperature was at or just above freezing. Scott noticed a six by ten foot shed that had been built back into the hill. Made of wooden M-14 shell boxes, a roof and a rough pine door had been added to the structure. Scott opened the door and found five guys sitting inside of this little shed and putting spent ammo into ammo cases. The little shed had a small heater.

Scott told the men that he had been sent to help and squeezed his way into the small sitting area. While they all bitched, they managed to find some room for him. Just like KP, no troop did work that he had not been told to do so obviously this man had been told to help them. They settled in and just kept filling canisters with spent ammo. A couple of guys finally got too claustrophobic and hit the air. That made the job more comfortable and still blessedly warm.

Scott made several trips out to find Bob, to no avail. Each time he returned he would slide into his previous position. When they noticed that the firing had stopped they started to close-down the shed.

They were just gathering the casings to fill the last box when the door opened. Two baby blue eyes crisp and sparkly from the cold night air peered into the heated sanctuary. Scott was crushed when Bob had the audacity to say, "Why am I not surprised that you would be in the only heated place in all of Ft. Ord?" Scott tried to defend himself by saying that he had gone out to look for him. Bob was not buying it.

Squad Training

Scott kept working on Bob to put himself before everyone else. While Bob had made some progress, he was still the nicest person that anyone could know. Scott had a feeling that his work was not yet done.

During the last days of AIT, the company was taken to a new part of Fort Ord. The serious part of their combat training was about to take place. The trees in this area were taller than twenty feet, and the rough terrain was used for squad tactics.

Two squads of men would line up at the bottom of a hill and hard charge up a very steep hill. On the ridgeline, there were silhouettes of the enemy. The two squads would fire their M-14's (with blanks) at the silhouettes as they ran up one hill after another. The cadre emphasized how these tactics would help them survive in Vietnam.

With only two weeks of AIT left, the training got harder and closer to reality. On this day, as the squads started up the hill, firing and moving, it erupted with men in defensive and camouflaged positions. When Scott's company started up the hill, the trees were shoved aside. Real men, not silhouettes, started firing their M-14s at the squads. They even had M-60 machine guns, firing blanks. Explosions rocked the terrain and rocks and dirt fell onto the trainees. All the noise and confusion caused a lot of disorientation.

The trainees were being pushed up the hill by training cadre barking commands and running. The earth was shaking with explosions and the infantry squads still had to maintain their discipline and training in order to take down the enemy positions. When one hill was taken, the company reassembled and hard charged another hill. This training went on non-stop.

After a long morning, the cadre gathered them into platoons and hiked them to another combat training area. There they were tested to see what they had learned with the morning's exercise. After taking the tests, they were reassembled at the bottom of another hill and this exercise continued, just like real combat.

They took several more hills before 1700 hours. At last they were formed up as a company formation ready to hike the many miles back to the post. There was precious little gas left in anyone's tank, a daily occurrence in combat. Soldiering On was one of the lessons of the day. No matter how tired, beat up, or exhausted, the soldier had to Soldier On.

The company was just getting ready to move out when a small stake truck pulled up. A Specialist 4th class climbed out of the cab and jumped up on the bed of the truck and asked, "How many here have had some college?" Scott's hand immediately went up and he instructed Bob to raise his hand.

Bob mumbled that he had only had a semester or two. With a clenched mouth Scott commanded, "Raise your damned hand." By that time, it was too late, nine troops, including Scott, climbed aboard the truck and it headed for the post.

When the truck got to the H-2-2 headquarters, they were given the tests that they had taken earlier, to correct. Correcting the tests took them fifteen minutes. Scott gave Bob a hundred.

Once they completed this "tough" assignment, they were allowed to store their gear, clean rifles, take a shower and go to chow. As the sun set on the ocean, the rest of the company hiked back into the company area. They stacked their rifles and headed for the mess hall.

Each man was covered with brown dust from head to foot. From his vantage point, which was forty feet away, Scott could see those baby blues piercing out of the brown-caked dust that covered Bob's face.

The Blue-Eyed Stare

Scott said, "Boy, Bob, it's a good thing that you did not raise your hand! I mean to tell you that without my many years of college, I do not think that I could have handled the task." By now their short-lived friendship was coming to an end.

Bob said, "What did they bring you college people back to do?"

"Fair question," replied Scott. "Do you remember those tests we took before lunch?"

"Don't tell me that you corrected those tests?"

"Okay," said Scott, "I won't tell you that that is what we

did, but you got a hundred per cent." Scott would always remember "the look" that he got from his California friend as
he headed on into the mess hall.

Escape and Evasion

*"Scott had no time to get off the small path, as the underbrush
was too thick and there was no place for him to go. He simply got
down on the ground and pushed his head and shoulders into the
underbrush.*

The E and E course was taken very seriously by the military. They devote an entire day to prepare the company to
run the course. They dedicate several hours of each trainee's
time to *actually run* the course. The course, 3/4ths of a mile
long and a half mile wide, sat on top of a plateau which was
eight-hundred feet higher than the area around it.

At the end of the course was a wire-enclosed Prisoner
of War camp. Inside were a couple of small buildings and
several bamboo holding cells ten feet long, five feet wide, and
four feet tall. When an AIT soldier was captured by the enemy, they were brought to the enclosure and questioned and
stuffed into the small cells with as many other prisoners as
possible.

While waiting for the course to begin, Bob and Scott
found an old foxhole which had been dug many years before.
It was fifteen feet across and three feet deep. Over the years,
the scrub trees had surrounded the pit and it could not be
seen from any direction. Scott had found the pit by accident.

They were joined by Chuck Farman, one of the men in their platoon.

On the way into the course, the cattle trucks had taken them by the E and E Course. Scott saw the POW Camp and the small cell enclosures scattered around the barb wired POW camp. He knew that on the course there were two companies of basic trainees whose job was to capture the AIT trainees and take them to the POW camp. To ensure that the Basic Trainees did their job, when they took someone prisoner they could then go into a warm tent and drink hot coffee.

Getting captured was a certain proposition, as was being put into one of those bamboo cells. Scott's claustrophobia was in high gear and he decided to escape the course and take a different route to the end. He told Chuck and Bob, "When they call for a formation to start the course you guys go ahead. I am going to escape."

In training, the cadre had told them that if they were ever captured, they needed to get away before the enemy got organized. Scott figured that if he did not go on the normal course, then he could make it to the far end without being captured.

As the makeshift plan unfolded, Bob and Chuck decided that they would go with him. They immediately started to reconnoiter the area to get a better lay of the land. Night was closing in, and they needed a visual of the mountain.

To make this work, they had to use the military mind to their advantage. No one would dare to do what they were planning. No one had told them that they had to run up the hill; they had only said that the goal was to get to the far side of the course without getting captured. They simply would not be running up this hill with all the rest of the company. They would wait and take a more oblique path to the end of the course.

As dusk set in, the sergeants called for everyone to move out into the open area at the foot of the hill. No formation was called. The rest of the company was standing out at the bottom of the long hill in a long-ragged line.

The sergeants waited for the last vestiges of light to leave the sky before blowing the whistle to start the course. When the whistle blew, over one hundred AIT trainees started yelling and hard charging up the long incline. As they crested the hill, eight hundred feet above, the games began.

The enemy soldiers were waiting to capture an enemy AIT soldier to tote him off to the POW camp. The waiting enemy could hear the AIT Company yelling as they hard charged up the hill. The number of enemy waiting doubled the number of men trying to complete the course.

While all those men hard charged up the hill, the three men stayed in the foxhole with their camouflaged faces and camouflaged green clothing melting them into the earth. Scott was certain that each of them was thinking that the cadre, only a few feet away, could hear their hearts beating.

The three men did not move. They heard the cadre as they lit cigarettes and chewed the fat. The discussion turned to getting in on the fun at the POW camp. They all got into vehicles and headed for the camp. The three men stayed in the foxhole as the jeeps and trucks pulled out. So far so good. The kid who was always looking for a way to make it better had made it past the first round.

When they were certain that the entire cadre had left, they did a military type surveillance of the area before sitting up to talk and smoke. They sat there for well over an hour while they listened to the sounds of the E and E course off in the distance. The road they had taken to get to the jumping off place ran right by the course and two hundred meters from where the course began, the road took a hard left. At the bend in the road was a guard shack which they were told would be manned. On the outside chance that there was someone in the guard shack, the E and E Escapees had to plan a route that would eliminate the possibility of being caught.

They decided to hike to the top of the hill and come down to the road, well past the guard shack. Once there, they would move to the far side of the road and use the scrub oak to keep from being seen and make their way to the far end of the course. From the far end, they should be able to watch what was happening at the POW camp and slip into the formation at the end of the night course.

They saddled up with their back packs, picked up their rifles, and started to work their way to the top of the ridgeline. Once they got to the top of the very steep hill they found a foot path that led off to the left, a hundred meters from the north side of the course. They found the path to be small and closed on both sides with the scrub oak trees. The undergrowth was very thick. As Scott headed up a twenty foot rise he saw that an enemy patrol was coming over the hill right towards him.

Fortunately, the patrol was above him and could not make out anyone in the darkness below. Scott had no time to get off the small path as there was no place for him to go.

He simply got down on the ground and pushed his head and shoulders into the underbrush. There was not enough time (nor any room) to get his legs off the trail. Scott's knees were smack dab in the middle of the trail.

With the patrol bearing down upon him, he spread his legs as wide as possible and prayed that they would step over the large tree roots on the trail. Then he just had to lie there and wait. In seconds the first troop reached his position and stepped over Scott's legs, as did the other four men. No one had clipped his legs with their toe or boot heel. He let out a sigh of relief. After the patrol had moved farther down the trail, he softly called for Bob and Chuck who had managed to get off the trail. That was close.

After that scare, the rest of the "plan" started to unfold. They made their way to the left edge of the course where they found something that Scott had not noticed. When Scott was looking at the POW camp, he had missed the very large chain link fence that ran the length of the course. This was a new wrinkle. What if this fence was also on the north side of the course? Since there was no fence on the south end, they figured the north end would be fence free. If there was a fence, they would go to plan B, which they did not have.

From the end of the fence line they took an angular trek to the right, down to the road and ended up fifty meters past the guard shack. They all sat and listened for a while to ensure that there were no cadre or enemy troops around. When they were sure that they were clear, they slipped across the road ten meters into the wilds. They turned right and headed towards the end of the E and E course.

Walking past the Prisoner of War camp and up a long

hill, they stopped well above the POW Camp and were relieved to find that no high chain link fence ran along the north end of the Course.

Inside the barbed wire which surrounded the POW camp, they saw a lot of H-2-2 trainees being interrogated. They also saw the men who had been recently captured treated pretty badly by the Basic Training 'enemy'. Scott watched as they put men into the bamboo cells. His spine shivered at the thought.

They sat on the hill and watched for well over two hours. They knew that the exercise was completed when the captured troops were let out of the prisoner bamboo cells. The three escapees headed down the hill and slipped into the formation in time to make the company roll call.

Without a doubt, they were the cleanest and least sweaty of any of the troops in the entire formation. They just stood behind their camouflaged faces and talked a good game. Scott knew that his older brothers would have been proud of his ingenuity.

The escapees had succeeded because they had a plan, and everyone worked together. They learned that no plan was without a hitch. You just had to use your god given talents to deal with it. None of the men told anyone about what they had done, or in this case not done.

The upshot of that exercise was that three guys walked away from that night with a better can-do attitude than they had had in all their training. He hoped that it put a little larceny into Bob's gentle heart. There was a takeaway that would be a part of the rest of Scott's military career. Always take roll call when you are a member of the cadre in a training company. Some kid from Iowa might just out-think the system.

Hawkeye's Inspection

"Scott walked into the barracks with Hawkeye dead on his heels. The entire platoon was watching as Scott ran the spinner around his combination lock. He knew that the end of his great weekend was now just seconds away."

Every weekend Bob and Scott headed someplace. This particular weekend they were going north to Santa Cruz as soon the Saturday inspection was done. Scott normally missed the Saturday inspections by going on sick call. This gave him some time to himself and by-passed what he thought was a waste of time and energy.

On this Saturday, Scott had headed off to sick bay to get some aspirin for his headache or whatever ailment he used for the day. He had a ticket in his pocket for Santa Cruz and thoughts of another great weekend in his head.

Since Scott was never there for an inspection, everyone used his locker to store excess stuff. Everyone in his barracks knew Scott's combination padlock code. Scott's bunk was the first one in the barracks, as was his locker. Before the inspection that locker was standing open with a lot of extra stuff hanging out.

The 1st Sergeant known as "Hawkeye" chanced to stick his head in the barracks before the inspection began. He saw that Scott's locker looked like a disaster zone.

He asked, "Whose locker is this?" They told him it belonged to Scott Ledbetter who was on sick call.

Hawkeye indignantly demanded, "I want to see that man as soon as he hits the company area!" as he stormed out of the barracks.

Scott came back with his obligatory envelope filled with aspirin. Instead of going into the barracks, he went into the orderly room to sign back into the company. Hawkeye followed him to the barracks.

Scott stopped and asked, "Can I do something for you First Sergeant?"

Hawkeye said, "I want to inspect your locker, private."

As he walked the few feet to the barracks, Scott was sure that he was not going to Santa Cruz or anyplace except the mess hall and some kind of KP duty. He knew that his locker, while normally squared away, had all the platoon's junk. With the first shirt dead on his heels, he had no chance to square the locker away.

Scott walked into the barracks with Hawkeye two feet behind him. The entire platoon was watching as Scott ran the spinner around his combination lock. He knew that the end of a great weekend was now just seconds away. As he opened his locker he could not believe his eyes. It could only be described as squared away. The poncho was exactly eight inches by eight inches. It looked like Scott was ready to head to West Point.

With a picture-perfect wall locker in front of him, Hawkeye knew that he had just been beaten by a Private E 1. He turned on his heel and exited the barracks. Hawkeye barely cleared the front door when laughter burst out. Scott laughed with them but had no idea what he was laughing about. Then his locker began to pivot one hundred and eighty degrees. The locker he was now looking at belonged to the man in the next bay.

Scott's bay mate Phillips had seen Scott going into the orderly room instead of coming to the barracks. He and his buddies had replaced Scott's locker with the man's locker in the next bay. They switched the names on the front of the locker. The padlock was just settling into position as Scott walked through the door.

Having passed his second inspection in AIT, it was off to Santa Cruz with Bob.

Santa Cruz

"One character they met was a long-haired dude, who turned out to be an Air Force type. He was wearing a multi-colored hippie kind of hat. On the inside, there was a long brown curly wig."

With the "inspection" behind them, Bob and Scott beat a path to Santa Cruz on a Continental bus. This was one of his first warm California experiences. They rented a room at a Best Western that set a couple of blocks back from the beach and just cruised the boardwalk area.

One character that they met was a long-haired dude, who turned out to be an Air Force type. He was wearing a multi-colored hippie kind of hat. On the inside, there was a long brown curly wig. In one second, his military short hair cut was replaced by hair that came down to "there, here hair, there hair, everywhere hair". Welcome to the 60's in California.

They found a liquor store that sold Coors. At that time, Coors was not available everywhere in the US. Consequently, everyone wanted Coors. Scott and Bob bought two cases to sell to the trainees at a better price than the other beer vendors. They would use this money to pay for their motel room, which was twenty-nine dollars a night.

They sold cans of beer for a buck each. They also discovered that the trainees who were not from California thought that they could sleep on the beach. Since California beaches are colder than a well digger's ass in Alaska, they gladly paid two dollars apiece to sleep on the carpet in a warm room. Bob and Scott had people sleeping all over the room and easily paid for a great weekend.

That evening, they went to an old boardwalk amusement area which Scott believed was one of the most beautiful places that he had ever seen. No fiberglass was used to build the rides; only wood that was beautifully crafted and shiny as glass. He believed that the same carpenters who worked on the benches on the old ferry to Sausalito from San Francisco must have worked on the boardwalk. It was a great weekend.

San Francisco for the Weekend

"Scott felt like he was in a car wreck with everything around him moving in slow motion. His life slowed down and was a part of a dream sequence."

The Playboy Club

A truly great weekend in San Francisco will be in Scott's memory for the rest of his life. When they arrived in San Francisco, Bob's aunt and uncle took them on a tour of the city. They visited the Crookedest Street in the World, Nob Hill, and the art galleries which are all part of the world's most beautiful city.

That evening Bob surprised Scott. Two young ladies, friends of Bob's aunt and uncle, went with them to the San Francisco Playboy Club. Bob had a key. Scott had never known anyone with one of these keys. For the young man from Iowa, this was a night of nights. Scott and Bob and their dates arrived at the club at eight PM and walked into a world of true make believe.

In college, Scott drank beer drawn from a tap sitting on the tailgate of a pickup truck. He could have counted the number of hard drinks that he had had in the last couple of years and not used both hands. A good dish of fresh peanuts was considered living pretty high on the hog. But on this night, he was walking into a legendary bar in the world's most beautiful city. He saw more class poured into the atmosphere than he had seen in his entire life.

Hugh Hefner had put the word class into simply serving a drink. The Playboy Key, like everything in the club, was wrapped with gold. Scott felt like he was in a car wreck with everything around him moving in slow motion. For a little while, his life was a part of a dream sequence.

Scott had heard how the bunnies delivered drinks with the little dip and he sat there in the booth and witnessed all this happening around him. The rest of the weekend was mostly a blur. Never did he think that he would walk through the door of anyplace like the San Francisco Playboy Club.

No Orders, Again

On the last Saturday of AIT, there was a graduation formation where the cadre said good-bye to this batch of trainees, now soldiers. When they got back into the barracks everyone was packing the last of their sierra and heading to training all over the country. Bob was headed for Ft. Benning and Officer Candidate School. Scott and several others who were supposed to go to OCS had not received orders.

Vehicles were coming and going with troops bound for the bus station and places all over the country and for some, headed directly for Vietnam. After everyone with orders left, there were twenty troops standing outside the barracks with no place to go. The cadre were headed home, and the men just waited for whatever was next. It seemed that they missed the memo about training being over.

Monterey Jazz Festival

"When Count Basie found out that Scott was in the Army and heading for OCS, he called him by his first name and wished him Godspeed."

Vehicles finally arrived to pick up the left-over trainees.

The men were driven to a Military Police Company where they were put into another formation and told that they were going to be assigned temporary duty until their class started. They secured their belongings in a barracks and returned to the orderly room. A sergeant asked if any of the men would like to make extra money, working as security guards for the Monterey Jazz Festival. The pay was seven dollars and fifty cents per hour and Scott almost broke his arm waving it back and forth.

The festival was held in a large municipal park with a beautiful pavilion that must have been built back in the depression. Behind the stage was a large concrete shell that stood thirty feet tall and surrounded the outdoor pavilion. That beautiful shell was painted light blue and pink. Scott was assigned to guard a closed and padlocked gate that was in the back of the park.

The pay was the same, so he just sat and watched the people gathered in the back of the park. They were smoking pot and playing guitars. To get into the festival they had to pay, but the park was free. As the hours wore on, the marijuana smoke was heavy as both the people smoking and the security guard were getting a pretty good buzz on. Scott was in charge of a bunch of people that did not need to be watched or could give a shit why he was there.

Sitting in a park beat sitting in some the barracks for one hundred and thirteen dollars a month. He was going to make in a few hours what he made for a month's army pay. At 1500 hours he took a 'well-deserved break" from all the pot heads and headed for the main festival complex.

As a theatre major in college, Scott was fascinated by all the activity backstage. He went into the break room for a

soda and saw one of the men from the post. He had a cigarette hanging out of his mouth and in a deep southern twang
he asked, "Do yuu, lik this shit?" Scott offered to trade places
with him and assured him that he would not be able to hear
the music from his post. The guy was elated to get away from
his post in front of the stage and the godawful music.

Before heading for his new duty station, Scott wandered
backstage with his little "I am one of the good guys badges."
A man stepped out of a dressing room and Scott almost ran
into him. He recognized Count Basie. He managed to say,
"Hello, my name is Scott Ledbetter and I love listening to
your music."

Count Basie did not miss a beat, when he said, "Hello,
Scott, and thank you for the compliment. I hope that all is
secure."

Scott said, "This is a temporary job, sir. I am in the Army
and heading for Officer Candidate School."

The Count said, "Bless you son and I hope that you can
avoid going to Vietnam."

"I will go wherever I am asked to serve, sir," Scott replied.

Count Basie paused for a few seconds and said, "Scott,
that is good to hear, and if you go to Vietnam, I wish you
Godspeed." He shook Scott's hand and continued on his way.
Scott had officially met his first celebrity. He would never
forget the experience.

Scott took up his new position right in front of the stage.
Along with making such a great hourly pay, he was able to
watch jazz stars come on stage to sing or play. Some he knew
and some he had never heard before, but it was all good. Finally, it was time for Count Basie to come out and close down

the evening of jazz. To say that he was impressive would be an understatement. He was not a tall man, but he stood head and shoulders above everyone else on the stage. He simply took the audience on a wonderful musical journey that went far beyond any place they had been.

At the end of his first set, he asked that the house lights be brought up so that he could see "his" people. He spoke to many of his friends and fans in the front section where Scott was standing. When he spotted Scott, he said, "Hello, Scott." He treated Scott just like he was one of his pals. He was the most elegant person that Scott had ever met.

At the end of the weekend, Scott was both tired and happy. He had a check for over a hundred dollars and memories of Sheila McRae and, of course, Count Basie. After a full weekend of listening to real jazz and seeing people and things that he had never seen, it was back to the barracks.

On Monday, Scott and all the temporary people repacked their bags and waited by the orderly room for their assignment. Some stayed right at Ft. Ord to be go-fers for some company. Scott was being sent to Camp Hunter-Liggett, a one hundred and eighty-thousand-acre forest reserve that sat behind Randolph Hearst's Estate, seventy-five miles south of Fort Ord.

At 1300 hours he boarded the green Army "tour" bus that was headed to his new post. While he was excited about going someplace else, he knew that his weekends in San Francisco were done.

He had never had the chance to move about the way he was able to in the military. The trip to this camp was yet another beginning of another adventure. He did not have any idea where he was going or what he was going to be doing when he got there. This made the trip even more exciting.

He thought about his military career and how something seemed to keep getting in the way of his training. From the time he had signed up to join the Army, he had spent close to three months not being training. He wondered how long his stay would be before he headed for OCS.

Camp Hunter Liggett

"The next morning, after picking up the Scout and their blankets, they headed for the old barn. They parked the Scout inside of the barn and slid the door closed behind them. They broke open a couple of straw bales and caught a couple hours of sleep."

Hunter-Liggett sat in a valley surrounded by nice sized hills, not mountains, but eight hundred-foot hills on the east side of the Sierras. The best description would be laid back or laconic.

The officer's quarters were built in the Spanish style. The rest of the troops lived-in single-story barracks that were plain Army ugly, built for WWII. There were no officers assigned to the MP unit. The commander of the MP Company was Sergeant Frank, who was an E-7.

The MP Company was made up of seventeen Military Policemen. When Scott arrived, he met David, another slick sleeved private. He, like Scott, had no orders for whatever school he was to attend. He had gotten to Hunter Liggett the day before and while they had no training they were put behind the desk at the MP station.

Poaching Patrol

After a week at Hunter Liggett, an E-6, Sergeant Mahoney, took David and Scott to the motor pool. He wanted them to start to patrol one hundred and eighty-thousand-acre timber and look for poachers. There were not told what to do with these "bad guys" should they find them. They were not given a radio or any way of communicating with anyone. They were just supposed to go out on patrol.

Those California poachers must have been early risers, because he ordered them to leave on patrol at 0430 hours. He would be checking the Motor Pool log to find out what time they had left. Apparently, he thought that two men in a single Scout could cover a hundred and eighty thousand acres.

Since they were in the MP's, the Motor Pool Sergeant must have assumed that they had military driver's licenses. Neither did, but when Scott had taken driver's training at Fort Ord, he had learned how to fill out a Scout requisition form. No one asked about their military license.

On the first day of their patrolling mission, they checked out at 0430 hours. The Scout had no roof or side windows and the early morning was extremely cold. They thought about heading back to the barracks to wait for sunlight but figured that the sergeant would find them. They did take Army blankets to ward off the wind chill.

After driving three miles, it was still very dark and cold.

They found a massive rock overhang where they parked the Scout. The rock slowed down the wind and the overhang seemed to give them some comfort. They wrapped in the blankets and shivered for the next couple of hours. As daylight filled the valley, they headed back to post to get some chow.

A half a mile up the road, they checked out an old barn setting thirty feet from the road. It had a sliding barn door on the side away from the road and inside a pile of straw bales. The farm kid from Iowa had found a home. Tomorrow they had a place to go until the sun was up and it was time for breakfast.

Back at Hunter, they ate breakfast and waited until the sun was higher in the sky before heading back out into the timber. They talked to the men at the fire station who gave them a topical map of the area. At least it had some trails marked and showed where the mountains started to climb toward the sky. They drove all day until 1500 hours and headed back to the post.

The next morning, they headed for the old barn, parked the Scout inside, and slid the door closed behind them. They broke open a couple of straw bales and caught a couple hours of sleep. They repeated this routine every day. They never went by the MP desk for fear that someone would want to know what they were doing. After a few days, they figured out that there was really no one in charge of them. The sergeant who assigned them this task had never talked to them about their patrol.

With no one in charge, the two men started to set their own hours. Tuesday and Wednesday were now their days off. Sergeant Frank signed passes and left them in a box at the MP counter. They would go in on Monday morning to pick up their passes for Tuesday and Wednesday. The two men did not go on patrol on Monday as they had to catch the bus back to Ft. Ord at 1500 hours. That let them start their two-day pass on Tuesday morning.

On Wednesday afternoon, they caught the bus from Ord to Hunter and arrived at 1300 hours. They would wait until Thursday morning to go back out on patrol. As slick sleeved privates, this was the best duty on Army earth. Sergeant Mahoney never asked them about the patrols and Sergeant Frank never knew what they were doing.

Thursday through Sunday the two men maintained their daily schedule. They would sign out the vehicle at 0430 hours, catch some sleep in the barn, and head in for chow. After breakfast, they headed for the toolies. The only time they came close to the MP station was when they picked up their passes. Since there was only one man on duty, no one had any idea where these two temporary men spent their day. Using the map from the firefighters they would figure out where they had not been in the timber reserve and head out to see new sights.

Poachers 1/2 mile away

… when Scott keyed the mike again he said, "Stop, you are under arrest for poaching!" The words bounced off mountains for miles.

The two men had spent over two months driving around the mountains and valleys of this forest reserve. Both men were from the Midwest and had stayed on the lower trails that skirted the mountains. Scott had seen a trail that went up the side of a fairly tall mountain and they decided to drive up as far as they could with the Scout. They got sandwiches from the mess hall as they would not make it back in for noon chow.

The trail started out with the normal dual tire tracks heading up the mountain, but eventually ran out and they had to make their own way up the mountain. Scott shifted down into the Granny Gears, to crawl closer to the summit. They got close to the mountain top with the Scout and then climbed to the mountain top. The view was stunning.

They were sitting on the rocks looking west toward the Sierra Nevada's and then back east to valleys of California. The wind made the only noise. A sudden roar came from the valley to their south. Scott turned to see an Air Force F-4 fly by, at eye level. If the pilot would have turned, Scott could have read his name tag. The noise was deafening, but it was a phenomenal site. It made the trip up the side of the mountain worthwhile.

They spent most of the day exploring the top of the mountain. Scott used a military issued .22 rifle and shot two huge pinecones out of the tall pine trees to send them home before leaving for OCS. They found a vantage point on the large rocks close to the mountains edge to eat lunch. Dave was using binoculars to scan the area when he saw a red Jeep on the far side of the valley. He watched as the jeep slowly worked its way down into the valley and crawled all the way down to the creek that separated the valley. Two men got out and took their rifles out of the back of the jeep. *Scott and David had just found two poachers!*

A loudspeaker was bolted onto the side of the Scout. The

speaker belled out, some two feet and was six inches from the top to the bottom. The speaker was made of tin and had a connected amplifier. That amplifier was kept charged by the Scout. They carried the speaker, amplifier, and microphone to a large flat rock. By the time they got everything set up, the poachers had walked quite a distance from their Jeep. Scott blew on the microphone and a huge shushing sound rocketed out across the valley. The men stopped walking and looked around trying to figure out what on earth they had just heard. Scott keyed the mike again and said, "Stop, you are under arrest for poaching!" The words bounced off mountains for miles. It seemed as if he had yelled it ten times.

Scott thought that the men were going to kill themselves getting the hell out of the area. They ran as fast as their little civilian legs could carry them through some serious ground cover, threw their rifles into the back of the Jeep, and headed south, out of the reserve.

The trip from the mountain top to the stream had taken the two men over thirty minutes. On the way out, they were heading over the far mountain top after ten minutes. Scott and David were laughing hysterically. David told Scott that he was crazy, but that was one of the funniest things that he had seen. When they finally got all the equipment mounted back on the Scout, Scott realized that it was getting late and they needed to leave for the base.

Scott had learned a lot about four wheeling over the past few weeks but getting down off this mountain was going to take some serious four wheeling skills. As they peered down the mountain, it appeared that they were about to drive over a cliff. The mountain was very, very, down. David, who had not sworn one time since they started to work together, mumbled, "Oh, Shit."

Scott tried to act like this was no big deal, but he could see them rolling this thing down the mountain. There would be hell to pay if something happened and the Army found out that neither of the men had a military driver's license.

Scott put the Scout in double granny and drove over the side of the "cliff". Somehow the Scout stuck to the rocks and for the next two hours they crawled back down the mountain. As they made it to the road, darkness was closing in and the gear box and transmission were so hot you could not touch them.

If he shut it down and let it cool, they could be stuck out there all night. This would have been a big problem, because no one knew where in hell they were. When they got to the road, he was able to shift up into the regular gears. When they arrived at the motor pool, the transmission was less than a thousand degrees and no one was there to check them in. The next morning, they waited until the motor pool opened and asked for a different Scout, making an excuse that theirs needed an oil change.

San Francisco every week

Scott figured out how to use Army transportation to get to Fort Ord and put San Francisco back into his itinerary. Each Monday Scott would have his AWOL bag packed and after picking up their pass they waited for the 1500-hour bus for Fort Ord. The bus always stopped at the Monterey Bus

Station and Scott would buy a roundtrip ticket to San Francisco.

Scott would get to the depot in San Francisco at 2030 hours. He stayed in the hotel where he had stayed on his first visit to the city. His $4.00 "suite" was always waiting for him. After a few weeks, he was given a room that actually had a chair and a desk, only a door away from the bathroom.

He normally paid for his room one night at a time. He found that there was a netherworld of people who had no home address. Many of these hippies simply did not have a specific place to lie down at night. Where they slept one night could be totally different than the previous one. Scott did not know that this level of society existed.

When Scott first arrived in San Francisco from Fort Riley, he had breakfast at a small diner close to his hotel. That diner, much like the one in Peoria, became his breakfast place. Everyone knew his name, and they would welcome him each week. Like the young priest in Peoria, these people were used to serving people who had no hope. When someone young, with a whole life in front of him, came in the diner, they were more than eager to talk.

Haight-Asbury

This was a time in Scott's life when responsibility was held at bay. He did not have to concern himself with what others wanted to do; he could just do as he damned well pleased. The intersection at Haight and Asbury Street was peopled with the hippies of the day. On his first visit to the area, Scott sat down with such a group of young people. He was the only one with a short haircut and clean clothes. One very large dude started questioning why a guy in the military could or would sit with his group.

The big man asked, "Why do you think that you can just come in here and sit down with us. You are acting as if you belong here!"

Scott returned his question with one of his own, "Do you understand space?"

"What do you mean, space?"

Scott replied, "Aren't you here because you want your own space?"

The man looked at him like he was from another country and said, "Ya, I want my own space."

Scott went on to say, "Well, I like my space, just like you. And that space happens to be in the military."

A long minute of silence passed as an intelligent thought cranked through the guy's under-used brain and the man smiled and said, "Hey, you are alright."

With that, he slapped Scott on the back, and Scott officially became a part of the group and included in the more esoteric discussions on the meaning of life.

This was a wonderful time in his life. Scott could sit with a new friend in some back-water tavern, tossing back bourbon, water by, until the light of a new day crept slowly into the city. Much like his new hippie friends, he was totally mobile. His bag was in the locker at the bus station and there was a bus ticket in his billfold. He always kept enough money to cover the cost of a taxi. While Scott never imagined he could be living this type of life, here he was.

Little Alioto's Tavern

There was a restaurant on Pier 39 called Alioto's. The prices at that restaurant were more than Scott made in a month. When Scott read the posted menu and saw the prices to eat, he started looking for other options. An old Budweiser sign hung outside a small tavern up the street, it was referred to as Little Alioto's.

When he walked in he found an old German, complete with Lederhosen, playing an accordion very badly. He had a monkey on a leash. The monkey had on a little red coat and a hat that reminded Scott of a man on an old Phillip Morse cigarette ad. The monkey had a small tin cup for collecting tips.

When Scott walked into the bar, the monkey came up to him. He had a tin cup in his outstretched arm. He started screaming and banging the cup on the floor. Scott dropped a quarter into the cup. Obviously that coin did not make enough noise. The monkey took the quarter out and kept screaming at him and banging his cup on the floor, but Scott ignored him.

The old German's name was Hontz and both he and the monkey were drunk. Hontz sat on a bar stool, just inside the door, and played mostly off key. If he did not like the person who came in or heaven forbid, they said anything derogatory, he would cuss at them. Apparently, the old German had been a part of this tavern for a long time.

On the far end of the building was a cafeteria. It was separated from the bar by huge pilings set in a row and decorated with the obligatory ship's rope and netting. In comparison with its expensive neighbor down the street, Little Alioto's offered good food and beer for a reasonable price.

On his first night there, he met tourists from all over the world. Even the local patrons and bartenders treated him like he was part of the family. He had found a home and made this place his office for future visits. He found that Mr. Alioto was a big supporter of the military.

Scott was now making a "grand total" of one hundred and twenty dollars a month. When he came back to the tavern for the third week, he asked the bartender if he would sell him a pitcher of beer, one glass at a time. A pitcher yielded four glasses for two dollars and seventy-five cents. A single beer was a dollar. At first the bartender said he wasn't going to do that. But after a while, Scott wore him down so he could pay for a pitcher of beer one glass at a time. Some days a pitcher of beer would last all day as Scott roamed the city.

Old Ferryboat

A permanently docked ferry boat sat next to Big Alioto's. Built back in the 1800's, it was the main link between San Francisco and Sausalito on the other side of the bay. It had been decommissioned when the Golden Gate Bridge was built. The local historical society had taken it over and used it as a tourist attraction.

Scott found the boat on his first day on the pier and fell in love with its beautiful old wooden benches that were more comfortable than a sofa. He could sit on the boat and stare out at the bay and the Golden Gate Bridge. The volunteers took a liking to the young soldier and would let him come on board without paying. Each week he would find time to visit the pier and the boat.

If the people running the attraction needed to take a break, they would leave him on board and put up a "closed sign" and leave. Scott had his own favorite seat on the bay side of the boat where he would sit in the sun and read. Because of the reflection of the glass, no one could see him from the outside. That seat became his personal hideaway. While he did not know what heaven was going to be like, he hoped that this seat would be there.

Monterey by the Bay

"This mug had a half inch of frost on both the inside and outside. A degree above freezing, the beer crackled in his dry throat as it slid down his gullet."

On one trip north to Fort Ord, Scott had to go to the infirmary for a cold, so San Francisco had to get along without him for a week. As he walked in the cold air and fog that was Fort Ord, he decided to head for the sun and warmth of Monterey.

Since the bus to Monterey was not running, he decided he would walk the beach to get to the sun. As he walked the beach his low quarter shoes sunk in the dry sand. When he walked on the wet sand, the waves washed over his feet.

After the long miserable beach experience, he did reach the wharf area of Monterey and the sun was shining. He walked out of the wharf area and into a normal residential area. There were no businesses and no place to buy a beer or a soda. A guy out turning the rocks in his front yard directed Scott to a tavern a couple of blocks away.

The signs outside the bar advertised the coldest selection of beer in California, a beer lover's paradise. They had well over fifty beer taps. The mug had a half inch of frost on both the inside and outside. A degree above freezing, the beer crackled in his dry throat as it slid down his gullet. He nursed that mug for a long time. Lord, have mercy, was that a great beer.

While another beer would have been great, his budget was still tight, so he caught the bus back to Hunter Liggett.

Last ride to Hunger Ligget

He was watching southern California slide by the window and recalled all his California experiences. He thought about the hippies and draft dodgers. He had met many men dodging the draft and one who was being chased by whoever chases civilians who are draft dodgers.

It was like he was doing research for a social studies class. He observed the making of the next generation from an interesting vantage point. The undercurrent in America was very strong with demonstrations against the government and Vietnam, a part of the daily news.

He had discussed the war and the government with his friends in the Hippie community. Those discussions only solidified his thinking on the war and his government. He understood the war from a standpoint of stopping the spread of communism though he was not sure that the present administration had any idea how to go to war and to win that war. The only president who had understood how to do that was Eisenhower, who was no longer in charge.

Scott was in a unique position. He worked for the government and was positive that he would end up in Vietnam. When asked by his hippie friends why he did not go to Canada, he answered that he was not raised to run away from responsibility; he was doing his duty as an American.

Everywhere that Scott went in the city by the bay, someone or something was testing all of life's rules. Rules that had been passed down to him by parents and grandparents were being broken or discarded everywhere.

The hippies had social rules, but they were very well covered with long hair, funky clothes, and a risky lifestyle. They had an utter disregard for those who had established the social mores, whoever they were. They did teach Scott that you could exist in society without following any rules.

The flower children taught him that rules were guidelines handed down by those who have gone before. Scott reminded them that their parents were passing down their best observation on life and the next generation should not dismiss what they were saying without giving it some thought.

Scott was certain that the things that he learned on the streets of San Francisco had become a part of his philosophy. He believed that there were rules that needed to be followed as well as rules that were little more than obstacles to progress.

To the hippies and flower children, Scott must have

appeared to be from a different time zone. He artfully wove his way in and out of this society and back into the military. He had been born three to four years before most people he met on the street, brought up on Tommy Dorsey, Jimmy Durante, and the music from the 40's and early 50's.

His midwestern college had none of the demonstrations rocking the rest of the country. The administrators were still considered to be omnipotent. It was his belief that future generations will be spanked with the repercussions of yesterday's decisions.

A desire for cheap labor brought us slavery, which in turn brought us the civil war, deep racial hatred, and the tearing apart of an entire race. By destroying the black family unit in the mid-1800s, an entire race of people had to re-establish roots without knowing what the seed looked like. The black race has had to establish itself with rules that have been made up as they went along in a racist America.

From the racial discord that rocked his world, there were places like Selma, Alabama. Rather than being some sleepy backwoods place, it was the first place mentioned when race was discussed. That place and that time gave rise to Martin Luther King and an era when racial issues, which had been kept under the rug, were given light.

Scott's time in San Francisco was a time of reviewing what society looked like from the eye of a theatre major. What he was a part of will never happen in the same way again, as an entire section of the country's future was in upheaval. They were spurred on by an unpopular war, an unpopular government, and a new drug culture that had never existed.

There was so much testing going on that it was impossible

to pin down all the cultures and counter cultures that were a part of the time. Scott wondered what America would be like when his generation was passing down the "rules" for the next generation.

The war in Vietnam had two support groups in the country: Both either worked for the military or the civilian companies who supported the military. The rest of the country was more than just apathetic. The young man from next door who was conscripted to fight a war in Vietnam would be turned into a baby killer and dope addict by an uncaring media.

Scott felt that he had an ace up his sleeve that separated him from the hippies he met in San Francisco. He had a strong belief in God and in his Catholic faith. Both kept him planted in the reality of where he had been raised.

When a young person was out on their own, it is easy to ignore religious beliefs. The only person who knew if he was attending mass or a church service was the individual. Through all the life events that surrounded Scott, he was kept on the straight and narrow with a devotion to his parents and an example by the Catholic priests, in particular Father O'Brien.

When he got back to Hunter Liggett, he found a note to report to the MP station where the desk sergeant handed him a manila envelope. The contents of the envelope meant that his days in San Francisco had come to an end. It contained his orders to Officer Candidate School at Fort Benning, Georgia. Both he and David were leaving the next day and leaving behind a really wonderful part of their lives.

His time at Hunter-Liggett had given him a chance to

catch his breath after months of military training. He had been able to drive through thousands of acres of back country with no supervision. He was able to go to San Francisco on a weekly basis and observe one of the most significant cultural upheavals in a country's history. He wished that this part of his life would have gone on longer, but it was time to get back to real life.

As Scott looked back on this time from his hospital room in Chu Lai, he realized that his time at Hunter-Liggett had added another three plus months to his time in the Army. He was more convinced than ever before that he was destined to be on the Castle Hill. He had to be there to restore the broken link in the chain of command. It was up to him to bring Bravo off that mountain.

4. Officer Candidate School OCS

*"If he (God) would go through all of that, to get Scott
through OCS, then Scott needed to put his ass in the air
and nose to the grindstone. He decided that he was staying in OCS and becoming a 2nd Lieutenant."*

"Welcome to Fort Benning"

Scott flew from San Francisco to Atlanta on his way to Fort
Benning. He was in the window seat as they lifted off so he
could once more see his beautiful city. What was lying in
front of him? In truth, he did not know. He had heard about
the officers called Ninety-Day wonders in WWII. Those men
were put through a three-month course, and a lot of them did
not make it through the war. The Officer training program in
WWII was only three months long. The men that they were
sending into battle were too young and when youth was coupled with inexperience, bad things happened.

When they reported for duty they were immediately in
heavy combat and the results were far from stellar. A lot of
those young lieutenants never made it back. That thought

stuck in his mind. He was certain that he was going to Vietnam, and he figured he might as well get paid for his time as an officer.

The airport at Atlanta was nothing like Chicago but both were enormous. Somehow, he managed to find his duffle among several hundred in baggage claim. He never let loose of his AWOL bag as that contained his orders and all his personnel and medical records. At the airport, he found a bus service that would take him to Columbus, GA where he took his first cab ride to 65th Officer Candidate Company.

As the cab entered the post, the driver asked him about the program he was going into. The man shook his head when Scott told him OCS. They drove for a couple of miles, past military buildings and pine trees, with little being said.

Scott had seen the Ronald Reagan movies about West Point, and Benning did not look like anything that he remembered. The cab pulled up to the curb in front of a large three-story concrete block building. Before getting back in the cab, the driver shook Scott's hand and wished him luck. The driver gave him one of the most "knowing smiles" that Scott had ever seen. He then got back in his cab and drove away.

He stood there along the side of the road with everything that he owned in a seventy-pound duffle bag, laundry bag, and an AWOL bag. It was 1500 hours on a hot Georgia day in October and Scott was already sweating profusely. In front of him were two side-by-side, three story concrete block buildings. In between the buildings, he saw a line of men with duffle bags. They were lined up and Scott assumed that this is where he was supposed to report.

Scott got to the sidewalk centered between the buildings.

The line of men stretched for thirty meters and at the end of the line sat two eight-foot tables. Everyone had three bags with him. Each time someone got signed in and headed for the barracks, everyone had to reach down and move three bags forward, stopping when the man in front him was an arm's length away.

A troop would sign in then pick up his stuff and head towards the three-story concrete block building. The time it took for that troop to get to the building, thirty feet away, might be thirty minutes. More than seventy blue helmeted senior candidates were hovering around all the soldiers in line. Some number of those senior candidates were hollering for the man who had just signed in, to do push-ups, straighten a gig line, or just for standing there. Scott now understood the reason for the smile from the cab driver. The cabbie knew what the OCS candidates had to put up with to make it through this training and walk out as officers.

By the time Scott figured out what was taking place in front of him, he was unceremoniously attacked by some number of senior candidates. In fact, every person standing in line was under constant attack by them. An hour later, Scott had only made it halfway to the sign in table. He had pushed out several hundred push-ups, and his head ached from the constant stream of scream.

His dress greens were soaked with sweat, as was his dress hat. He was not certain how long he was in the line. He could not imagine the hell that would have been created if he would have looked at his watch. That would mean more senior candidates bringing more wrath upon his by now—very sorry ass.

The sun was setting behind the barracks before Scott found himself at the first eight-foot table. An easy task had been turned into a nightmare. Scott was to learn that this was OCS: take the smallest task and make it larger than anyone would ever imagine.

The senior candidates were doing the Army's bidding. The harassment was designed to get rid of as many weak candidates as possible. When these Blue Candidates arrived at OCS, they had undergone this trial themselves and by all that was unholy, they were going to get their pound of flesh.

Scott finally signed into the company and then signed for his M-14 and several other forms whose importance he had no idea. He signed for whatever they were "issuing" him so he could make it through OCS. When he went to the second table to get a platoon and room assignment, there sat Sergeant White, a closely cropped 1st Sergeant. Scott stopped directly in front of him and looked him squarely in the eyes, and asked, "Why do you let this go on?"

The question shot all the way down to this man's enlisted soul. The sergeant looked down and said nothing. As Scott was trying to get to the door with many blue helmeted SOBs on his backside, he glanced back and saw the sergeant head towards the mess hall.

Inside the barracks, the treatment only got worse. While four senior candidates were yelling at him, he had to take off his low quarters before entering the building. Now he had something else to carry. His billets were on the second floor, and he was certain that he would not get there in time to collect Social Security.

The Blues never let up as he climbed the stairs with all his gear and walked sideways down the narrow hallway with his sierra. The yelling continued. Once inside his room he found no roommate: he was the single target of opportunity. No matter what he sat down, it was in the wrong place. They actually had him lie down on his bed and make the bed while he was in the bed. He managed to maintain his composure. He was determined that no blue helmeted SOB was going to "out his ass."

At long last, the Blue Helmets left the floor, leaving a 2nd lieutenant in charge. He was more than capable of picking up where the Blues had left off, but there was only one of him and thirty men in the platoon. Somehow Scott was able to get his things put away and get into bed. At 0430 hours, the yelling started all over again.

OCS Morning

Scott had been in many training barracks and every one of them had some self-enforced morning bathroom time. In OCS, the shower was a run in, lather up, wash off, and out the door. Washing hair was not an issue as everyone had a buzz cut.

In the OCS barracks latrine there were five mirrors, and thirty guys to use those metal mirrors. A candidate had to get right next to the mirror to see if he was shaving his face. The guy two feet behind the candidate is yelling at the guy at the mirror to hurry. Scott lathered his face and started scraping the lather off when he was in front of the mirror. Then it was twenty seconds of vigorous brushing with his toothbrush and out the door.

Even though Scott had been in the military for months and had been through two training cycles, he did not understand the rules of OCS. OCS went deep into your soul, grinding away at the candidate through six full months until the candidate quits, is tossed from the program, or graduates as an officer. OCS in the sixties spent little time teaching the candidates how to be a good officer, it just taught them to make it through to the end of the course, under extreme duress.

The candidate had to come to grips with the fact that the program demanded that he focused one hundred percent on a myriad of insignificant details. Those tasks included floors, furniture, windows, and everything else small and every day. These items were made monumental tasks on the road to earning a gold bar.

OCS Hallways, Spit and Polish

The hallways had five and a half, eight-inch floor tiles. The candidates only walked on the middle tile and only in stocking feet. No candidate "Ever" wore boots inside the building. By the end of his first month, Scott had callouses on both little fingers from pulling up his boot laces. He pulled on them each time that he fell out for a formation or left the barracks for any reason. When he returned, he had to take off his boots before entering the building, which made his fingertips sore. There were days when he would leave and re-enter the barracks eight to nine times. That meant his boots were tied and untied eight or nine times.

When two men walked towards each other in the hallway, both would be on the middle tile. Both would lean to their right and step around each other. You would not step off that center tile. The other tiles in the hallway have a high gloss shine. If those tiles were walked on, they lost their shine. Candidates would have to get on their hands and knees and shine those tiles with a diaper and a can of Butcher's Wax. Everyone stayed off those tiles around the clock.

The challenge came when thirty men were scurrying to get ready for early morning formation. Thirty men are walking both ways on one line of eight-inch tiles and OCS always goes at full speed. That was especially true in the morning. In the morning, the hallway looked like a giant engine with the pistons going up and down.

Floors

All the tiles in their room also had an extremely high gloss shine. If they were walked on, then the two roommates would have to use Butcher's Wax and a cloth baby diaper to buff out boot prints. As a result, the only tile that they could walk on was the first full tile in the doorway.

When a candidate got to his room, he would step from the center tile in the hallway to the middle tile in his doorway. then he would step onto the single Army cot inside the room. If he was fortunate to have that first bunk, he stayed on that bunk and slid out his footlocker to get everything that he needed to study and live. At no time did his feet touch the floor any place outside of that first tile in the middle of the door frame.

If you were the poor soul on the far side of the room, you had to step onto your roommate's bunk and pull out his footlocker. Crawl out and lean over and pull out your footlocker. Then you stood up and stepped from one footlocker to the other. You would then step onto your bed and that is where you would live.

The candidates sat on their bunk to write letters, study, polish shoes, get undressed for bed, and dressed for the day's training. When it was time for the sheets to be changed, it was all done while kneeling on the footlocker. To make making the bed easier, candidates put large safety pins through the blanket and the sheets on the wall side of the bed. That way he could kneel on the foot locket and make the bed without worrying about the other side of the bed. All the day's activity was done without one foot touching the floor.

The Butcher's Wax on the floor was so thick that if you walked on the tile with your boots on, you could read the name imprinted on the bottom of the boot heal. When the Platoon Tactical Officer (TAC) inspected rooms many times during the week, he kept his boots on so Scott and his roommate had to hand buff his heal marks with a baby diaper and apply more Butcher's Wax.

To keep the footlocker from damaging the wax build up on the floor, ten women's Kotex pads were glued to the bottom of the footlocker. Kotex pads were also glued to the bottom of the 2x4 that was on the bottom of the bunk legs.

Scott thought that whoever came up with the use of Kotex pads to be a genius.

They used baby diapers to put on the wax and hand buff the floors, so it was not unusual for an unmarried young guy to head to the PX for diapers, Kotex, and pantyhose. Pantyhose were used to put a high shine on boots and low quarters.

Furniture

Each room had two beautiful mahogany desks that were never used for studying. The desks had a beautiful leather desk pad that was unusable because it had a thick layer of Butcher's Wax. One-time Scott made the mistake of signing a paper on the pad. His signature was now on the pad, backwards. He spent a long time to get that signature buffed out of the pad.

The desk lamps had a long base with two stems holding up a fluorescent lamp. The cord was so tightly wrapped around the two stems that it looked like it was glued to the stems. These old lamps had never shined on a single book.

The two wall lockers were never locked and in fact the wall locker doors were always open for an inspection. It displayed the seventeen fatigue uniforms for each candidate. Those uniforms were starched and pressed by the Army laundry.

The four dresser drawers were never closed. The bottom drawer was pulled out twelve inches from the dresser, the next by nine inches; the next by six inches; and top drawer open by three inches. Having the drawers open at those exact measurements enabled the Tactical Officer to stand in one spot and see all the squared away clothing at one time.

Windows

The windows were ones that you unlatch on the bottom and shove out. They stayed open twenty-four hours a day, seven days a week, and were all uniformly opened to eight inches, no more, no less. This meant that the building looked uniform from the outside. It made no difference how cold or warm it was, these windows remained permanently open.

Directly across the street was the Army's parachute training facility where a thousand plus jump school trainees spent the day running and jumping. The dust they raised constantly attacked the candidate's rooms. When they returned from a day of training, the entire room had to be dusted. They would lie down on their footlockers and hand dust the floor and furniture. Then they would step from locker to locker to dust the top of the furniture. The Tac Officers did not care how much dust came in the open windows, they wanted everything dusted.

Letters of Reprimand were given by Tactical Officers who saw:

A string hanging from a buttonhole
A sock with a hole
A Candidate sleeping before lights out

A candidate up after lights out

A candidate sleeping in class

A Candidate eating anything in the barracks

Any of these infractions resulted in the candidate typing a letter of apology for their lack of discipline. It was a lot like writing on the school's black board "I will not talk in class" one hundred times and it accomplished the same thing, nothing.

The reprimand letter had to be typed, not handwritten. This wasn't easy as there were no typewriters in the room. The inanity of these letters was never more evident than an incident involving Scott's Army dress shirt.

The Cracked Button

Pugil stick training was a lesson on how to club someone into insensibility. A Pugil stick was a three-foot piece of round oak wood with padding on the last six inches on either end of the stick. In the training, two trainees were paired off and they attempted to defend themselves from the other by jabbing or parrying with this padded stick. Scott had been through this training at both Ft. Riley and Ft. Ord. By the time he got to OCS, he had learned how to keep from being beaten to death.

At the Pugil stick training at Fort Benning, Scott's company was just starting the last training session at Benning when he was called to the platform and was directed to meet with his captain, Capt. Willows. The sergeant pointed to a waiting jeep a hundred meters from the training field. Scott ran across that field with all sorts of bad things going through his mind. He imagined that this was very serious because his company commander had come at least five miles from post to talk to him. Perhaps someone at home had gotten ill or had been injured, Scott had no idea.

As Scott got to the jeep, he saw that Captain Willows was accompanied by three tactical officers. Scott stopped by the driver's side, saluted, and yelled, "Sir, Candidate Ledbetter reporting as ordered, Sir." Willows returned Scott's salute and then stared at him through the booze lines that made up most of the surface of his eyes.

Scott waited, still at attention. Willow's asked, "Do you see what I have here in my hand?"

Scott did not look down until the captain told him to be at ease. He saw that he was holding a tan, long sleeved Army dress shirt.

Scott said, "Sir, Candidate Ledbetter requests permission to speak!" He was given permission.

Scott said, "Sir, you have an Army issue tan long sleeved dress shirt!"

With that apt description of what he was holding, the Captain began a diatribe about this being Scott's shirt. An unannounced IG inspection found this shirt with a cracked button, third one from the top, in Scott's dresser drawer. The company had flunked the IG inspection because of Scott's broken button.

The dress shirts were in the second drawer of his chest of drawers and no one looking through a six-inch opening could have seen a cracked button on the shirt, let alone the third one down.

'Look at this, candidate," the captain barked menacingly.

"Sir, Candidate Ledbetter requests permission to look at the cracked button on my tan Army issue long sleeved blouse, Sir!"

With permission granted, Scott looked down at the pathetic button that had caused the entire post of Ft. Benning to come to a halt. The owner of this button was such a miscreant that four officers had gone to the motor pool, signed out an Army jeep, and had driven five miles to confront the sorry assed soldier, who had perpetrated this grievous affront to military bearing.

Scott damned near lost his grip. His insides lit up like a kid who had just been given a pound of candy. It was all that he could do to keep from breaking out in fits of laughter. He had been afraid that some blue helmeted SOB would get him kicked out of OCS for clocking his ass. Here was a broken button in the hands of a drunken captain that was going to get him shanghaied.

The captain commanded Scott to have a five-hundred-word letter of reprimand on his desk, first thing in the morning explaining how this had happened and why he was so lax in his military bearing. As he returned Scott's salute, the captain put the pedal to the metal and wheeled the still running jeep around and headed back to post. He came an inch from running over Scott's feet.

The captain's departure had happened not one second too soon. As Scott headed back to training, he believed that his body had been possessed by laughter. This was the most preposterous and stupidest thing that he could imagine happening to an adult. When he got back to the training area, the company was already seated in the bleachers. He stopped and put on a sober and sorrowful face.

The sergeant in charge of training stopped talking as Scott got to the bleachers. He motioned for Scott to approach the platform. Scott walked to the platform carrying his tan Army shirt. The sergeant wanted to know what had happened. Scott knew that he had to watch himself as some candidate would sell your soul to get on the good side of the brass. Scott handed the shirt up to the sergeant and as sorrowfully as he could say anything, said, "Sergeant, last week they put a new mallet in the washing machine at post laundry and that mallet hammered my shirt extra hard. The third button from the top could not take the pressure and it cracked. In my hurry to put things away, I neglected to notice this errant button.

"Today an IG inspector found it and gigged the entire company. The gig was so heinous that the captain and three TAC officers drove many miles to the Pugil stick training site. They parked a long way from the site so that the candidate would have to run to get his ass chewed out. Disciplinary action against the perpetrator has been doled out and a letter of reprimand will be on the captain's desk, first thing in the morning," Scott said without laughing.

When he was done talking, he went to the bleachers and sat down. The sergeant stood there for a couple of seconds trying to hold back laughter. Then he just fell apart. He gave Scott's shirt a place of honor on a chair on the platform. He retrieved his shirt at the end of the training session and listened as the sergeant told the rest of the training staff about the shirt. He was laughing so hard that tears were streaming down his face.

That night Scott used an old manual typewriter he kept in a parked car on the OCS parking lot. He sat in the shower and "quietly typed" a five-hundred-word Letter of Reprimand for his grievous sin. This was done after lights out and after he had spent the evening preparing his uniforms for the next day, hand buffing the floor, and dusting everything. If he would have been caught for being up after lights out, he would have had to type yet another letter of reprimand.

Long after lights were out at the barracks, Scott took the letter down to the permanent charge of quarters. He asked the specialist to put this on the commanding officer's desk. The specialist asked for permission to read the letter and laughed at its ridiculousness.

Pogey Bait

Unauthorized food was strictly banned in OCS. One rainy night Scott's platoon was caught with pizza brought and delivered to the barracks by one of the married guy's wives. The ladies would pick up the pogey funds and make a run to a pizza place. When they returned, two candidates with a clean garbage can would meet them and secretly carry the pizza to their floor.

Getting the garbage can filled with pizza into the building before the food was cold took some real planning. They had tried tying ropes to the can, but it beat against the side of the building. They ended up posting a guard at the end of each floor to watch for the TAC on duty.

On this particular evening, they had made it to the floor

and were just about done eating when the TAC busted them. He made the whole platoon fall out wearing a helmet with no liner, one boot, a T- Shirt, and a pair of shorts and do close order drill with their footlocker. As they cleared the door, a rainstorm began. They did calisthenics and those close order drills for thirty minutes. When done everyone fell back into the barracks and began planning the next Pogey Bait Party.

Uniforms

Scott had seventeen fatigue uniforms. There were at least five in the "we smash um" post laundry. He thought that they must use a mangle to do the uniforms as they looked a little worse for wear at the end of each week. Scott had a hard time keeping up with his uniforms because it was so costly to have them cleaned and there was no way to launder or iron uniforms. There were no facilities for laundry in the barracks.

The candidates were given E-5 pay, three hundred dollars a month. By the middle of the month, that money was gone. The cost of uniform cleaning and upkeep wiped out their paychecks. The men were issued three of the required seventeen uniforms and had to pop for fourteen fatigue uniforms. They had to change uniforms anytime they came back from doing any physical activity, which could happen multiple times a day.

Food Glorious Food

Army chow wasn't exactly gourmet but when you are in physical and mental training, eating was damned important. Instead of letting the candidates eat and go and prepare for the next day, chow time was looked upon by the TAC Officers as a target of "oppoor-tunity".

Like basic and AIT, the candidates stood in line outside the mess hall and counted off by five to enter the mess hall, which was a military tradition. In OCS, the tradition continued except that the Tactical Officers prowled the chow line looking for any infraction of their rules. It was nothing for a candidate to pump out a couple hundred push-ups, sit ups, and pull ups while they waited for chow.

When the candidate made it inside the mess hall, the harassment only got worse. The chow line went past a table filled with TAC Officers. They were just waiting for an errant or supposedly errant move by a passing candidate. At the smallest behest, the candidate and their appetite would be outside doing push-ups, the low crawl, or pull-ups.

This harassment had gone on for weeks. One night, Scott had made it to the table filled with TACs when one of the lieutenants took him and nine others back outside. He marched them to the steam plant which was one hundred feet long and fifty feet wide and had them low crawl, on their backs around the steam plant until he got tired.

They were at this for well over a half an hour and by then the green grass stains had become a part of their fatigues. When they were sent back to the mess hall, the TACS still sitting at the table said that they were not fit to be officers.

The chow line was closed. The mess sergeant scraped up something for the men to eat. Scott made the decision to skip evening chow line. He simply could not stand the harassment and decided that if he was not in the chow line then no one could screw with him. This decision predicated the purchase of pizza so they would have something to eat. Screw the rules.

If a candidate made it through the gauntlet to the actual chow line, eating was a complete misery. The chairs had a bright blue strip painted six inches from the front. The candidates had to sit on the front six inches of the chair, at attention, and square each bite that they took.

Squaring your meal: The candidate sat at attention while he ate. To take a bite of food the candidate could look down and select the bite of food. He would put the fork into the bite of food and bring it straight up from the tray. When it reached eye level, he would bring the food directly to his mouth. While chewing, he would put the fork down on his tray, at a ninety-degree angle, tines down. When the candidate had properly chewed and swallowed his food, he would repeat the process.

Because of the TAC officer harassment and squaring their meals, a lot of the candidates simply stopped going to the mess hall. The mess sergeant told Captain Willows that he was throwing away food, as very few were eating. Willows gathered the entire company around the barrack's steps for one of his drunken diatribes. This time he lectured them on eating to stay fit for training. After blithering on for some time, he concluded the lecture by giving them a direct order to go to the mess hall and eat.

The next evening over ninety percent of the candidates did not go to the mess hall for evening mess. The student company commander was called in to ask why the candidates were not eating. He told them that the harassment had far exceeded anyone's desire to eat. Scott stood and watched those who braved the TAC Officer gauntlet to go to evening mess. He wanted to go down and eat but the trip around the steam plant had pushed his resolve to low ebb.

Congressional Team

An event took place at the 65th OCS Company that contributed to the demise of many long-standing military traditions at OCS. The event happened one evening when the company returned to the barracks from training. The candidates were standing in a downpour, taking off their boots on the steps outside of the barracks. Then they ran sock footed through the water and into the barracks.

Scott was shocked to see people in the dayroom, and they all had on boots and shoes. The candidates could not use the Day Room. The floor was covered with Butcher's Wax and its shiny floor was simply a show room for the commander. Each day a platoon was assigned to dust the day room and to polish any marks out of the Butcher's Wax. That ensured that the Day Room was inspection ready.

When Scott got to his room, there was a memo that had been uncharacteristically pitched onto his bed. He wondered what slovenly SOB would just throw a piece of typing paper onto a bed. The memo read: You are requested to come to the company Day Room to meet with members of a congressional investigation committee.

The coconut telegraph was humming with the news that this committee was here to talk to the candidates about living conditions and disciplinary tactics in the Army's OCS program. Scott was the second person in line. He was instructed to sit at the far end of a folding table where he talked to a young man in a blue uniform. Scott had no idea what corps this group represented.

Before they started asking questions, Scott asked the young man why all the people in the room were wearing shoes? The young man was surprised by the question, so Scott pointed to all the marks now streaking the floor. He explained that an entire platoon would have to spend hours hand buffing the floor with Butcher's Wax. Which meant that they would not get a full night's sleep. The candidates still had to spend hours preparing for the next day's training.

He was asked, "How do you keep from marking up the floors with your boots?"

Scott said, "We do not wear boots or shoes into the barracks, ever."

The young man continued, "Do you take your boots off before coming into your barracks?"

Scott told him, "I have never put a boot or a shoe print inside of this building, and I have been here for six weeks. Rain or shine we put our boots on outside of the barracks, even in a driving rainstorm."

Scott told them about Butcher's Wax and what they had to do to keep their floors shining at an extremely high gloss. He told them that they had to buy the Butcher's Wax at the

PX as it was not provided by the military and about all the Kotex pads that cushioned the furniture.

He told them, "We never set a foot on the floors in the room. We never study at the desk because the desk pad is laden with Butcher's Wax. We could not sit in the chairs because there were no wooden "boards" with Kotex under the chair legs, because the chairs would not fit under the desks."

"Candidate, do you feel that your inability to study is having an adverse effect on your grades in OCS?" the man asked.

Scott said, "Sir, studying is a far distant third at OCS. Spit-shined floors and harassment are the rules that we live under."

"What harassment is causing the biggest problem?" he wanted to know.

Scott related that the number of TAC officers in the chow line harassing the candidates waiting to get into the mess hall was the top misery. He told them about having to low crawl on their backs for thirty minutes, in the middle of trying to make it to and through the mess hall.

The guy was incredulous, when Scott told him about the Steam Plant incident. He asked, "Why would anyone do that?"

Scott said, "They do it because they can do it and the candidates can do nothing but obey or they are thrown out of OCS."

Scott told about them having to sit on the front six inches of a chair to eat a square meal. He talked about the five-hundred-word letter of reprimand over a cracked button on a dress shirt and having to sit in the shower to type quietly because lights were out.

Congressional Decree

There must have been some very serious meetings going on in Washington on this topic. To graduate an OCS Lieutenant, the Army allegedly shelled out $75,000.00. At least that is the figure that Scott had heard. Given the facilities and the wash out rate, he did not doubt that this was true.

For the next two weeks after the visit, TAC officers were a pretty mellow bunch. Two weeks later the company was ordered to fall out and gather on the south steps. This was one of about thirty of these step top rants that the candidates had gone through from the drunken captain.

The candidates were all gathered around the base of the steps when they were called to attention. The captain came through the door. He put the company at ease and then started pacing back and forth on the top of the steps. He did this for five minutes without saying a single word. Then he reached in his back pocket and pulled out a six-inch jack knife and opened the blade. He started walking down the steps with the knife handle pointing toward the candidates. No one stood their ground. A company of candidates backed up in unison.

The captain got to the bottom step and he held the handle of the knife out to the company and asked, "Who amongst you is willing to take this knife and plunge it into my back?"

He stood there for a long time looking through the drunken road maps, which served as his eyes. Fortunately, no one said anything, although the thoughts were certainly running amuck.

The Congress of the United States had decreed that from

that day forth there would be no hand polishing or shining of any floors with any kind of civilian wax. The wax used would be the normal US Army issue that was to be buffed with an electric buffer, with pads supplied. Boots would be worn into the barracks. No one would need to take them off until it was bedtime.

Desks were to be used for studying, and the electric desk lamps would be plugged into the outlets provided so that the candidates could sit at the desk and study. The desk pad would be stripped of all wax. The floors in the candidate's room would be buffed with the buffer. The candidates would be able to walk on their floors, with boots on their feet.

It was decreed that the candidates would no longer have anyone harassing them in the chow line. Squaring meals was totally outlawed, starting today. A work order would be issued to have all the blue lines taken off the mess hall chairs. This work was not to be done by the candidates. It would be done by the US Army maintenance staff.

There would be no harassment of the candidates during mealtime or study time. In fact, the officers were not allowed to eat in the mess hall with the candidates, effective immediately. Disciplinary action would be taken for any officer not obeying this directive.

Then the final blow was delivered. There would be no more disciplinary measures resulting in letters being written or typed by the candidates. Discipline was to be done with directives found in the Universal Code of Military Justice. The mission of OCS was to turn to academics and military conditioning, not harassment.

You would have thought that they had torn the heart out of the captain. He rambled on for the better part of thirty minutes about desecrating sacred rituals. Scott figured that if the captain lived long enough he would make it to a detox farm or spend the rest of his life inside of a Jack Daniel's bottle. When he finally stopped rambling, he turned on his heel and went inside to cry or have a drink.

When the company was dismissed, Scott was the first one through the door and up the stairs with his boots on his feet. He grabbed the buffer out of the closet where it had been setting for years and wheeled it down the hall. By the time the rest of the platoon got to the floor, Scott was busily buffing fifty years of Butcher's Wax with a real electric buffer.

For the first time in six weeks he was standing on the waxed floor with his boots on his feet. He knew right then that there really was a God. He may have been in Washington DC, but he was real.

Pay Day

A Jody Song was sung when a company was marching to or from training: "They say that in the Army the Tea be mighty fine, they gave me 300 and took back 299. Oh, Mom I wanta go, but they won't let me go, HOME." This marching song had been a part of the military for generations because it is very close to the truth.

It was the end of the month and Scott's funds were riding on zero. He was elated that pay day was finally here. OCS candidates were given the temporary rank of Specialist E-5 so that they could pay them more money. OCS was a very expensive proposition for the individual soldier.

With no facilities or time for a candidate to do his own laundry, Scott had to pay post laundry to clean his seventeen sets of fatigues plus all of his underwear, consequently there was literally no money left the last week of the month.

Payday was here and he was about to get three hundred and thirty dollars in cash. Scott received his pay from one of the Tactical Officers and the 1st Sergeant asked, "How much are you giving to the United Funding?"

Scott said, "I am giving nothing to anyone as it's taking all of my money just to pay for my laundry."

Scott knew immediately that he had just committed the most heinous crime, even worse than the cracked third button.

The words had barely cleared his mouth when no fewer than five TAC officers jumped on him with both boots. He had no warning and no time to throw up any kind of defense. With close to two months in OCS, he could normally dial out screaming and yelling, but today they had caught him a little short on "Whoa."

In a loud voice, he asked permission to speak and it was granted by his tormentors. The mess hall got silent and he gave the silence a one thousand one, two, and three count. Then he asked at the top of his lungs to be escorted directly to the Post Inspector General's office.

No one in the military messes with the Inspector General's office. A sergeant working for the IG could bring a full bull colonel to his knees. The words were barely out of his mouth when all the TAC officers melted into the woodwork. Scott turned back to Sergeant White and asked, "Do you need anything else, First Sergeant?"

Sergeant White answered, "No, Candidate Ledbetter, I believe I have had all that I can bear."

Scott wanted to ask what that meant, although in his heart he knew that beneath that shock of white hair was an old Korean War Vet who was either smirking at or cheering for this incredibly stupid candidate. It was apparent to the sergeant that this man was more of an enlisted man than anyone on the base.

As Scott walked out of the mess hall, he heard the guy behind him also decline to give anything to the United Funding. As it turned out, few if anyone behind him paid the tariff for this charity. Scott just smiled and headed on to his room. He would not give to any charity who took advantage of the most underpaid employees in the country.

The United Funding: You have to be in the service to understand what his lack of cooperation meant to the company commander, his commander, and so on up the line. The Army was adamant on getting 100% participation in the United Funding drive. Every troop was expected to donate money to the United Funding or face the wrath of the 1st shirt or company commander.

Scott understood what would happen if he had stayed in this OCS company: he would be tossed out of the program for some infraction, real or dreamed up by the officers. Come Monday, he would be out of this chicken shit outfit. He was scheduled for surgery on his left shoulder.

On Saturday, he cleaned out his room and said goodbye to his fellow candidates. He was not sorry to leave this company or its cadre.

First Casual Company

Scott left the OCS barracks and was driven to the First Casual Company which was housed in the old clap board barracks from WWII. Its only purpose was to house troops who had been injured in training. A troop hurt, having surgery, or in rehabilitation was assigned to a Casual Company.

The only time you found a casual company in the Army was when there was a large contingency of troops being trained. At Fort Benning, the men being trained included a Basic Training Battalion, an Advance Infantry Training Battalion, a Paratrooper Jump School, and an OCS battalion. Scott imagined that there were close to ten thousand people being trained at Benning at any one time.

The old wooden barracks that Scott was assigned to was over the Day Room, just like when he was at Fort Riley. The barracks was filled with twenty-five OCS candidates with every kind of break, bruise, and cut. Every day someone was coming in from or heading back to OCS.

The company was run by a cadre who were being mustered out of the service for the good of the service. This included sergeants and the captain, who must have peed in somebody's Wheaties bowl. The only one that was not being tossed out of the military was the company clerk. He was working with a bunch of people who were no longer needed by the military and had been asked to leave. The attitude of the cadre had morphed to the company clerk as he did not give a damn either.

When Scott reported to the hospital on Monday, he found out that his surgery had been pushed back a week.

He headed back to his barracks to wait another week. His bunk and locker were pathetic, and he decided to improve his sleeping situation. There was a cadre room not being used by anyone. The door was locked with a padlock, and Scott had to find a key, or a hack saw to get in.

A trip to the orderly room got him a ring with one hundred and fifty keys. He pulled up a chair and started going through the glob of keys. Thirty minutes later he struck gold. He had found the key to a padlock that had not been opened in years. The room had a new bunk with a very thick mattress, a small bookcase, and a table with four chairs.

In the real Army, this room would have been for an E-6 NCO or higher. Scott cleaned it up and stored his sierra in the wall locker and dresser. He now had a private room. The next Monday he once more reported to the hospital and was told that his procedure had been pushed back two more weeks. Scott had grown tired of carrying a bulky key to a padlock with him so he "Jerry-rigged" the padlock to make it looked like the room was padlocked, when it really was not.

Six weeks after leaving OCS 65, his surgery was finally scheduled. He came to in the recovery room and discovered that no operation had occurred. The surgeon had tried to dislocate his shoulder before operating, but it would not totally dislocate. It was decided to do nothing. His shoulder now hurt like hell because of all the pulling done by the surgeon and it was still partially dislocated.

He figured that the hospital would tell the OCS battalion that they had not operated, and someone would contact him. After a few days, he realized that that had not happened. He was the only one who knew his status. Life in the Casual

Company was infinitely better than what was going on behind the walls of those concrete block buildings. Scott decided to give it a few more days before letting anyone know that
he was ready to go back to training.

A Three-Day Pass

Three-day passes were very unusual for the Army. Normally
they were only issued for special occasions. At First Casual
Company, no one gave a damn about the soldiers or where
they were. The Company Commander would sign a box
full of passes and leave them with the company clerk. Scott
would take a pass from a tin file box, fill in the dates, and sign
out Friday morning for a three-day pass. He would sign back
in on Sunday evening when he got back.

Two of the other escapees from OCS invited Scott to go
with them to Destin, Florida for the weekend. Early on Friday morning with their three day passes in their wallet, they
headed south from Benning. Scott had never driven through
the south and his eyes were opened to a whole new layer of
society. They drove past a house that he could see through the
house into the back yard without looking through a window
or a door. The boards on the front and the back of the house
were gone.

He also saw a scene right out of an old Civil War movie. In a field alongside of the road was a hayrack filled with
close to twenty black men. They were all standing up holding
shovels and hoes and were headed to the field to hoe weeds
in some crop. If they all sat down on the wagon, it would not

hold all of them. The wheels on the hayrack were rubber. If those tires would have been wood, the scene could have been from the 1800's.

Destin was the first place where Scott saw white sandy beaches. They stayed at a hotel on the beach which was nice without costing a lot of money. Destin was so nice that the three of them made the trip three times over the next few weeks. Here it was in December and Scott was able to walk out of the hotel and go for a swim in the ocean. He kept pushing his return to OCS off as life was pretty good. It reminded him of his time at Hunter-Liggett when it seemed that the Army had forgotten about him.

Late in December, one of his Destin buddies told him that an E-6 from OCS had been asking about a Candidate Ledbetter. He told the sergeant that he did not know who the candidate was, but he would keep an eye out for him. Scott's private room kept him from interacting with the other OCS candidates on the floor. Only two or three knew that he was living in his own private room.

Scott would sign in and out of the company and was always accounted for on the morning report of the First Casual Company. Each day Scott would sign out of the company before the company clerk arrived and then sign back in after the clerk left the always open orderly room. Normally he would sign out and just go back to his room and read.

At Christmas time, an Army post pretty much closes down. Scott requested and got a two week leave and headed for Iowa. When Scott returned, he got to know some of the men on the floor of the barracks. They used his nice table to play cards.

On a Sunday afternoon towards the end of January, the guys were playing cards in Scott's room. The door, which was normally closed, stood half open. The door was shoved open and there stood Scott's favorite Sergeant E6.

He said, "Candidate Ledbetter?"

No one said a word.

Scott raised his hand and said, "Yes, Sergeant."

The sergeant said, "You know that I have been looking for you since before Christmas."

Scott said, "Sergeant, I have been here all along."

When they walked out of the room the sergeant stopped and looked at the padlock hanging locked on an open door. He looked questioningly at Scott. Scott closed the door. When he did, the padlock looked like it was secure on the door frame. The door while it looked padlocked, was not.

The sergeant said, "Well I'll be damned."

On his visits to the barracks he had seen the ugly padlock and dismissed it as a totally locked room.

Everyone who was playing cards helped Scott and the sergeant load his gear into the sergeant's jeep and waved as they pulled away. On the way over to the OCS battalion, the sergeant looked over to Scott and said, "Ledbetter, if you make as good an officer as you do an enlisted man, some company is going to fare well in Vietnam."

Scott just smiled.

To OCS or to not OCS

The sergeant had policed up his ass at 1300 hours. At 1600 hours he was signing into the 56th OC Company. It was Sunday and there was virtually no one in the barracks. As he carried his sierra up the three flights of stairs, he had a great deal of trepidation about returning to OCS. He had been living the good life. He had even given thought to staying at First Casual Company until his enlistment was over. He had heard about this happening during the Second World War and thought it might just be possible.

There was no one to tell him where to bunk so Scott took the empty room at the top of the stairs. He knew from his previous company that this room might belong to the platoon at either side of the stairwell. It all depended on how many candidates were still in the program. He figured that this would give him time to decide if he wanted to stay in OCS.

He stowed his stuff in the wall locker and the footlocker and padlocked both. This was against all OCS rules which stated that the wall locker would always be left open for inspection. When his gear was all stowed, he closed the door just as he had found it. The room now looked just like it had for the past few months, empty.

When Scott went down to the chow hall for evening mess, there were no TACS to yell and scream and no blue line painted on the chair seats. He was able to sit back and eat like a normal person. Here he was in an OCS mess hall and did not have to eat a square meal or do a single push up. So far it was a stay.

Scott laid out his uniform for the next morning and tackled his boots which had grown very "grolly" over the past several weeks and required some of the skills that he had learned from Carl Toban back in basic training. He did all this work with his door closed. No one knew that there was a new kid on the block.

Map Reading

"This many-hour misery finally ended with the company back on those same metal bleachers and the same steady rain coming down. They handed in their tests. Scott knew that he was toast..."

The next morning Scott was up and showered before anyone was out of bed. The platoon fell out for the early morning formation at 0430 hours. Scott was already outside in the dark and just got into formation with the platoon. He was certain that everyone wondered who Ledbetter was when he answered the roll call.

He found out in the formation that they were going to take the Map Reading final test that day. Good Lord, Scott had missed a lot of map reading classes. He had left in the eighth week and this company was in their tenth week. They had started and completed map training during his absence from OCS.

Scott had to rely on what he remembered from a few weeks before and from map reading at Ft. Ord. After formation, they headed for breakfast and when they mounted a deuce and a half for the trip to the map course, it began to rain. In the Army, rain only means that it was going to be wet as it would take a real storm to make the Army blink in a training situation.

By the time they reached the map course, the downpour had subsided to a steady rain. They sat on steel bleachers with no cover as the cadre droned on about the importance of map reading and their compasses.

The map course covered two square miles which was covered with trees and red sticky Georgia clay. Posts were scattered across this huge expanse. Each post had a large white board with a black number painted on it. The distance between posts might be a hundred meters or it might be five hundred. It all depended on the map problem being solved.

They wanted to test the candidates' ability to use a compass and a map. First problem: Scott started at post number 749. He was to shoot a 160° azimuth from post 749 to his next post.

When he got to the area, there were three numbered posts within thirty meters of each other.

Using the map that he had marked and the azimuth from the first post, he was to select the correct post number and write that number on the test. If Scott selected the wrong post at any time during the test, the rest of his test would be wrong.

The map was wet, and the day was wetter, and he found himself second guessing his decisions.

The red Georgia clay stuck to his boots and each of his feet was a foot wide. He wallowed in the red clay all day. If he got to a post that happened to be on several test papers, the area surrounding that post was pure red muck soup. This many-hour misery finally ended with the company back on those same metal bleachers with the same steady rain coming down. The five-page test was handed in and they climbed back on the trucks to go to the barracks.

Scott knew that he was toast and started planning where he was going to be the next weekend after they tossed him out of OCS. When they got back from the map course, Scott slid into his room, unnoticed, and closed the door.

Even a Blind Squirrel

"He told the formation that the committee had stacked all the test papers, which were wet, on top of one another and they had all dried together."

The next morning the sun was up shining brightly in the early morning sky. It was a beautiful Georgia day. While the rest of the world was shiny, Scott was not. He knew that the tests would be graded, and they would find a candidate who could not find his ass with both hands.

He went through the motions of going to class at Infantry Hall and then double-timing back for lunch. When they got back to the company area, the company commander came out to talk to the formation. The young captain stood up on the platform in front of the gathered company formation. He said, "I have some bad news." Scott thought he was going to announce his score. The Captain continued, "The map reading committee stacked all of your wet test papers on top of each other before they left the training site last night. This morning all the test papers were stuck together and could not be pulled apart. The company will have to retake the map reading test. The time for the retake will be next Saturday." Scott could not believe what he was hearing. He had been given the opportunity to retake a major examination. Everyone was really angry, except for Scott.

Every waking moment of the week Scott was inside the map course instruction booklet. He got a compass from the training room and shot azimuths at anything that was nailed down. On the next Saturday morning the sun was shining, and the red Georgia Clay was its rock-hard self.

Scott went through that course like a dose of salts. At the end of the day the map reading committee had them wait in the stands while they immediately graded the tests. They not only graded the tests, they called out the scores for each candidate. Scott sat there in disbelief when they announced his score, ninety-six percent. He was elated.

He considered all that had to happen for him to be able to retest the map reading course. It had to rain all day and soak the test papers. Then someone had to stack all those tests into a pile so they would dry together. This was too much to be considered as happenstance. His guardian angel must have been pulling her hair out to get Scott through this test and on through OCS.

Scott sat there in the warm Georgia sunshine and determined: *if the good Lord would do all of that to get him through OCS, then he needed to put his ass in the air and nose to the grindstone.* He decided that he was staying in OCS and was going to be an Infantry Lieutenant."

Ranger Training in the Swamp

"He got the Wait a Minute vine to release his rifle and when he stepped backward, he fell over Gordon Ireland, who was already in his fart sack."

When they got back from the map course, Scott found out that they were heading out on a two-week Ranger Training course in some swamp somewhere in the south. He spent the night getting ready.

The five-hour ride in the back of an uncomfortable deuce and a half to the training course was long and monotonous. When they arrived, it appeared that there were a lot of plans that had-not or did-not come together. They reached the night laager as the sun was setting. When you are in the swamp, the sun quickly drops out of the sky.

When the column came to a halt and the Rangers indicated that this is where they would spend the night, all the platoons started moving into position. Scott had made an adjustment to his pack and when he looked up everyone in his platoon had become dark shadows. He found his Tactical Officer and told him that he was new and assigned to the second platoon. The man pointed Scott across a small opening and told him to look for some guy named Ireland. There was no moon and every step found him running into some piece of nature that refused to yield.

There was a parasite vine, called a wait-a-minute-vine, that grows from the trees down. The size of the lead in a pencil and is surrounded with hook needles that will hook clothing, skin, or anything that it touches, even the sight of an M-14 rifle. Scott got to the far side of the clearing and called for Ireland and a voice said, "Over Here!"

Scott turned to walk towards the voice and was attacked by several wait-a-minute vines. They hooked his rifle, pack, and field jacket. Those vines are hard to see in the daytime and impossible to see in the dead of night. He just about made it to the voice when he got tangled up in another vine. He finally was able to get the vine to release his rifle. When he stepped backward, he fell over Gordon who was already in his fart sack.

Scott apologized and began to unpack his air mattress and sleeping bag. The two of them talked but were not formally introduced until the next morning. Gordon was from some place called Broomall, PA just outside of Philly. Now there were two more Irishmen working together for the good of something. What, he did not know.

Swamps are Shaggy and Nasty

"He kept wading through the swamp and suddenly he sank down past his belt buckle. He then knew why the all the pissing and moaning was happening."

The company spent "ten fun filled" days hiking the low-lying hills and forever swamp. No one ever knew exactly where they were, but based on the geography and the extensive swamp, Scott believed that they were in the Okeefenokies swamp, in southern Georgia and northern Florida. No matter, as swamp was swamp; its location was of no consequence.

After a full day doing Army maneuvers they walked into the swamp at 1900 hours. For the first mile or two, the water was up to their knees. It was neither cool nor warm and their feet and legs adapted to the temperature of the water. Up ahead, Scott started to hear some bitching and great amounts of pissing and moaning. He kept wading through the swamp and suddenly he sank down past his belt buckle and knew why the all the pissing and moaning as " the boys" had just gotten wet.

The farther they went, the deeper and colder the water got. In one area, the water reached his mouth. The troop in front of him was a kid named Burman who was shorter than Scott and the water was to the top of Burman's forehead. He was doing well keeping both above water when he stepped on a branch that was angled away from his body. The tree branch carried his boot out to where it hit the trunk. Both Scott and Burman went underwater. When Scott regained his footing, his helmet floated off into the swamp. He was trying valiantly to keep their heads above water and retrieve his helmet before it turned over and sank. In the middle of all this, Burman yelled, "Dammit, Ledbetter are you trying to drown me?"

At long last they began, as his Cajun friends in Louisiana would say, to "unclimb" the bayou. Slowly the water went down, or the earth came up and they walked out of the water onto dry land. While everyone was getting settled in for the night, Scott, as the "f'n new guy" was "picked" for guard duty.

The Slasher

Scott was sitting on the perimeter staring out into the night. He was wet and tired. When he came to, the first light of day filtered into the swamp. As he was packing up his gear, one of the men in the platoon told him that he needed to check a mirror. Apparently, a Ranger NCO had used a red marker to "slash" the throat of anyone sleeping on guard duty. Scott had been "slashed". Before Scott headed for the chow line, he had to scrub off the red marker. Anyone who went to chow with a slashed red throat was treated badly by the TAC officers.

Water Moccasins

Scott was picked for patrols early and late. He was always out ambushing some enemy patrol or spotting enemy movement in some far-off place. One afternoon the company had stopped for a break, and he was resting in the sunshine when he was "picked" for a reconnaissance patrol. The company had to cross a swampy river twenty feet across and chest high. It was his patrol's job to secure the area on the far side so the company could cross without being ambushed by the "enemy."

It was late in the afternoon and the coolness of water felt good. The company made it across safely. As they were getting ready to move out, Scott realized that his gas mask had fallen out of the holster on his leg. The company waited while he went back to retrieve his gas mask.

On the way back to the company, he entered the water

and felt something smack his boot tops. He thought that he had stepped on a tree branch and it had turned and slammed into the top of his combat boots. However, the pounding on his boots picked up speed. Water moccasins started popping their heads up out of the water. There were twenty snake heads above the water and Scott did his impression of walking on water. As he got to the far side, three men had their hands out to pull him out of the swamp. The company decided to take a different trail back to their night laager.

Green Eggs and Ham

One-night Scott was "picked" to go on another recon team. They left the base camp at 0330 in the morning with a box of breakfast "C" rations. When they reached their recon position, they set up a small perimeter to watched for the "enemy". Just before dawn, Scott decided to eat something. With no light and no fire, he decided to eat the cold "C" rations. He was reminded of WWII movies with guys eating cold food in the jungle.

He used his trusty P-38 can opener to open the largest can, normally the main course in a "C" ration meal. As he pushed the spoon through the contents, he could hear the sound of the spoon peeling off some of whatever was in the can. It did not sound good. He took one bite and shoved the can aside.

When the sun rose, he discovered they had given him ham and eggs. Scott now understood where Dr. Seuss had gotten the name for "Green Eggs and Ham". That can, with just one spoonful taken out, is still buried in a swamp in the southern US.

Extra Strength Excedrin

At the end of their ten days in the swamps, the rains came. It turned from a not-too-great-of-a-place into just plain cold and miserable. Through the day, Scott had begun to run a fever. When it got dark, the company stopped. No one gave them a command to set up or move out. They just stood in the pouring rain, waiting. Scott's fever was getting worse and he was shaking so hard he could not stand it anymore.

He found a bottle of a new aspirin product in his pack. It was called Extra Strength Excedrin which he had never taken before. He took two of them, hoping to get a little relief.

Not far from where they were waiting was a large tree that had been blown down in a storm. With no word from anyone on what they were doing, Scott used that tree and his poncho to get out of the rain and wind. He could quickly move out if they told them to saddle up. He draped his poncho over a tree branch and sat down with his shoulders against the tree. That gave him protection from the rain and slowed the wind down. Then, to his surprise, the two Excedrin took him out.

When he came to, he could hear them yelling his name. It took him a while to figure out where he was. He crawled out of his hide away and asked why they were looking for him. The cadre had made the decision to set up here and when Scott did not answer during roll call they started searching for him. Suddenly he was both loved and cursed by everyone.

Standing out in the wind, Scott shook as his temperature spiked. He needed medical attention. He was taken to Fort Benning where a doctor prescribed some real medicine and the lieutenant took him back to the barracks.

The next day was the last day of the Ranger training. While Scott was lying in his bed, the rest of his company was bouncing their way north in a cold and damp deuce and a half. Somewhere in southern Georgia, there is a tattered old poncho hanging on the fork of a very large old tree.

OCS is broken into Three Parts

- Junior Candidate—Week 1 through Week 11
- Intermediate Candidate—week 11 through Week 14
- Senior Candidate or Blue Helmet—Week 15 through Week 18

As a Junior Candidate, you ran everywhere, and everyone took a run at your sorry ass. At the end of eleven weeks you were judged to see if you are worthy to continue in OCS. If you pass muster, you move onto being an Intermediate Candidate. A scarf worn with the fatigue uniform reflected your advanced status. You were no longer required to run everywhere.

An Intermediate Candidate was up to his backside learning to be an Infantry Officer. If you are not going to make it to your commission ceremony, you would know at the end of the fourteenth week. If you are not cut at the end of the fourteenth week, then you are just three weeks away from being a 2nd lieutenant.

OCS Blue Helmet

"They were both sure that their Tactical Officer was not going to let a couple of miscreants, like Ireland and Ledbetter, become officers and gentlemen, even by Act of Congress."

On Saturday at the end of their fourteenth week, both Scott and Gordon sat in Gordon's room and discussed where they might go during the next weekend. They were both sure that their Tactical Officer was not going to let a couple of miscreants, like Ireland and Ledbetter become officers and gentlemen, even by Act of Congress. They figured that they would be cannon fodder in Vietnam within two weeks. They might even make them E-4's. Scott told Gordon about the good times they had in Destin, Florida and that was a good destination.

Scott went down to look at the list of wash outs on the company bulletin board at 0900. There was nothing posted. Then after chow they checked the board again. Another hour passed, and Gordon headed down to the bulletin board to see if the list was posted.

When he came back, he just smiled and said, "We cannot go to Destin, Florida next weekend. We were not cut!"

Scott in disbelief said, "What? Seriously we are not on the list? Lord, have mercy we are going to be Blue Helmets."

On that day, in that room, were perhaps two of the

happiest senior candidates that ever had gone through OCS. They knew that if they did not pee in someone's In Basket for the next four weeks, they were going to be 2nd lieutenants.

That Sunday they went to the supply room and were issued newly painted Baby Blue helmets with an OCS sticker centered on the front. They were also issued white scarves with a beautiful gold and black OCS emblem sewn onto the middle. When wearing fatigues, that emblem was in the center of their open shirt collar. They were also given blue felt for the back of their gold OCS pins. That blue felt replaced the black felt that had been issued when they made Intermediate Candidate status.

When a new OCS class arrived later that day, most of the men in the class went out to get their pound of flesh from these newbies. Scott had not forgotten how miserable he was on that day, fourteen weeks earlier. He chose to sit in his room and watch the circus from his window. He never harassed anyone in his civilian life, and he did not feel that a blue helmet or a gold bar gave him the right to do that in the military.

The Blue Banquet

"Scott, I did not know that you could bring your mom."

At the close of seventeen weeks, the OCS Battalion sponsored a Blue coming out dance held at the post officer's club. It was to be a fantastic affair with all the spit and polish the Army can muster. The single guys were expected to have a date, and married guys could only come with their wives.

The problem was that there had been zero time to meet anyone to ask to the dance. A list of women who would go to this dance with a candidate was passed from one OCS Company to another. Scott took the list and a handful of dimes to the hall telephone and started calling. A check mark indicated the woman already had a date. Scott did not know how a woman got onto this list and he was sure the women had no idea of such a list in the first place. After several calls, Jo Ann said that she would love to go to the dance.

When he was still at the First Casual Company, Scott had bought an English Ford from a soldier shipping out to Vietnam. He gave two hundred dollars for the car and it sometimes would run. Throughout OCS he used the car for storage space for his civilian clothes, his old portable type-writer, and anything that would not fit in his footlocker. It sat on a parking lot behind some deserted barracks for several months.

The license plates were from whomever owned the car before him. The plates were expired, but since the car never left the parking lot, that was no big deal. Scott did not have the money to have it registered and licensed. The car just sat on the parking lot, full of his stuff. He could find no other rides to the dance, so Scott enlisted the old Ford. He cleaned it up, put all his junk into the trunk, filled it up with gas, and hoped that it would make it back and forth from Columbus.

He got to the big dance just as everyone was being seated. All the tables were full when they arrived. There was a table for the married men whose wives had not made the trip, and

Scott found two chairs at that table. Jo Ann was older than Scott and most of the men in the room. One of the married men leaned over and quietly said, "Scott, I did not know that you could bring your mom."

Scott was twenty-four and his date was twenty years his senior. Despite the age of his date and illegal car, Scott made it through one of the biggest social events of his young life.

By Act of Congress

"Out of one hundred and fifteen candidates who started the course, seventy new lieutenants put on their gold braided hats and walked out of Infantry Hall."

In the next week, they were fitted for their dress greens and their gold braided officer cap and hat. They were issued gold bars to be pinned on by their parents at graduation. The ceremony for graduation was done to the "NINE's". The morning of the graduation, the 56th OC Company was on the parade field marching while a military band played. When the outside ceremony ended, the candidates were formed up for their last OCS formation and marched into Infantry Hall.

Scott's Mom and Dad and his brother Rick had driven down to Georgia, and Scott was so happy to see them. They were already in Infantry Hall waiting when the company of candidates marched in and took their seats for the thirty-minute commencement exercise.

At last the pomp and circumstance was over, and the brass

saluted the newest class of 2nd lieutenants to graduate from OCS. At that moment, the class stood up, let out a yell, and threw their enlisted hats into the air. They came down, no one cared where. Seventy new lieutenants put on their gold braided hats and walked out of Infantry Hall. For many, this was the last time that they would ever be in the Infantry Hall.

Out in the sun, Scott's Mom pinned on his gold bars. A friend whose parents had not made the trip asked Scott's mom to do the honors, and she was very proud to do so. Today was a red-letter day for her family.

Gordon and Scott had both been assigned to Ft. Polk, LA. They said their goodbye's and looked to see one another in a couple of weeks. On the way to the car, Scott saluted Lt. Robert Tarr, his Tactical Officer and said, "Bob, thanks a lot," With the pinning of his gold bar he was now an equal with his Tactical Officer. Rank among second Lieutenants, does not exist.

Scott and his family headed for Iowa. Several hours into the trip, he remembered the English Ford which was sitting on a parking lot not far from his OCS barracks. There was nothing of any value, save his old portable typewriter, so he just drove on. One day it would be towed, and no one would know its story.

5. Going Home from OCS

"When they got to Millersburg, Scott found that most of the people that he had grown up with had moved away."

The four Ledbetter's headed home via St. Louis. They stopped on the outskirts of St. Louis where they stopped at the Coral Courts Motel, an old Route 66 Motel. The ate dinner and went to visit Gas Light Square which was a major tourist attraction with folk singers and small coffee shops in abundance. Scott took his folks to a coffee house where they heard a young lady with a crisp and beautiful voice sing the songs straight out of the hippie generation. The songs were all protest songs that he knew his folks would not understand. They just loved listening to young people sing with their beautiful voices.

They walked around the various shops on the square before Scott headed the weary travelers back to the motel. The next day they headed on home. When they got to Millersburg, Scott found that most of the people that he had grown up with had moved away. Others who stayed in the area were married and had little time for a single guy who had not been around for a long time.

Scott and his Dad went out looking for a new car. Scott bought a white 1963 Ford two-door hard top. On the last Saturday of his leave, he loaded up the car and headed for Ft. Polk, LA. That was to be his first duty station as a commissioned officer.

Fort Polk, LA 1st Officer Assignment

"Sergeant Loftin: "I h'ain't been around the world but Seven times, Three Times on a bicycle, three Times on a Tricycle, and One time in a Peanut Shell, "most uncomfortable." Do you know what I learned from all those trips around the world, in all of those conveyances? I learned what Bull Shit sounds like and son, this is Bull Shit."

Scott arrived at Ft. Polk on a Sunday, the first day of August and was assigned a temporary officer's billets. The building was an old barracks that had been fitted with rooms for visiting officers. Unfortunately, there was no air conditioning to abate the excessive heat and humidity that is Louisiana in August. A huge fan set out in the hall and it looked like it could lift an airplane off a runway. Scott left the door open and let the fan move the hot humid air.

Already sweating profusely, he decided to head to the Officer's Open Mess for something to eat and for a place to cool off. By the time he got back to his room, he was running a temperature. He tried to sleep, but the heat was too oppressive.

When he set out to find the hospital, all he had on was

a pair of shorts and some flip flops. He was burning up with the "fevers." They admitted him and put him in an air-conditioned ward. They gave him something for the fever and to help him sleep. The doctors believed that the stress of the past few months in OCS and being assigned his first duty as an officer had caused him to get sick. He stayed in the hospital for four days.

After being on post for a week, Scott was assigned to a Basic Training Company, D-1-2, as a training officer. His commanding officer was Lt. Ed Smith from South St. Louis. When he arrived, the company was halfway through its basic training cycle. When he reported to the company, Ed sent him to the training facility where the trainees were learning about the M-14 rifle.

Non-Commissioned Officers

Scott found the training area late in the afternoon as the Louisiana sun hammered down on the humid air. Five NCOs wearing Smokey the Bear hats were standing in the shade of an old training shelter. As he approached, the tallest one (Sergeant Halder) stepped out from under the roofed area and cut the air with a salute right out of the NCO academy. Since most of his time as an officer had been spent in sick bay, Scott had only experienced a few salutes. He managed to return the salute without looking like a numb nut.

OCS had given him the formal training and a gold bar, but these men were the real deal. Over the next few months they would teach him how to be an officer.

"I Hain't been..."

Sergeant Loftin was the First Sergeant at D-1-2. He lived in an un-air-conditioned NCO room in the barracks. He spent his time off duty in his room. There was always beer in an apartment sized refrigerator.

Scott and the sergeant became good friends. He was a mentor and helped Scott understand the military and how to be a good soldier and officer. He was as real a man as Scott would ever meet in his life. One of the sergeant's favorite sayings:

"I Hain't been around the world but Seven times,

Three Times on a bicycle, three Times on a Tricycle, and

Onct in a Peanut Shell, "most uncomfortable."

Do you know what I learned from all those trips

around the world, in all of those different conveyances?

I learned what Bull Shit sounds like

and son, this is Bull Shit."

Scott carried that down-home thought and that saying with him wherever he was to go.

One Friday at the end of a five-weekend month, Sarge invited him up to his room. He gave Scott a cold beer and the two men sat and talked in the afternoon heat.

Sergeant Loftin asked, "Lieutenant, where are you going this weekend?"

Scott said, "This is a five-weekend month and I do not have money to go anywhere."

Sergeant Loftin reached into his back pocket pulled out his billfold and handed Scott forty dollars. Scott refused. Sergeant Loftin would not hear any of his objections. Sarge said that he could repay him on Monday, which was payday. He told Scott that he was too young to stay around this f'n place over the weekend. Sarge said, "Lieutenant Ledbetter, the world is waiting outside of the gates for young men like you. Leave the post to old guys like me. You can take charge when you return on Monday".

On Saturday, Scott and two others headed for New Orleans and arrived well before dark. After checking into their hotel, they were walking down Bourbon Street when they came to a very wide alley with tables, chairs, and three young ladies sitting and drinking hurricanes. The three men sat down at an adjacent table and before long the two tables joined together. The night got a whole lot more fun for everyone. The next morning found Scott at mass with a hangover.

After mass, they stopped at the Café Du Monde for coffee and beignets. With the sweetness of New Orleans still in their mouths, they headed for Fort Polk. This was the first time that any of them had ever been in New Orleans and it had lived up to its reputation for laid back living and great experiences.

That Monday, Scott was the pay officer and when Sarge came in for pay, Scott palmed him forty dollars. The man just nodded and walked out.

Full Colonel's Impact

One day on the firing range, Scott did something totally wrong. His timing was top of the mark, because Colonel Reed, the battalion commander had arrived minutes before.

The colonel led Scott off to the side and reamed out ten new rectums. He never raised his voice. Scott locked his heals and saluted when he was done. Col Reed returned his salute and left for the next firing range.

Several weeks later, Scott came in the back door of the Officer's Club, racked his helmet, and went into the dark tavern area. As he walked towards the bar, he saw Lieutenant Moran sitting in a pool of light and as Scott approached Moran said, "Ledbetter, you appear to be putting on a little weight around the middle, ha ha ha."

Scott not- so—"jokingly" said, "Moran, you name the place and mileage and we will saddle up and I will walk your ass into the ground on my worst day, ha ha ha." Out of the darkness on the other side of the table came a command voice that Scott had heard before.

"Yes, Lieutenant Ledbetter, I have heard that that is a true statement." Colonel Reed invited Scott to sit and have a beer. This was the first time that he had ever been in the club with a high-ranking officer. The colonel taught him how to be social and fit in with all levels of men in the Army. He also taught him how to be an officer and a gentleman.

Alamo Platoon

Scott had gotten to D-1-2 in the fourth week of an eight-week cycle. As a company executive officer, he spent the next four weeks learning about training men from the command side. The cycle was in its final days when Lt. Smith and Scott were summoned to the office of Colonel Reed.

Colonel Reed started the meeting by thanking them for their good work that they had been doing. The company troops had scored very high on the rifle range and in the Physical Combat Proficiency Test. They chit chatted for a while and Scott was beginning to think that when that other shoe fell, it would take off their heads. He was pleasantly surprised with the announcement that D-1-2 was getting the Alamo Platoon.

Colonel Reed told them that D -1- 2 had been "picked" to train the Alamo Platoon because of their outstanding performance in the last few Basic Training Cycles. The Alamo Platoon was made up of fifty-five men who were recruited from San Antonio. That city was celebrating its 150th anniversary as a city. A recruiter got "giggy" with the anniversary and recruited an entire platoon of men to join the Army and gave them the moniker of The Alamo Platoon.

He promised these men that they would be kept together through basic training at Fort Polk, LA. Now that promise was to be kept by D-1-2. The Colonel wished them the best and a warning to keep the good name of his training battalion in the forefront of their thinking.

The Alamo Platoon Arrives

The fifty-five members of the Alamo Platoon arrived as all basic trainees arrive for Basic Training—on a cattle truck which is an open-topped semi-trailer that is pulled by a large truck. The Ft. Polk Post and a paper from San Antonio were there for this PR event. Even with this company, the training cycle began just like all the other cycles. There was a great deal of yelling from the Drill Sergeants as they got the civilians (in military clothes) into a formation. Everyone expected that their basic training was going to be miserable. With the help of the experienced Smokies, this cycle started like all of the rest – miserable indeed.

The Drill Sergeants had eight weeks to turn men who cannot march or run in a group to be able to do all with precision. They would also be able to fire an M-14 rifle well enough to take down a target from as far away as five hundred meters.

In basic training you would find men who are literally from every part of the country. Their backgrounds were as varied as any you would ever see. Some were raised on dirt farms back in the hills while others were city born and raised. Rich, poor, and everything in between were living elbow to elbow.

This diversity was intentional to keep AWOLs (Absent Without Leave/Permission) down to a dull roar. If Harold from Pin Hook, Arkansas decided to go AWOL, he would be heading there all by himself because the guy in the next bunk from Chicago would have no interest in going to Arkansas. The Alamo Platoon was different because the entire platoon was from San Antonio and most of them grew up together.

It was the job of the cadre to get all the trainees to come together as quickly as possible by getting all of the trainees to hate the cadre. The faster the platoon came together to show this sorry Son of a Bitch that they could take whatever he dished out, the faster they would become a working platoon.

The men started pulling together to show these son-of-a-bitches that they were tougher than the cadre. After eight days of training, this bond started to work in the cadre's favor. Suddenly the two-mile morning run was not so bad; the cadre began to resemble human beings.

By the middle of the second week, the company began to form into an Army unit. Scott would not trust them to take a hill in combat, but they were starting to come together. In the Jody songs, they learned all about Jody and they were able to stay in step as they ran for miles in formation. In the first fourteen days, the trainees would go from hating the cadre to respecting them for getting them in the best shape of their lives. When the cycle reached this stage, the Army training lessons started to sink-in.

Sergeant Danny Botman and Scott were the caretakers of the Alamo Platoon. Sergeant Botman was in tremendous shape. One day two trainees walked by Scott and did not salute. When he looked back, both troops were lifted off the ground in the grasp of Sergeant Botman. He had simply grabbed both of them by their fatigue shirts and lifted them straight up in the air. While suspended, he explained to them that they would salute officers. Scott was certain that he had gotten their attention.

The Alamo Platoon was ninety percent Hispanic in all kinds of shapes and sizes. The largest of them was a kid who stood 6'3" and weighed over three hundred pounds, he needed a lot of conditioning. On the first day, Scott had the men doing sit ups and push-ups and the man could not get his head off the ground. Scott nicknamed him Fluffy.

PCPT

On the first Saturday of Basic Training the cadre marched the company down the street to the battalion Physical Combat Proficiency Test (PCPT) area. The rules were the same for these men as it had been for Scott when he went through his training. A trainee had to get three hundred points from doing five different exercises.

At the end of the first PCPT, the company had thirty-five men below the passing mark of three hundred points. Come Monday, the company marched to and from a training area in the rain. There was a company formation, the training schedule for tomorrow was announced, and Scott called out the names of the men who had a score less than three hundred. He had them form up into a formation in the company area.

The rest of the company was dismissed. Scott got up on the platform and looked at these sorry assed people. He reminded them that while the rest of the company was getting ready for chow in a nice dry barracks, they were standing in formation, in the rain. Scott asked the sergeants to march the men to the company low crawl pit.

Prior to this, Scott had pulled two men who had finished the physical training course with a perfect score of five hundred and asked them to fill the company's low crawl pit to the brim with water. The sergeants marched the group of thirty-five men around the barracks and halted them five feet from the pit.

As they stood a few feet from the pit, Scott talked to them about getting in shape. He knew that some of the men in this formation had chosen to blow off the event as unimportant.

He told them he did not know who could or could not pass the test and he needed to find out. Scott told them that each night after the day's training that they would enjoy additional training. If they passed the PCPT on the next Saturday, they would not have to do extra training.

Scott said, "Gentlemen, when you pass the PCPT test, you will be able to stand in the barracks and look down on the men who have not put out the effort. If you look up at the barrack's window on either side, you will see all your buddies. I want you to look up and wave to the men in the windows."

Scott concluded the talk: "Gentlemen, I would be ecstatic if I could leave immediately after the day's training was done. However, your lack of caring is causing me to do extra training that I do not need. I will be here every night doing extra training until every man can pass PCPT."

Scott stopped talking and entered the low crawl pit and low-crawled the length of the pit and got out. He never asked a single man to do what he would not do. No trainee could complain that they were singled out to do this training because an officer was going through the same low crawl pit.

He told the cadre to start the men into the pit. After the first wave of four troops went through the water, it looked like a very large hog wallow on his Iowa farm. Scott had the men low crawl three times. When they finished their third swim, he asked the sergeants to march them back to the company formation area.

Scott got back-up on the platform and said, "Gentlemen, I hope that this evening's training will help you to understand how much the Army and Lieutenant Ledbetter wants every man to be in shape and pass the PCPT. I have decided to give this training group a name. That name will be Led-better's Rangers."

The next night, Scott had one of the young E-5's, who had played high school and college football lead the Rangers in calisthenics. Scott was in the group doing the exercises and they were a bitch. Sergeant Botman and Scott took then them out on a two-mile run. They repeated this schedule for three more nights. On Friday night, Scott took them out on a four-mile run.

As they ran, Scott was counting cadence. That meant that the entire formation was running in step. That was one of the hardest things for new troops to learn. Not only did they have to run for miles, they had to do in cadence while singing Jody songs. Scott would turn around and run backwards for long periods of time, passing the Rangers who were running forward.

The next Saturday morning the company held another PCPT. At the end of this second test, Scott went from thirty-five soldiers down to nineteen troops. Now he could work with the troops who could not pass the test. On Monday evening, he had all thirty-five men get into the Ranger formation.

He called out the name of each man who had gotten over three hundred points on the PCPT, he thanked them, and dismissed each and every one of them. When he was done excusing those who had passed the PCPT, there were nineteen men in his group. The men were expecting to hit the low crawl pit. They were relieved when they were wheeled out onto the road and a two-mile run, when they returned, they did thirty minutes of football drills.

Each Saturday, Scott would lose from one to four soldiers as they got themselves in shape. After four weeks, he was down to six guys. One of them was a man who was way overweight and to help him get in shape, Scott appointed him to be the permanent Road Guard for the Alamo Platoon. Normally this "honor" rotated. A Road Guard never stopped running from the time the company goes out on the street until they arrive at the training area.

When an infantry company was on the street and an intersection approaching, the NCO in charge would yell, "Post Road Guards." The road guards on either side of the column would run out ahead of the company to stop traffic from both directions. When all platoons have marched through the intersection, the road guards ran to catch up with their platoon. The road guards stayed in the formation until the next intersection. On a normal day, the company might pass ten intersections and Scott's permanent road guard was posted at each intersection.

At the end of the seventh week, Scott's road guard was able to pass the PCPT test. Ledbetter's Rangers was down to one man who could not pass the test. That man had tried as hard as he could but could not get more than 250 points on the test. He had been through all the training that the company had done, plus all the training done with the Rangers.

On this final Monday of the cycle, Scott retired the Ledbetter Rangers. He announced at the formation that Ledbetter's Rangers was being disbanded. He told them that no matter what they would do in the up-coming PCPT test and the rest of their military career, that they were the ones who would make the difference.

Scott told them, "In the coming years you can tell your relatives and friends that you graduated from Basic Combat Training and where you learned to be a good soldier. That is what the sergeants and officers at D 1 2 have been trying to accomplish in the last eight weeks. We want each of you to be good soldiers."

The sergeant dismissed the company. When he did, all nineteen Ledbetter Rangers formed up in the Ranger formation. At first Scott did not know what they were doing. Then he realized that he was being thanked by a group of men who had no other way to say thanks. He took off his fatigue shirt, as did all the men, and they wheeled out onto the street and went for a three-mile run. When they got back, none of them were even breathing hard. Scott knew that he had made a difference in the lives of these men.

When they returned to the company, the men got back into their formation and Scott told them how proud he was to be able to work with them. Before dismissing them, he saluted them, put on his fatigue shirt, and headed for a beer at the club. He noticed that the drill sergeants had all stayed in the company area. They were standing on the sidewalk that led to Scott's car and each saluted him as he walked by. That was one of the most meaningful displays of gratitude that he had ever felt. As Scott drove to the Officer's Club, he was a very happy man.

Final PCPT

"Six guys from Ledbetter's Rangers grabbed him and stuck him back up on the ladder. He fell off the ladder four times and each time his Ranger buddies stuck him back up on the ladder."

All the tests during Basic Training were run by the cadre of D-1-2. To graduate from basic, each troop had to pass the test that was sponsored by the Fort Polk PCPT committee. On the day of the Post PCPT, Scott could only encourage, as his job was done. As the event was winding down, he noticed a large crowd of troops gathered around the parallel ladder. The last man to attempt the ladder (the ladder had fourteen rungs and the trainee had to go down and back), was the kid who had never been able to do the parallel ladder. He had never passed the company's PCPT test.

The parallel ladder was based solely on upper body strength. While a lot had been done to get the Rangers in shape, there was only so much that could be done in a short amount of time. As Scott walked up, the young man was just beginning his first trip down the ladder. He made it to the fourth rung and fell off. Six guys from Ledbetter's Rangers grabbed him and stuck him back up on the ladder. He fell four times on his trip down and back. Each time, his buddies grabbed him and stuck him back up on the ladder. When he finally got to the last rung, every man in the cycle was cheering him. He had completed something he had never done before.

Scott walked over to the sergeant in charge of the event and told him about the young man and how much he had improved since arriving eight weeks before. Certainly the sergeant was impressed by how the company had come together as a unit for this young man.

The sergeant looked at Scott and said, "The manual says that the trainee has to touch all 28 rungs; there is no mention about having to touch them without falling off."

He continued: "What have you been feeding these men? In all of my years, I have never seen anything like D-1-2."

Scott replied, "We have been teaching them to be good soldiers and to have one another's back, and the proof appears to be in the pudding."

The sergeant passed the young man and the whole company gave out a yell. Scott stood away from the large group of trainees gathered around this jubilant young man. He wanted him to have his fifteen minutes of glory. Scott knew that this young man had never had so much support from his peers. He had never had as many friends who cared for him. Today he was a hero and Scott felt pretty damned good that he was a part of the victory.

The Can-Do attitude of Ledbetter's Rangers had permeated the company. It was the company who helped the young man win and because of their giving spirit, they also won. The NCO's all felt a special pride in this group. More than likely there will never be another Basic Trainee group that will be of the same caliber as this one.

Basic Trainees Graduation

Most of San Antonio made the trip to Fort Polk for the graduation. The Army gave certificates for different achievements, including the most improved trainee of the cycle. Scott had chosen his ladder man for this award. To make the award even more special, Scott went out and bought a trophy for the young man. He had no doubts that this was the only trophy he had ever won.

Colonel Reed was the main speaker at the graduation and in charge of handing out the awards. The most improved trainee of the cycle was the last award given. Colonel Reed called the young man up and gave him his certificate and trophy. At the close of the graduation ceremony, Reed looked at Scott and gave him a thumb's up. Scott cherished that action all his life.

After the graduation, Scott walked through all the barracks wishing the men good luck. When he got to the Alamo Platoon, the young man who arrived out of shape and overweight was packing his clothes. He called Scott over. Scott saw that the man was standing with both legs in one leg of the pants, that he was wearing on his first day of training. The other pants leg was hanging limp. His mother may not have recognized him when she came to the graduation. More importantly, he now recognized himself as a new man.

This young man and Scott's ladder man had succeeded with a winning score in the PCPT because a training officer and an NCO had taken the time to do what had to be done. All the letters and other awards given by the Army were as useless as a Zippo lighter with a misspelled name, these two men were the real deal.

Heading Home to Iowa

Scott arrived at his trailer park late in the afternoon on his last day at Fort Polk. The trailer was at best utilitarian. Its only saving grace was that it was better than the Bachelor Officer Quarters on post. Next door to Scott's trailer a young soldier and his wife lived in a trailer that was very small, and very old. He doubted that it would ever be pulled anywhere, except to a junk yard. Scott was going to get ready for a party for all officers leaving for Vietnam.

The lady next door was out playing with her son next to their trailer. He had not seen the husband for a couple of weeks but assumed that the Army had shipped him to another post or someplace for training.

Scott went in to take his shower, no water came out. The kids in the park thought that shutting off people's water was a fun game. He pulled on a pair of walking shorts and went outside to turn on the water. As he was making his way back out from under the trailer he saw a pair of nicely shaped legs standing by his porch. It was the lady who lived next door, and she was holding little Ronnie.

Scott asked if he could be of help. To which she replied, "I suppose you think that Larry and I are married."

Scott said, "Yes I had figured that."

"Well, we ain't and now the SOB has taken off on me."

Scott could tell that the end of this story would have him

listening to "ain't" and "Y'all" and little Ronnie for a long time—and God knows what else.

He said, "Ma'am, you're a very pretty woman I'm sure you will find someone to take Larry's place. I am engaged to a pretty lady up in Iowa, and she would be very disappointed if I changed direction at this stage of the game."

She thanked him and said that she understood. With that, she and little Ronnie boogied across what passed for a yard, back into that little bitty trailer. There was no little lady in Iowa, but Scott had to think fast to discourage the gal.

At the farewell party, Colonel Reed gave him a Zippo lighter with the battalion's insignia and wished him well in Vietnam. He also recognized him for getting every man in his basic training company to pass the Post PCPT. Scott was amazed at how much Reed knew about the test results. He even knew about Ledbetter's Rangers.

Scott and Gordon were heading for Fort Lewis, Washington. They would be a part of the "A" Packet, which was made up of four hundred men who would be shipped as a unit to Vietnam. Once in-country, the packet would be dissolved and the men would be assigned where the Americal Division wanted to send them. The report date at Fort Lewis was the fourth of January 1968.

The next day, after giving his head time to clear from the farewell party, Scott packed his car and headed north to Iowa. He made it all of ten miles before he started feeling sleepy. He stopped at the Advanced Infantry Center at North Fort Polk for some coffee. The NCO on duty poured him a cup and wished him luck in his Vietnam duty.

Scott drove through the night and was driving through

northern Arkansas the next day. As he passed a cotton field, he saw a farmer on his large cotton-picking machine on the far side of that field. Scott realized that he had never seen a cotton plant ready to be picked. He pulled off the highway and walked into the field and picked one head of cotton and waved at the farmer before heading on up the highway.

An Old Friend

He drove east to St. Louis where one of his friends from St. Ambrose was going to school and Scott was going to stay overnight with him. The two men had been drama majors. During college, Scott had gone with George to visit his parents on the South Side of Chicago. They had left on Friday afternoon on the six-hour drive to Chicago, which consisted mainly of two-lane roads. They went through small town after small town where they slowed down to the twenty-five miles per hour speed limit that was strictly enforced by the one-man police force. The cop funded his job with fines from the city slickers heading to or from Chicago

George lived in what is known as "The South Side". You did not need to add "of Chicago" because that was understood. The word South did not sound like that. It was pronounced more like "Soutt" side. His home was a brown stone which never made any sense to Scott as it was made from brown brick.

They arrived in time for dinner and it was like taking a step back in time. The table was covered with a beautiful tablecloth and the meal was delicious. Soon after supper was over, George and Scott hit the air and went to some of the local taverns.

Since neither of them had much money, they stopped at a small grocery store where George bought twenty-four cans of Bull Frog Beer. The beer came in a plastic net bag, and the cans were loose in the bag. It cost fifteen cents a can and was simply godawful. After tasting his first can, Scott figured that the beer had to be one degree above freezing for someone to drink the liquid. They spent the night visiting some of George's old friends.

They headed back to Davenport the next morning with tons of goodies from George's Mom. They came into one small town where the few buildings were on the left side of the highway. They were set back a hundred feet from the road. Between the buildings and the highway were several acres of gravel and abandoned vehicles.

When they reached halfway through this town, the motor caved in on their car. George coasted onto the dead vehicle parking lot with his dead car offering. The car had one thing in its favor, it looked really nice with no rust or dings. The only problem was that George was not one of those people who did that oil thing.

The sun was setting in the western sky, and they were fifty miles from Davenport. Scott looked across the highway and up a gravel road to a house with a bunch of cars in the yard. He left George with the car and walked up and knocked on the screen door. The man of the house came to the door wearing his bib overalls buckled on one side.

Scott told him of their plight. He had noticed the bunch of cars that were setting around his house and wondered if he would like to trade for a really nice car with a blown engine? The old man buckled up his other bib strap, put on some old work shoes, and they walked down the hill talking about farming and living in a small town.

When they got down to the car, they found George, looking very much like someone from Chicago, sitting on the right fender. The bibbed-gentleman took a walk around the car and allowed that the car was sure in nice shape and he might make a trade. They all walked back up the hill together. Scott and their car savior walked well ahead of the city slicker. They looked over the twenty or so cars around his house to decide which car they would haggle over. They finally found a 1952 Plymouth that was the pick of the litter.

It started and the transmission was pretty tight. Actually the car was in pretty good shape. Between Scott and George, they had seventy-five dollars. They negotiated a trade for the new car and sixty dollars as they needed some money to buy some gas.

Before they headed down the hill, the man came around the front of the house with a five gallon can of gas. He said that they should be able to make Davenport with a half tank of gas. Titles were exchanged and they drove down the hill to George's old car.

George pulled his license plates off his old car and put them on the new one and as they headed west they waved goodbye to the man. They had been in that little burg for just over an hour. George could not believe that Scott had pulled a trade for a car with a blown engine for one that ran.

Scott was going over that trip in his mind, as he pulled into St. Louis. He was able to find George's apartment building. It had been built back in the early 1900's and set not too far from both St. Louis University and Gas Light Square.

George was going to college and paying his rent by working for a St. Louis taxicab company. After he picked up his cab, he picked up Scott to ride with him. He had an extra hat for Scott to wear and he introduced Scott to his passengers, as a trainee cab driver. That night Scott was introduced to a whole new level of clientele. George's taxicab area was in the old part of St. Louis: they picked up whores, pimps, and winos. After four hours, Scott grew tired of his taxi gig and George dropped him off at his apartment.

St. Louis and Claire

The next day they traveled the city before it was time for George to go back on his taxicab duty. When George left to go to work, Scott headed for South St. Louis where he had "sort of" a date. Scott's commander at Ft. Polk was from South St. Louis. When he found out that Scott was going to stop in St. Louis to visit friends, he told Scott to call Claire and she would show him around St. Louis.

Earlier in the summer, Ed had taken a two-weeks leave and had gone home. He had asked his friend Claire if she would mind meeting Scott. She figured that nothing would ever happen and said yes. Scott called Claire and introduced himself as a friend of Ed. She asked Scott where his friend's apartment was located. He told her he was close to a very big intersection of Grand and Lindell. She said that she had no idea where that was, but if Scott wanted to meet her that he could come to the South Side Bowl, where her bank team was bowling.

South Side Bowl was filled with women's leagues, he knew that Claire bowled for Federal Bank and that there were two leagues from the bank. He found them both. They were six lanes from one another. He had no idea what Claire looked like other than she was blonde.

A lady wearing a Federal Bank bowling shirt was talking to a man that was sitting behind one of the teams. Scott introduced himself to the man and the man said, "Oh you must be Claire's date." Scott offered that he was, and the man asked him to sit down with him. At the end of the first game, a disheveled looking man in tattered clothes and scraggly beard came and stood right behind Claire's team. He stood there for most of three games. Along with his clothing the man's personal hygiene wasn't the best.

Scott's new friend figured out that the women on the team thought that this young man was Scott. Sure enough, the women would look at the man and start whispering to each other. They had decided to tell him that Claire had gotten sick and did not bowl, while she made her get-a-way.

The man finally left his place behind the team and the women were watching to see if he would come back, which he never did. As the women were getting ready to wrap up the 10th frame, Scott's friend took him over and introduced him to Claire and all her Federal Bank team. They had seen Scott sitting there but had no idea that he was the date person. After the games, both teams went to the bar and had drinks.

Scott and Claire went to Shakey's Pizza Palace so Scott could get something to eat. A banjo and a piano player were playing the oldies and they had a great time. Shakey's reminded Scott of Your Father's Mustache in San Francisco and he felt right at home.

This was the first real date that Scott had had in months. At Ft. Polk, single women would go out of their way to stay away from soldiers. That was especially true of anyone going to Vietnam. Since that included just about everyone on base, dating chances were pretty sparse. The women in the area around an army post knew that the chances of someone coming back from Vietnam were slim and damn well none.

Before the weekend was over, they had been all over St. Louis. He wanted to go to the newly completed St. Louis Arch. While he did not say anything, he knew that there was a chance that he might never see this tourist attraction. The day that they went it poured rain. The wind was blowing so hard that Claire's umbrella turned inside out. They did go up in the arch, even though they could hardly see the ground when they got to the top.

Claire asked if they could stop by to visit her sister Mary and her husband Larry who lived in South St. Louis. They stayed the whole evening just visiting. Larry said he was a glazier. Scott had no idea what a glazier did, but he figured if he listened long enough he would be able to figure it out. He never did. The only glazier that he could think of was a guy who put shiny stuff on donuts. Since Larry worked on some kind of construction, that description did not fit.

When they left, Scott asked Claire, "What does Larry do for a living?"

She told him that he was a glazier, to which Scott replied, "I know that. Now what does he do for a living?"

She told him that he put glass in commercial buildings. In Millersburg, population 125, there had been no new construction as long as he lived there. The buildings had the same glass that they had when they were built. Obviously, St. Louis had more new construction than Millersburg.

On Sunday, they went to Mass and had a Sunday meal. He got a taste of the South Side Dutch and how they lived in these little houses with neat concrete steps in front. After they ate, Scott said his goodbye's and headed for Iowa. As he left, he thought that he would see Claire and her family again. He knew that he was looking at a year of being in harm's way and rushing was not in anyone's interest. His immediate future was going to have him staring at some jungle path a long way from St. Louis.

Time at home

Scott enjoyed his time at home. The last few months had been a major turning point in Scott's life. All the heartache of the last few years had been gratefully washed away in that one moment of elation at the OCS graduation. By decree of the United States Congress, he was now an officer and a gentleman.

The leadership that he had been taught by his dad, brothers, cousins, and the good people of Millersburg was starting to shine through as he progressed with his new rank. When he left Fort Polk he sincerely thanked all his cadre at D-1-2. They had taken a raw recruit of an officer and made him a better man. He had learned how to work with both NCO's and the enlisted men. The men that he had worked with at Fort Polk would long be the salt that helped cure this raw young man.

He was even thankful to the men of Ledbetter Rangers because he learned what he was to practice when he was in a field command. He had worked side by side with the Rangers as they went through all the extra training hours and was able to develop a philosophy of working with the men in his command. Scott did every exercise he asked the men to do. This experience would serve him well in the coming months.

December 1967 was rough, not only because of the cold of Iowa but also knowing that Scott was headed for Vietnam. The war was unpopular with the people in the United States. Scott's folks had seen so many young men go off to war and never return. They also knew of men who had returned from war but could no longer relate to society.

In Scott's eyes, he was as ready as was possible. He had been through nine months of lethal combat training and then pushed Basic Trainees for another five months. While he was respectful of combat, he was not afraid of being a combat soldier. At this stage of his life, going to Nam was not his duty; it was his obligation. At least that was his thinking at the time.

Fort Lewis Bound

On Christmas Day 1967, Scott drove to Cedar Rapids to pick up Gordon at the airport. They had decided to see the country by driving to Fort Lewis, Washington. Scott had spent time in California in AIT but had never been across the country. Gordon had never been to California nor had he ever traveled across the US. They decided to take two weeks of their leave to make a road trip.

The day after Christmas 1967 was a very awkward day. Scott's folks were trying to act as if everything was normal, and yet their number three son was headed for war. His mom and dad stood with him on the front porch and cried. His Mom held on as tightly as she could. With one final hug, Scott headed for the car. As he backed out of the driveway, he looked at the small gray house with the front porch door and its six small windows. His mom and dad were framed in that six-panel storm door, both crying. They knew that this might be the last time that they saw Scott alive. He would keep that picture in his mind forever.

Scott's tears for their aching hearts were streaming down his face. When he and Gordon reached the brick on Main street, the howling of the tires across the old red brick was the only sound permeating the sad silence. The car was quiet for a long time as both young men were lost in the moment. It was sad that what was planned to be the greatest trip of their young lives was the start of a time at war. They crossed the old steel bridge north of town and headed for the interstate. As that bridge faded from sight, the trip started to pick up the pace.

For the first time since forever, neither had any responsibility save keeping the car between the ditches and getting to Ft. Lewis a few days after New Year's Day 1968. Beyond that, they only had the safety of themselves and those driving with them or toward them. Given the time of year, there were not a whole lot of people driving towards them and damned few heading their same direction.

They were going to Denver to stay with a buddy of theirs from OCS, David. The winter had Iowa well in its grasp as they traveled across I-80 to Omaha. They looked at the map and determined that they would drive to the middle of Nebraska and drop south when I-80 reached the southern-most point in the state.

When they reached the halfway mark, they dropped down to I-70 across Kansas as that seemed to give them the straightest line to Denver. They drove through an enormous amount of slush during the day, slush that quickly became solid ice as they drove along at seventy plus miles per hour. At 1700 hours the right front retread tire from Louisiana had all the damned cold that it could take. The tread broke loose and was trying its best to drive a hole through the cowling around the tire. They pulled over and Scott used a pocketknife to cut away a six-inch piece of rubber.

The rubber did not want to be cut of course, and Scott's hands were almost frozen by the time he got back in the car. With a chunk of rubber obviously missing from the left front tire, the ride became a monotonous thumping existence. They looked on the map and saw that they would be coming into Joe's, Colorado in less than one hour. That was the only town on that part of the trip.

Scott just hoped that the rest of the tread did not come off because the sun and daylight were gone. They were left with nice frigid winter air. Joe's, Colorado appeared in their headlights at 1800 hours. As luck would have it, they found an open gas station where they were able to buy a tire. Scott pulled the car with its additional layer of eight inches of ice into the bay. The young man put the car on a lift in order to put on a twenty-five-dollar tire.

As Scott and Gordon waited up front they heard a tremendous crash from the back of the service station. They ran back to find that all that ice had just fallen off the car.

They continued on, less the thumping of that right front tire, toward Denver. At long last they came over a rise and they could see Denver in the last elements of the day. When they arrived, Dave's family had a much-appreciated hot meal waiting for them.

Dave took them on a tour of the bars in the area, but Scott was starting to come down with a cold. A cold on top of a twelve-hour day of driving through the Midwest winter had Scott pretty well strung out. Dave said that he would drive, and that Scott could sleep on the way home. When they got to the local hang out, Scott decided to soak his cold with a double bourbon, water by. He had heard that this would work but had never tested the theory. They stopped at three places before a final stop at the first bar they had visited. Scott ordered another double bourbon, water by. The waitress was amazed that he was still going, so was Scott.

When they got home, Scott was out before his pillow got warm. At 0400 hours, he came to life and found that he was soaked with sweat. The bourbon had cleaned out every pore in his body. He had sweated through the sheets, bed spread, and quite likely the mattress pad. Scott had crushed his cold.

The Rockies

The next morning, they got their first real look at the Rocky Mountains. That was an unforgettable sight, a sight made more unforgettable because they were driving through those mountains on December 26th. To say that this was a thrilling ride would have been a misconception. It was downright scary.

In the early part of the day, they were able to keep their speed at a manageable level. They crawled up from the mile-high city to some big peaks. For several miles, they followed a snowplow which threw a massive snow arch out into eternity only a few feet from Scott's extremely small 63 Ford. Some people with serious brass gonads passed them and the snowplow. Scott just kept on driving.

At noon, they came to a road pointing up to a ski resort. When he turned, Gordon looked at him like he was nuts. Scott had only seen people ski in the movies and on television and he wanted to watch real people slide down the snow on bent boards. This might be something that he would never see again.

The road was amazingly clear and they made it to the top of the mountain to a ski lodge where they got a hot cup of Joe and some sandwiches. They sat in the window seats to watch this skiing phenomenon. The skiers were standing around outside like it was summer. Scott walked out to see if there was heat coming from someplace he could not see. Just as he thought, it was colder than a well digger's ass in Alaska. He decided that skier people were truly crazy.

With a good lunch under their belts, they made it back

down to whatever highway they were on and headed west. Through the day, they wended their way through endless mountains and switch backs. They stopped for gas late in the afternoon and a truck driver asked Scott if they were heading for the Western Slope? Scott had no idea what that meant, but he said yes. Sometimes it was necessary to just go with the flow.

Gordon pulled over when they reached the top of the western slope and woke Scott. Within a few minutes of starting to drive, Scott tipped the car over the top of the slope and drove down the two-lane highway for the next five hours. In those five hours of driving, he did not take one turn that was not headed down. Sometime after 0600 hours, the sun started to rise in the eastern sky and it was beautiful.

The sun's rays were bouncing off the fog that filled the sky above them. The rays changed the colors and hues of the early morning mountains and valleys. The blues turned amazingly azure blue. Cold against the early morning mountain made everything crisp and fresh. For the first time in his life, he understood psychedelic painting. The greens were a bright yellowish green that followed waves of all sorts of green colors. This color phenomenon lasted for over twenty minutes. When the fog closed in, there was only gray.

The Diner

Through the fog came a blinking sign that said "Eat." He pulled into the parking lot of the small diner and parked next to the only other car on the parking lot, which belonged to the owner and cook. She looked like a mom or a great Aunt Maggie. She took their order and disappeared behind a small wall that did not reach the ceiling. While she was cooking, she talked to her two new guests. She wanted to know where they had come from and where they were going. She could not believe that they had driven from Denver and had gotten there so early in the morning. She thought they were crazy for driving all night.

She continued to talk and cook. The stack of flapjacks that came out of that little kitchen stood nine inches high. Each pancake was as light and fluffy as the last one. If they had said they wanted more she surely would have made them for these two lads on their way to Vietnam

"A place where they should not be," she said. Scott did believe that she was right, but that did not change the fact that that was where they were going.

Salt Lake City

When they left the diner, Scott turned the keys back over to Gordon, who by now should have been the most rested person in several states. Scott fell into a very deep sleep and missed his chance to see the purple sage that Zane Grey talked about in his books. Gordon, who could not remember if there was any such a thing on the trip, was pulling into Salt Lake City when Scott came back to life.

All his life Scott had dreamed about what this town would be like with its plains, mountains, and Mormon attitude. They found winter about where it had always been, on the ground and on the windshield. They drove into downtown Salt Lake City where they found the streets that Scott had read about. They were wide enough to swing a wagon and two teams of horses from one side of the street to the other.

They found the Mormon Cathedral and where the Tabernacle Choir rehearsed. Coming from a church where the tabernacle was only big enough to hold two or three chalices, Scott was having a hard time calling a choir a tabernacle choir. They visited a center with a forty-foot statue of Christ. A ramp was built around the statue and they walked to the top where they looked into the eyes of Christ. They were impressed. At the choir's rehearsal hall, they sat and listened to the large organ.

The recital hall, a large domed building, reminded Scott of a tent that was stretched to form a perfect concert hall. There was a true master on the organ, and they settled in for an hour's break from driving. After so many hours on the road and still getting over the flu, Scott heard maybe three or four minutes of some beautiful music. As the last chords were being coaxed out by the organist, Scott woke up.

Gordon asked him, "How did you like the performance?"

The chilly air brought Scott to life and they headed for the car and their next stop, Reno, Nevada. Just a few miles out of town they came to a sign for, The Great Salt Lake. Scott exited and followed the lonely highway several miles to a closed swimming area that featured a closed saltwater taffy stand, set thirty feet from the lake.

Scott walked past the stand and through the open gate to the water's edge. He stuck his forefinger into the lake and tasted the water. He got back in the car to the sound of

Gordon laughing his ass off at someone so anal as to test the water in the Great Salt Lake.

"Hey," Scott said, "I'm from Iowa and I never understood how saltwater got so lost as to end up in Utah." He just wanted to make sure that it was in fact salty, which he could now attest to. They made it back to the highway and headed west for two solid hours without seeing anything but desert. One hundred and thirty miles from Salt Lake City they came upon a sign that read, "You Are Now Entering the Desert." Scott wondered what they called the area they had just driven through.

Hour upon hour they drove themselves across the desert. The AM radio only played Spanish stations, so that was what they listened to for hours. It got so boring that they slowed down to a set speed for a set number of minutes. They counted the telephone poles and fence posts in that time frame. Once the counting was done, they would do the math to figure out how many board feet of lumber made up that number of poles and posts. It was a silly game but that was how boring the trip was.

There was one small moment of excitement when they got to the Nevada border: slot machines. Scott had never seen a slot machine, let alone play one. At the gas station where they stopped to fill up, they had six slot machines. He lost his first dollar to the gas station slot machine and then got back in the car and headed for Lake Tahoe.

Lake Tahoe

It was December 28, 1967 when they got to Lake Tahoe at 2100 hours. Much like skiing, Scott had never seen anyone gamble. As they made their way into the first casino, Scott noticed a man in a small area with thirty slot machines. The man was playing ten machines at one time. He just went from one to the other, dropping in fifty cents and pulling the handle before going to the next slot machine. Scott was amazed at how much money he was throwing into the machines. They ate a late supper at the casino restaurant which cost less than two dollars each. Scott had heard about how cheap the meals were at Reno and Vegas, and by gosh they were.

You could walk out of one casino and into another without knowing that you had just walked between two buildings. Scott was walking down a carpeted aisle and hit a little sidewalk. When he looked to his left and right he saw that there was less than three feet of space between the two buildings.

Scott played the nickel slots and won eighty dollars. And like all good conservative Iowa farm boys, he quit playing. He looked all over to find Gordon and finally found him playing the slots. As they headed out to their car, they walked past that small area where the man was still playing ten slot machines. Scott had no idea how long he had been there.

It was 0300 hours when they got to their room. Scott was dumbfounded when he saw how late it was. They decided to stay one more night in Reno before going to San Francisco.

They were not sure that they could make it that far with so little sleep.

After two days of frivolity in Lake Tahoe, it was time to head for Scott's Mecca, San Francisco. It had been a long time since he had walked its hilly streets and felt the ever-present wind blowing off the ocean.

On the way they went through Sacramento, the first place where prices had already started to move toward the turn of the next century. They stopped at a Denny's kind of place for lunch and paid over five dollars for a cheeseburger and fries. It must have come from a specially treated California cow and not the ones they had left in Iowa where that meal would have cost three dollars. When you were only making three hundred and thirty dollars a month, five dollars is a lot of money. They left and made it into San Francisco in the middle of the afternoon on New Year's Eve, 1967.

San Francisco, New Year's Eve Night, 1967

As Scott drove into the city, he thought about how much time he had spent here with nothing but public transportation and of course, by Shank's Mare (walking). He thought about the people that he had met and the times that he had spent in SF. He had walked or ridden past the Hilton Hotel countless times. In his wildest imagination, he did not think that he would ever be staying there.

Scott had made reservations with military rates. The clerk told them that they would have to be in uniform to get the military discount. The regular rate was eighty dollars; their military rate was forty-five. Their uniforms were in the car, beneath layers of travel gear. Scott was not going to go and put one on so that some civilian clerk would approve a discount.

Scott took out his military ID card. As he handed it to the clerk, he quickly leaned back and searched the hotel lobby, as if looking for someone he knew. Then Scott lowered his head and had the clerk come closer. He explained to the young man that they were under cover as part of the military intelligence community. They would blow their cover if they had to wear uniforms. With this explanation, the clerk, who was now speaking very softly, agreed to check them in at the military discount rate. Scott took one more look around the lobby and then quietly nodded.

Meanwhile Gordon, who was standing right next to Scott, could not figure out what in the hell Scott was telling the clerk. Scott did not tell him until they got onto the elevator because he knew that Gordon would double over in laughter, which he did when Scott told him what he had said.

The parking garage was on the inside of the hotel and they parked their very un-white, grungy 1963 Ford next to everyone else's Cadillac or Lincoln before going to their room on the 11th floor.

They got situated at 1430 hours and Gordon wanted to hit the air to see San Francisco. Scott had been driving for a long time and really needed to catch some sleep. Gordon went out while Scott slept. Scott knew that San Francisco was a lot like Europe. People did not go out to dine until 2100 hours. Even though this was New Year's Eve, he was certain that that tradition would hold true. When he went out, he did not plan on being back to the hotel until sunrise.

Gordon came back and they headed for Chinatown. Gordon was amazed at how much Scott knew about getting around on the cable cars. He easily got them to Chinatown, and they searched for a good restaurant. Scott was not a big fan of rice, but they were in Chinatown. Gordon commented that several million Chinese had survived eating the stuff for a couple of thousand years. Scott went along with Gordon's idea of eating Chinese food and had to admit that the food was very good.

Outside the restaurant, the New Year's celebration was just starting to crank up. At 2000 hours the streets were filled with people. Normally the big celebration on New Year's Eve was held in downtown San Francisco, but they were building the new Bay Area Rapid Transit and downtown was all torn up.

This year the celebration was held in Chinatown where the crowds and the noise and piles of confetti were every-where. Scott was had been hit several times with confetti be-fore he bought his own bag. That bag was six inches across and a foot deep. The best time to throw confetti at someone was when they had their mouth open. He would wait for a perfect stranger walking towards him. When the stranger began to laugh, he would hit them with a handful of confetti. He learned this after getting hit with confetti several times. By the time he looked up, the culprit would be a block away.

The crowd in Chinatown seemed to be growing by the second. They were propositioned several times for "dates", but they just kept on moving. Scott thought about the night on Leavenworth Street when he was stationed at Fort Ord. He had gotten lost early in the evening. At the time, he did not know this street was the red-light district. He ended up walking through the area on the way back to his Suite D' Elegance. Explaining that he was dead broke kept the ladies harrumphing off to find a John with money to spend on their "merchandise."

It was approaching 2300 hours and Scott convinced Gordon to go to Pier 39 and to Little Alioto's. Gordon had heard Scott's stories about this place. He reluctantly left all the frivolity in Chinatown and got on a streetcar to go to Scott's special place.

"Go There and He Will Come"

Little Alioto's was a block off Pier 39. It was so unassuming that you assume there is no reason to go there. When they arrived, Scott began to doubt himself as there was only old Hontz playing bad accordion with his obnoxious monkey. The monkey still had his cup and was still banging it on the floor for a bigger tip. This looked like just another night at a local bar – only ten people were there and no New Year's Eve celebration anywhere in the area.

Gordon was pissed that they had left the huge party to come to this dump. They took a table next to the large pilings which separated the bar from the closed cafeteria. There was a row of lights above the pilings that shined on both sides. Both Gordon and Scott were thinking that there was still time to get back to China Town.

The rest rooms were on a wall at the end of the pilings. As Scott headed to the bathroom, he looked to his left on the far side of the pilings and there was a table filled with four young ladies. They were all dressed for a New Year's Eve party. Scott got Gordon's attention and motioned for him to check the other side of the pilings.

The Philly Irishman always had a gift of gab which Scott had seen over the two years that they had known each other. When he returned to the table, all four women were sitting at the table with a round of drinks coming; two beers and four soft drinks.

Scott never questioned why four very nice-looking women would choose little Alioto's on New Year's Eve. They came into an old Budweiser tavern and sat all by themselves in a semi-darkened cafeteria because they knew that Scott would come. Without knowing who he was or why he was coming, he would be there. Scott was sure of that.

In the days when he used this tavern as his office, he met several people who came and just sat and waited for him to come in, buy a beer, and ask if he could join them. He would sit down and spend hours talking to them. They would buy him beer and listen to his stories. They wanted to be his friend.

Tonight was just like it used to be. Destiny had brought the girls across the bay to Little Alioto's. Scott was certain that the girls had never met real servicemen. He was equally as certain that they had never met anyone on their way to Vietnam. The rest of New Year's Eve turned out far different than they or anyone could have guessed. If you knew Scott, then this was exactly what he thought was going to happen.

This was exactly what he lived for: to meet people and go with the flow.

The girls said that they were leaving soon to go to Midnight Mass at the University in Oakland. Scott asked if they could go with them as he was Catholic. Gordon was just going along for the ride.

Since their car was still at the hotel, all six of them got into a girl's sedan and headed across the bridge to the college. The college church was unique: the altar was elevated in the center all the way around. The concrete floors were smooth concrete, no carpeting. It was like someone used a giant donut to form the interior of the church and they pushed the donut down into the concrete and the center was pushed up. This was a very California experience.

On the way across the bay, Scott had asked about having a party at the girl's apartment. She said that sounded fun, not knowing what she was getting into. After Mass, Gordon and Scott stood outside and invited people to the party. Gordon was certain that the girls did not think that anyone would be so nuts as to ask perfect strangers to go to a party at 0100 hours on New Year's Eve, but they did.

Across the street from the church was a liquor store where they stopped and bought beer, snacks, and a bottle of bourbon. The apartment was not too small for the twenty people who showed up. The guest list included four college students, three priests who had co-celebrated the mass, a writer from the New York Times, Los Angeles Chronicle, and San Francisco Chronicle. There was also a small contingent of hippies who must have just wandered by the church.

Scott ended up in the kitchen sitting next to the sink. He

and the three writers had an intriguing conversation about Vietnam, the military, and the government. He could not remember having such a discussion since his time at St. Ambrose. Scott felt overmatched by the writers, but that did not stop him from diving into every conversation. They possessed a mind for what was happening at the time.

Scott wished that his old OCS roommate, Lou LaLonde, would have been a part of the discussion. His intellect was on a par with these guys. With nothing riding on the outcome, save some memories, Scott held his own for the better part of two hours. He figured that he was about forty IQ points shy of being on a plane with these men. Lou was the last guy who had made his head hurt during a philosophical discussion.

As the sun was coming up, the party began to break up as the hosts decided that the party was over. One of the girls gave them a ride back to the hotel and was quite surprised when she dropped them off at the Hilton. They thanked her for a great evening and for an equally great party.

This night had turned out just the way Scott wanted. They were riding a crest of uncertainty as they moved through the evening. He was so happy that Little Alioto's had not disappointed them. Who would have thought that two Army officers would find themselves at a Catholic Mass on New Year's Eve, 1968? Then to manufacture a party at a girl's apartment that they had met just two hours before was the stuff of legends.

The girls would never look at someone in a military uniform and not remember that they had met two Army types who were gentlemen. Yes, they had taken over their lives for a couple of hours, but they did it with style and grace. Every person at that party will always remember New Year's Eve 1968.

When they got back to the hotel, it was like they had just been through a dream sequence. Did they really spend the night having great discussions with people with a far superior intellect? Had they really been in San Francisco for New Year's Eve? It was a time that could not be duplicated, only remembered as something very special. They had made some new friends that they would never see again. So it was in the military.

In the military, you could not take a long time to get to know someone. If you waited, you would spend most of your time alone. When you met someone in the military you had twenty to thirty seconds to decide if you like them. If you did, you went with it. There was so much movement in the military and no time to spend deciding who to like or dislike. Scott never missed an opportunity to make or be best friends with the people around him.

The military taught him to see life as two ships constantly passing in the night. If you can stop to say hello, do so; if you cannot, at least wave and say a prayer for that other person. In San Francisco, Scott wanted to meet every person that passed by because each of them had a story to tell, a story that would have an impact on his life. And just the telling of their story might impact their lives.

The two men decided they needed to at least use the hotel beds to get a couple hours sleep before maid service woke them up. They then headed for the Presidio to see if they could bunk at the visiting Bachelor Officer's Quarters. That would give them more money to spend in San Francisco.

The Presidio was in holiday mode. No one was there except for the people who had to be on duty. The MP at the front gate gave them directions to the Visiting Bachelor Officer's Quarters. The sergeant told them that no visiting general officers were at the Presidio and he would put them in a visiting general's suite.

If a general showed up he would move their stuff to the lesser officer's quarters. They paid him the twelve dollars for two nights and booked to their new digs.

The Presidio sat at the end of the Golden Gate Bridge. The general's suite had two bedrooms, a kitchenette, living room, and was on the second floor. The bay window in the living room was four hundred meters from the end of the Golden Gate Bridge.

They spent the next two days in San Francisco bumming. Scott took Gordon by boat over to Sausalito and showed him where he used to sit and have wine, French bread, and cheese with the tourists getting off the boats. No matter how he tried to explain it, without taking the time to do this kind of thing, it was hard to explain how enjoyable it was.

Big Al's and Your Father's Mustache

Gordon had never been to a lady's dance club, so Scott took him to Big Al's. That was where they used to have a woman dancing in a plastic cage, ten feet off the street. Apparently, that had been abandoned or closed down.

Scott and Gordon walked into Big Al's and sat in front of what passed for a stage. Old ice cream chairs had been slammed against each other to maximize the number of men who could sit down at one time. Before the dancers came out, the waitress told Gordon that there was a two-drink minimum. He ordered beer. They were served two nine-ounce glasses of warm beer with a two-inch collar.

After one dancer came out weathered and worn, the two men left and headed to Your Father's Mustache. It was a Dixieland place filled with tourists enjoying the piano and banjo playing. When they walked through the door, Scott felt right at home. He remembered how often he came here when he was stationed at Fort Ord.

They bought a pitcher of beer and sat down at a table that had several Aussies at the other end. They were valiantly trying to sing the old songs and one man noticed that Scott was singing all the songs. He invited both men to join them. With Scott leading the singing, a crowd soon gathered around the table. The Aussies were members of an Australian airline and Scott hoped that they were not flying real soon, because they were all pounding down the beer.

Shortly before the Aussies left, ten Swedish Merchant Marines arrived. They saw where the party was and surrounded the table and took the vacated seats. The only word that anyone could understand was the Norse drinking word, Skoll. When Gordon and Scott headed out into the night, they left a large table filled with tourists and Merchant Marines Skoll-ing and singing.

Time to Leave

Finally, the morning arrived when they had to leave for Fort Lewis, Washington. It was hard to leave the General's Quarters, as that was the highest cotton that Scott had ever "stepped in". Sadly, they left the magnificent view of the Golden Gate Bridge and all that was San Francisco.

They drove north of San Francisco where Scott finally got to see the Redwoods. The area was filled with these magnificent trees, and it was as if they were in God's own cathedral. The silence was deafening, and the power of these trees was felt down to their souls. They stopped several times, just watching and listening to the sound of nature. Even when silent, it spoke volumes.

As they got to Eugene, the fog was closing in and they could see lights but could not make out if any of them were motels. They took an exit, found a Knight's Inn and called it the end of the day. When they got into the hotel, Gordon went to bed, but Scott was so wired from several hours of bad fog, that he went down to the bar area. He met eight others who were Seattle bound, but had stopped because of the fog.

The bar had two swinging doors that went out to the hallway. The bottom of those doors cut a perfect shadow across the carpet in the bar. Two guys started to pitch quarters to see who could split the quarter with the shadow of the doors. The one with just a half of the quarter showing won all the quarters pitched. Scott could not miss. He was certain that he could have banked a quarter off the wall in front of him, and it would split the shadow of the swinging doors.

By the end of the session, Scott had made ten dollars in quarters. The bar closed and one of the men invited three of the quarter pitchers to go for a sandwich at a local country club. For Scott, it was another chapter in his journey as the four ships passing in the night stopped to say hello. They pitched some quarters, had a few beers together before heading on to the rest of their lives.

The next day was a light day. All they had to do was to drive three hours north to Ft. Lewis and get signed into the unit. Washington State welcomed them with rain and overcast skies.

Fort Lewis, Washington

They got to Ft. Lewis in time to find their unit and sign into a unit called "A" packet. They met Captain Reeds, the commanding officer of "A" packet. They found him to be what could best be called a "winker". Someone who winks as they are talking to you. The wink indicates that this is just among us girls and that you and I are tight. Scott had learned long ago to back up and stay away from this kind of phony. They were only going to be with this officer for a short while. Once they got to Vietnam, he would be miles away and would not be a concern.

Gordon and Scott ended up at a really nice motel with two beds and a bathroom. That was their home away from home for the next month. They found out that there was literally nothing to do at Fort Lewis other than some obligatory training. The Army just has to train, because they are the Army.

One day they took all of "A Packet" to a classroom and introduced them to the M-16 rifle. Scott had only seen this rifle in pictures and knew nothing about its durability or rate of fire. Once they got done with the information class, they headed for the rifle range to fire the weapons.

The first position they were to fire from was lying on the ground covered with what the people in Washington state called "slain." This is a mixture of snow and frozen rain two inches deep. When you walked through slain, you could look back and see your footprints in the snow-filled water. As a trainee, Scott had all the wet and muddy that he needed. He decided to stand up and fire. He went to the next firing position. It was a round piece of culvert that had been set in the ground.

When Scott dropped down into the pit, the concrete was six foot three inches deep. All he could see was concrete. Men before him had thrown rocks into the pit, but the mud sucked the rocks down. His concrete hole was made for someone six foot four inches. Scott was six-foot-tall.

The range NCO said lock and load three rounds of ball ammunition. Instead of firing, Scott put his empty rifle up in the air and waved it back and forth. An E-7 NCO came charging over ready to have an enlisted guy for lunch. He stopped his normal tirade when he saw that the man waving his rifle was an officer. Scott looked up at him and asked him if he was the NCO In Charge of this range? When he said that he was, Scott asked him how in the fuck anyone could fire from this position. He then asked him why he did not fill in these holes with gravel.

The sergeant said that he would take care of that straight away. Scott thanked him and asked for a ladder so that he could get out of the pit. Scott hoped that he would carry through as this range needed to be made fit for the men who followed him. Scott was allowed to fire his three rounds from a standing position.

What turned out to be the weekend before they headed for Nam, four of the men who had graduated from OCS 56th OC Company went into Seattle. That was a day of days. They traveled up Puget Sound as far as the road would take them. At the extreme far north end of Seattle and the sound, they found a small open naval base with a working lighthouse. Puget Sound could be heard for blocks before they even saw the water. The waves were crashing against the rocks surrounding and protecting the fifty-foot light house.

The four men got out of the car and walked toward the lighthouse. A man wearing a pea coat and navy skull cap came out on the porch of the house. He gruffly informed them, "This lighthouse is not open; it is a government installation and not a tourist area!"

Scott walked over to the man and said, "We apologize for the inconvenience. We are Army guys who will be heading for Vietnam in the next few days. We are all from the Midwest and have never seen a lighthouse up close. We will head out and get out of your way."

The man asked, "Are all of you in the military?"

Scott had all the guys give the man their military ID's.

The man's attitude changed four hundred percent and he invited them to follow him into his lighthouse.

The waves made this fortress of a building shake constantly. They went all the way to the top of the working lighthouse and the man gave them explanations about how old the building was and how long he had been the caretaker.

When they left the lighthouse, the man invited them into his house for a cup of coffee. They politely declined. The man thanked them for their service and wished them God speed. As they were saying their goodbyes, he saluted them before they headed back to their car. They headed for Seattle and the Space Needle. As the Space Needle turned 360 degrees they were able to see all of Seattle during lunch. It was a fantastic view.

The next week, Gordon and Scott were looking for something to do on the next weekend. Gordon had met some pilots at the air base. These guys flew to Anchorage each week on a resupply run and said there was plenty of room if they wanted to ride along. They were looking forward to this trip the whole week. But on Friday they were called into Reed's office and were told that they were scheduled to be heading to Vietnam on Sunday. Scott could not imagine what would have happened if they had been in Anchorage as the unit left for Vietnam.

Scott took his car to a used car place and sold it for three hundred and fifty dollars. That price was two hundred dollars light, but it was sold. He sent a money order to Mom for $250.00 to pay off the car loan. Scott and Gordon moved from their motel into the barracks for the last two days. On

Sunday, they were loaded into buses and taken to McChord Air Base.

6. Vietnam Bound, February 4, 1968

They went to the air base on the morning of the lift off. There they loaded onto a C-141 that was to take them to Vietnam. The seats, while better than the nylon seats on the airplane that Scott had taken when he went to Fort Ord, were not that much better. He hoped that this flight did not require a navigator, like his flight to California. Scott climbed up into the cabin and the pilots invited him to join them in the navigator's seat.

Once seated, he found that he was in for a once-in-a-lifetime treat: a view of the vastness of the Pacific Ocean from the cabin of a huge airplane. He was not sure of the altitude that they were flying, but he could see hundreds of miles of dark earth surrounded by a halo of light. It seemed as though they were in some netherworld. Out in front of the plane he could see eight massive storm columns which stood a hundred thousand feet up in the sky. The pilots wove the plane between these massive storm columns like they were posts in a highway.

On the way to Vietnam they stopped at Clark Air Force

Base in Manilla. They arrived in Da Nang two days into the TET Holiday celebration on February 4, 1968. The North Vietnam Army and their Viet Cong guerillas were trying to blow the US troops back to the United States.

On February 12, 1968 Scott was on Landing Zone Baldy waiting for Company B 1/6th Infantry to come into the LZ. They were returning from a terrible battle at Lo Chiang, just outside of Da Nang. They arrived late in the afternoon and stayed at Baldy overnight. The next day they went on a combat assault on a village in the Rice Bowl. That was Scott's first combat assault and the day he earned his Combat Infantryman's Badge. The enemy in the village were firing at the chopper on the way into the village.

Over the next many months, he became a seasoned combat soldier. His uniform was faded, worn, and dirty, unlike that first day when his fatigues were new and very green. It did not take long to look like everyman in the company. The single night that the company stayed on LZ Baldy was the only time the company was out of the field. Every day they moved to a new night laager.

Scott's time in the field through February, March, and April—while not a cake walk—was only a precursor to what was to come in May and June of 1968. In Tet, 1968 the NVA had used all their war material in the south and did not get rid of the Americans. It had taken two months to resupply the troops in South Vietnam and in May of 1968 they started to push hard against the US Forces.

When those months hit, it was a new game. In the beginning of his tour, the NVA would make contact with Bravo and then break off the contact. While there was still some of that tactic being used, in May and June they made contact and stayed in contact.

Chu Lai Hospital

On his fifth day in the hospital, the doctors looked at his wounds. They wanted to watch them for another day before releasing him back to the field. On the sixth day, they determined that the wound was solid and would not allow infection to gain a foot hold. They released him from the hospital.

Scott called his company to pick him up. He filled his backpack up with rations and fresh ammunition and found out that his men were still on Baldy. The brass had decided to wait until Scott was back. There simply was no one to send to the field, especially on short notice. Scott found that his men were not getting along with the rear echelon types.

He caught a chopper to Baldy and arrived at 1500 hours. The major in charge of the Tactical Operations Bunker at Baldy was glad that Scott was back. He wanted Bravo off the LZ and back in the jungle. Scott never asked, and the Major did not tell him, all that had happened while he was lying in a hospital bed.

Scott was afraid that their mission was going to be changed and the company would be sent back out to work along the Laotian Border or back to the Que Son Valley. The Major, knowing how decimated Scott's company was, left their mission the same. They were still going to be Palace Guard. Their job was to keep rockets from being fired from what was called the Rocket Pocket. Bravo was to lift off at 1000 hours the next day.

Scott had time to sit down to have a beer with his company. They had ten f'n new guys to go back to the field. Scott worked with the sergeants and spread those men over the three platoons. Bravo was up to fifty-four troops. Those men put them at a strength just over the strength of a fully manned infantry platoon.

After a few brewski's with his men, Scott went to find a bunk. The men harassed him for being so damned spoiled. They were all sleeping on their air mattresses and Scott now needed a bunk. The mattresses at the hospital were a lot more comfortable than an air mattress.

Back to the Field

At 1000 hours the next day, the birds lifted off with Bravo Company. For as long as Scott could remember, he had not been inserted into the jungle, via a combat assault, when there was no enemy firing at the choppers. That was the biggest difference between being on Palace Guard and living in the jungle out by Laos.

The company was back in the jungle close to Chu Lai which meant a lot more people, but fewer NVA. The Viet Cong were a problem, but after spending so much time out by Laos with the NVA, the VC were not that bad. They had a couple of snipers shooting at them, but no open warfare.

One of the new tactics that had grown popular was

running Rat Patrols at night. Four to five men would move out long after dark and search for enemy activity. This meant that men who had been up all day were moving around the jungle at night with no training on how to work at night. The patrol would be out and moving for up to three hours.

Scott never asked anyone to do something that he would not do, so he went out on the first rat patrol. All five of the men had been up all day and now had to be at 100% alert as they moved. The area they were patrolling was made up of open rice paddies and jungle. If they were lucky, the moon would be out; if not they just hoped nothing would kill their night vision.

Scott and four men moved out at 1930 hours with five checkpoints to call into the company as they moved. They were moving down what was noted on their maps as a road. It really was two small strips where a vehicle may have driven in the past year.

They came upon several conical mounds that were three feet high, four feet across. A small corrugated awning, three feet by two feet, stuck out to one side. Scott had never seen anything like this in his months in the toolies. As he approached the first mound, something moved under that awning. He fired two rounds into the ground so the muzzle flash would light up whatever was under that awning. He saw a woman and at least two children huddled under that awning. Scott did not fire again and told everyone to keep moving. He could not believe how close he came to harming innocent people. That scared the heart out of him.

They continued for another half a mile before circling to a village marked on the map. They eased by an old French mansion. The Vietnamese lived in thatch huts around the mansions but never lived inside the buildings. They could hear the families talking as they slipped on into the night.

They were walking next to a bamboo thicket that ran along a rice paddy. A water buffalo had been penned in the water by the Vietnamese. The buffalo moved as they walked by and five rifles covered the movement. Someone whispered, "Water Buffalo" and five men raised their rifles and moved on down the trail.

They were moving through a jungle area and came upon a long, thatched building not displayed on the map. The hut was beautifully thatched with six to eight inches of thatching. All the villages that Scott had seen since coming to Vietnam had been ram shackled affairs. No new thatching had been put on the huts and the sides were mostly gone. This long house looked like something out of National Geographic.

A small fire on the stone floor gave Scott enough light to see that the house was filled with young Vietnamese women. This was an NVA whorehouse. The women were waiting on the men. Their men could not move in the day, but the night belonged to the jungle and the NVA.

Scott moved his patrol quickly away from the long hut, fearing that they were going to be ambushed.

By this time, Scott had seen enough to know this sneak around in the dark without any training or any night equipment was deadly. They continued to move for two more hours, going to each checkpoint and calling in their location to his platoon sergeant. On the way back to the company perimeter, a rice paddy dike collapsed on Scott. He fell in and was muddy from the sole of his boot to his crotch. When the dike gave way, it sounded as if he had just done a cannonball into a river.

As the Rat Patrol went hour by hour, the amount of alertness fell off precipitously. When Scott went into the water, he had stepped too close to the edge of the dike and it just gave way. The reason for the misstep was that he had been up since dawn and was just plain tired. By the time they approached the perimeter, all the men were at fifty to sixty percent alert. They had been up for eighteen hours in the jungle heat and they were spent.

They were talking to the men inside the perimeter by radio. The only place where there were no trip flares or Claymore mines around the company perimeter, was where the Rat Patrol had left the perimeter. Four hours later, that area looked like the rest of the perimeter.

One clump of trees that Scott had marked in his memory was directly in front of where they had left. They kept circling until he spotted what he hoped was that clump of trees. He used his pen light with a red filter and flashed it one time. A squad leader whispered into the radio that they should come back into the perimeter.

That was Scott's last Rat Patrol. He called in the grid coordinates of the whorehouse. Battalion thought that he was kidding, but he repeated the same warning. This was a village that was not marked on the map and it was nicer than any hooch he had seen in his months in the field. He recognized the talent that was standing around a lit fire.

Since they had no training or equipment to work the night patrols, the company stopped doing the patrols at night. They set-up ambush sites and kept a tight perimeter at night. Scott finally got word that he was being replaced by a captain. He also found out that the captain was bringing two lieutenants to the field with him.

With the company out of daily contact and new officers coming in, Scott felt that it was a good time to unass the field. The shoulder that had been slammed into the tree when he was wounded was giving him problems. The shoulder would hang up and Yancy would serve as Scott's chiropractor. He would push Scott's arm down and slam his shoulder with the palm of his hand. It was time to see an orthopedic doctor.

The day that the new CO arrived, the company was in the valley south of Hill 76. At 1800, the CO had Scott come to his Command Post. He was going to move the company two kilometers, after dark. It reminded Scott of the night that Reed's moved the company to attack a far-off mountain. He was beginning to see a repeat of stupid.

He gave Scott the coordinates for the new night laager. Scott had been having a problem with his compass. He no longer trusted what it indicated. He knew after months in the field that the compass was right, but for the past few weeks he had been second guessing himself. With a night move to an unknown area, he knew that he was in trouble.

He called Sergeant Rolling, one of his squad leaders and a damned good compass man. The two plotted the move and the sergeant took over. The company moved out at night and made it to the new night laager. When they got to the area they were on a flat plain. There was no advantage to this night laager. The laager that they had left was the highest spot in the valley. This laager was on flat ground. Scott went up and asked the man why he had picked a night laager that had no tactical advantage. He got an answer that sounded just like Reeds, "You do as I say!" Scott said nothing and went about setting the perimeter defenses in the dark.

Scott tried all night to tighten up his head. He felt like his wheels were wobbling. He realized that his time in the field had drawn to an end. He could not put up with any more stupid. If Scott did stay in the field, it would not fare well for either man.

The next morning Scott thanked his men for keeping him standing up during a lot of months of combat. He told them that he was going to see an orthopedic doctor and have them look at his shoulder. While his shoulder had become a nuisance, it was Scott's head that was giving him the most problem.

A chopper was coming in with resupply and as it turned out the two new lieutenants assigned to the company, were on that chopper. Scott was standing there when the chopper came down. He saluted both new officers and wished them well. He climbed on what is known as his "freedom ship" and headed to Chu Lai.

Da Nang

After a visit with the doctors at Chu Lai, he was medevaced to Da Nang to see an orthopedic surgeon. After arriving in Da Nang at 1600 hours, he caught a ride to the PX where he bought some supplies. He was standing out in front of the PX with his backpack, air mattress, ammo vest, and an M-16 rifle. It was the first time that he had not been responsible to a platoon or company. It was a strange feeling, but it felt good.

He was standing there watching the parade of soldiers with shined boots and no weapons as they headed to the PX. He even looked down at his unpolished boots, just thinking about how bad he must have looked to all the rear echelon types.

An E7 came up to Scott and asked, "You are infantry, right?"

Scott stuck out his hand and introduced himself and said, "Yes, Sergeant, I am infantry." He told the sergeant who he was and that he was going to be seeing a doctor the next morning.

"Where are you bunking, tonight?" the sergeant asked.

Scott said, "I thought I would go and see if they have a bunk at the hospital, or I will just lie down on my air mattress someplace."

The sergeant said, "No, you do not need to do that. I am heading to Saigon and will be gone for three days. You can use my hooch."

Scott followed the sergeant down into a tent city where they came to a small Quonset hut with a generator running. The sergeant gave him a quick tour and told him that there was beer in the refrigerator and one channel on the TV. The shower was just across the company street, and the mess hall was two streets away.

The sergeant said, "Sir, just fill the refrigerator up with beer when you leave. Strip the bed and throw the sheets down on the floor by the head of the bed. Those are clean sheets that are on the bed."

Scott tried to give the man some money for beer. The sergeant pointed to a tarp that was over a square of something. "Sir, that is all beer under that tarp, I will not take your money."

He showed Scott where the gas for the generator was located and gave him a salute. When Scott acknowledged his salute, the man turned sharply on his heel and headed on to Saigon. Scott watched him walk up the street and wondered, what in hell does an E-7 do that has a Quonset hut in a sea of platoon tents?

The first thing that Scott did was tap a beer and head over to take a shower. Then he just sat and drank beer and watched the little 12" television. After chow, he came back to do the same thing.

The next morning, the orthopedic surgeon gave him the option to stay in country with a profile or be sent to Japan for an operation on his shoulder. Scott opted to stay in country to finish his one-year commitment. He was afraid that they would fix his shoulder and send him back to the field.

Scott stayed in Da Nang for three days in the Quonset Hut. He drank beer and slept. He did not talk with anyone. On the morning of the third day he filled the refrigerator with beer, dropped the sheets on the floor, and left a sincere thank you to a man that he did not know.

He closed the door and filled up the generator with gas. Before leaving, he thought for a long moment about the happenings of the last couple of days. What force caused a complete stranger to offer his hooch before heading off to Saigon? How did he know that Scott needed some time to just be quiet?

When Scott returned to Chu Lai, he was assigned to the Chu Lai Defense Command as a Tactical Operations Officer. He was the only infantry officer assigned to Division Artillery. He worked twelve hours on and twelve off for the next four months. On February 4, 1969, he headed for Cam Ranh Bay and Seattle, Washington.

7. Going Home

On February 4, 1969 at 0100 hours, Scott's Pan American jet lifted off the runway at Cam Ranh Bay bound for Seattle, Washington. Scott was so excited about going home or at least to the US that he was unable to fall asleep on the twenty-five-hour plane ride. All he could think of was getting home and being away from people who wanted you dead and the people who would send you into a place where you could be killed.

Unfortunately, his welcome at SeaTac by the airport staff and fellow travelers made his homecoming less than a great experience. He arrived at 2300 hours the day before he left along with a plane filled with returning veterans. There was not one military person there to greet them. No one to help a plane full of returning veterans from Vietnam to make travel arrangements or arrange a night's sleep.

Scott feared that what he was seeing was an example of how the military took care of their own. These veterans were no longer a part of the war: they were simply ignored. He was to find out that this was the norm for the treatment of Vietnam Vets from the military and the general populace.

When they landed, there was nothing open at the airport. Everyone made do by sleeping on the floor or in a comfortable airport chair. Scott was beyond tired and decided to see if there was a bunk somewhere in the airport. He located a USO facility that was close to the ticketing area in the main building. They had six bunks setting in the middle of the room. The lights were left on all night and there was no place to secure valuables. He slept fitfully with his wallet under his body. He had his travel orders stuck under the mattress.

The next morning Scott felt someone's hot hand on his shoulder, he came to by leaping to his feet. He would forever feel that hot hand on his shoulder. He stood there next to the bed watching the young man who woke him, running away. He figured that his jumping up ready to fight, was caused by the long flight and lack of rest the day before. It took a long time for him to understand that he was not the same person who had flown to Vietnam a year earlier.

He slowly regained his senses and tried to find someone to help him buy a ticket home. He booked a flight to Cedar Rapids. The airline person could give a good God damn if he ever got home. As bad as his treatment by the airlines staff, he was to find that dealing with the traveling public was going to be worse. The airport customers thought of Vietnam soldiers as baby killers and hopheads. Some said the words through their actions; while others took a more direct approach.

Scott was still in his jungle fatigues as he walked to his gate. The reaction of the people to a soldier still dressed in battle fatigues was incomprehensible. Three college-age people accosted him, spat at him, and called him a baby killer. People were beyond awful.

While he was hurt by the verbal and physical abuse, he had to work hard to keep his cool. He had been trained to be lethal and remove a threat in any way necessary. Here he was being physically threatened by people in an airport. It was tough to hold back months of combat training and combat. He had to just put his head down and walk the long corridor to his gate.

When he got on the plane, not one person talked to him. He felt like he was an invisible person or had ended up some-place where service men were hated. The experiences at the Seattle airport and on his way home caused him to hide his Vietnam experiences for over forty-five years.

During his two-week leave, the only time he left the house was to go and visit family. He was in fear of what could happen if svomeone accosted him after he had a few beers, Scott opted to stay home with his parents and just chill. He reported into Fort Leonard Wood, Missouri and was as-signed to a Military Police unit. He had his left shoulder operated on prior to leaving the military in August of 1969.

Before the war, no one would talk to him about a job because he was going to be drafted. Now they would not talk to him, because he was a Vietnam veteran. After a lot of searching, he found a job with The National Cash Register Company as a salesman. He was to spend over forty years in sales.

Few, if any, knew he was a veteran, let alone a platoon leader and company commander in the field. Those who knew, never heard one story about Vietnam. Scott believed he had closed the door on combat and never brought up the subject.

Years went by when veterans did not talk to any other veteran. Vietnam vets were ostracized and that caused them to pull further and further back from the trauma of war. With no help from anyone, Scott found solace in a basement hideaway. He started writing his military experiences, out of self-defense. He needed to talk to someone, but with no one who he trusted, he just wrote his experiences down on paper. It let him get combat off his mind.

In his basement, he listened to his old LP Albums. He could understand the words and hear the melody. He could also turn the volume up as his hearing had been impaired by the mortar blast on that day in May in 1968.

He listened to the music from when he was young and had a life before him. He especially liked listening to Charlie Daniels sing, *"Still in Saigon"* on his old turntable. The words to that song presented by Charlie, were healing. They also condoned his sitting in his basement hideaway, writing all alone.

"Command at Dawn" is the result of writing to stay sane. By writing about combat, Scott was able to reduce his anxiety level a few percentage points. He still likes it when someone says, "Thank You for your Service".

The events and people in this book are fictional and do not represent any actual event or individual.

The Boy from Roy and Marge's Store

What happened to the boy?
We knew so along ago.
What became of him and where did he go?
He used to milk cows on his Iowa farm,
With his calloused hands and sun-tanned arms.

Hell, I remember him buying penny candy at Roy and Marge's Store.
Now we do not see him there anymore.
In '66 he joined the Army, where
combat training was lethal, and as hard core as could be.

In months, they taught him how to kill.
In combat he tested his newborn skill.
As a man in war, he had to stand tall,
As he watched fellow soldiers fall.

He came home changed
And we hope he is doing well,
But, haven't seen him, so we can't tell
If war got him or if he got war.

He grew up in peace and love
But combat's talons had killed the dove.
He knows things few men will ever know
He's kept it inside, believing that it did not show.

Now, he finds peace in a basement hideaway
Where he can play
Charlie Daniel's song "Still in Saigon",
As the words both heals and condones,
His hunkering down in a safe place, all alone.

He is filled with Anxieties' Fear
It has been by his side for fifty years
That boy from Roy and Marge's store
He is boy, no more.

As a man, he is journeying to see,
If he can find a way
To live, with PTSD.

—Mel Carney, 2019

CPSIA information can be obtained
at www.ICGtesting.com
Printed in the USA
FFHW022141181119
56086977-62120FF